The

Reference

Shelf

Religion in Politics and Society

Edited by Michael Kelly and Lynn M. Messina

The Reference Shelf
Volume 74 • Number 3

The H.W. Wilson Company
2002

The Reference Shelf

The books in this series contain reprints of articles, excerpts from books, addresses on current issues, and studies of social trends in the United States and other countries. There are six separately bound numbers in each volume, all of which are usually published in the same calendar year. Numbers one through five are each devoted to a single subject, providing background information and discussion from various points of view and concluding with a subject index and comprehensive bibliography that lists books, pamphlets, and abstracts of additional articles on the subject. The final number of each volume is a collection of recent speeches, and it contains a cumulative speaker index. Books in the series may be purchased individually or on subscription.

Library of Congress has cataloged this serial title as follows:

Religion in politics and society / edited by Michael Kelly and Lynn M. Messina.
     p. cm.—(The reference shelf; v. 74, no. 3)
    Includes bibliographical references and index.
    ISBN 0-8242-1012-3 (alk. paper)
    1. Religion and politics—United States. 2. Religion and sociology—United States. I. Kelly, Michael, 1972– II. Messina, Lynn M. III. Series.
    BL65.P7 R4355 2002
    291.1'7—dc21

2002025889

Visit H.W. Wilson's Web site: www.hwwilson.com

Printed in the United States of America

Religion in Politics and Society

Edited by Michael Kelly and Lynn M. Messina

The Reference Shelf
Volume 74 • Number 3

The H.W. Wilson Company
2002

The Reference Shelf

The books in this series contain reprints of articles, excerpts from books, addresses on current issues, and studies of social trends in the United States and other countries. There are six separately bound numbers in each volume, all of which are usually published in the same calendar year. Numbers one through five are each devoted to a single subject, providing background information and discussion from various points of view and concluding with a subject index and comprehensive bibliography that lists books, pamphlets, and abstracts of additional articles on the subject. The final number of each volume is a collection of recent speeches, and it contains a cumulative speaker index. Books in the series may be purchased individually or on subscription.

Library of Congress has cataloged this serial title as follows:

Religion in politics and society / edited by Michael Kelly and Lynn M. Messina.
     p. cm.—(The reference shelf; v. 74, no. 3)
    Includes bibliographical references and index.
    ISBN 0-8242-1012-3 (alk. paper)
    1. Religion and politics—United States. 2. Religion and sociology—United States. I. Kelly, Michael, 1972– II. Messina, Lynn M. III. Series.
    BL65.P7 R4355 2002
    291.1'7—dc21

               2002025889

Visit H.W. Wilson's Web site: www.hwwilson.com

Printed in the United States of America

Contents

Preface

The world's religions have always addressed the social dimension of faith, and social and political customs have always been affected by religious beliefs. Indeed, a primary meaning of the word "religion" is an *institutionalized* system of beliefs and practices, and some scholars argue that it is the social aspects of religion—its concern with ritual, morality, and community—that distinguishes it from the more solitary discipline of philosophy. (Others point to the rationalist character of philosophy, in contrast to religion, which often appeals to the emotions.)

While it is common to draw a distinction between the "sacred" and the "secular" in discussing the social impact of religion, such categories may not be universally valid. To an extent, they derive from the Christian heritage of the West: Christ's injunction to "render to Caesar the things that are Caesar's, and to God the things that are God's"; Christianity's early status as a minority religion persecuted by the Roman state; and, in the Middle Ages, the endless power struggles between kings and popes. Ever since the European Enlightenment of the 18th century, the distinction between sacred and secular has found expression as the principle of the separation of church and state, yet in much of the world, neither the distinction nor the principle is recognized.

Nevertheless, because of the great extent to which Europe and its former colonies have influenced world events during the last 500 years, the distinction between society and politics on the one hand, and religion on the other, is a valuable prism through which to consider current world affairs. The articles collected in this volume explore a few of the many ways in which religion informs, reinforces, and collides with social and political practices around the world. While no book of this size could hope to treat the subject exhaustively, *Religion in Politics and Society* does seek to provide a starting point for further research.

The book's first section examines a few of the roles religion plays in modern culture. We begin with Paul Marshall's commentary on the West's need to more seriously consider the importance of religion in international affairs. Next, Mark Clayton looks at a growing movement in the social sciences to reexamine the role of religion in society. In another article, William Breakey suggests that psychiatrists should open themselves to some of the methods of religious and spiritual advisors when counseling their patients. The section then moves to discussions of more specific religions, beginning with an article about the importance of Jerusalem to Jews, Christians, and Muslims. Then, Scott Appleby looks at the impact of Pope John Paul II on both the world at large and the Roman Catholic Church in particular. Michael Bordeaux next examines religious worship in present-day Russia, while David R. Sands outlines the various branches of Islam today.

If religion can be a force for compassion and social justice, it can also encourage political strife and violence—a fact that was underscored by the September 11 terrorist attacks on the United States. The second section explores the connection between religion and political violence in some detail, with several articles placing the attacks in a broad historical and philosophical context. First, Avishai Margalit and Ian Buruma address the notion of "Occidentalism," the standpoint from which many Islamic extremists view the West, while Harvey Cox comments on the new American war on terror. R. Scott Appleby and Martin E. Marty next discuss fundamentalism as it applies to both Christianity and Islam. The final two articles look at the battle between India and Pakistan over Kashmir and the war in the Balkans, two conflicts very much tied to religious factions in those regions of the world.

Because most religious traditions bolster their authority by pointing to the antiquity of their origins, we tend to think of the religious landscape as static and unchanging. But as Toby Lester argues in his article "Oh, Gods!" this is not necessarily the case. New religions are constantly emerging or dying off; and every now and then, a new religion gains respectability. The book's third section looks at several of these new religions, including Falun Gong and Mormonism. Articles on these religions are then followed by reflections on missionary work in two different parts of the world—Guatemala and Africa—where new and old religions compete for the souls of the native peoples.

Section four is devoted to an issue that has caught the attention of several religious traditions and which, in the view of many commentators, will assume greater importance in the coming decades: the confluence of religion and environmentalism. Faith-based environmentalism is of interest not only because it addresses such topical concerns as global warming and loss of biodiversity, but also because it represents a rare common ground for religion and science. The first article in this section, by Linda Ashton, provides an overview of religious groups taking a serious interest in environmental issues, while the next, by Michael J. Strada, compares the attitudes of monotheistic and polytheistic religions toward the environment. George Rupp then discusses the ways in which religious beliefs have influenced environmental attitudes.

The book's fifth and final section examines the intersection of gender and religion, including articles that focus on the changing roles of women in Theravada Buddhism, Islam as practiced in the United States, and in Orthodox Judaism, and on the situation of gays and lesbians in black Protestant churches.

Many people assisted in the production of this book. We would especially like to thank Jennifer Peloso, Sandra Watson, Gray Young, Norris Smith, Rich Stein, and Cliff Thompson.

Michael Kelly
Lynn M. Messina
June 2002

List of Maps

I. Religion and Culture

Editor's Introduction

As William James noted in his classic study *The Varieties of Religious Experience*, religion is a notoriously fluid cultural phenomenon. It is, he wrote, "a field of experience where there is not a single conception that can be sharply drawn. . . . Things are more or less divine, states of mind are more or less religious, reactions are more or less total, but the boundaries are always misty, and it is everywhere a question of amount and degree." In other words, it is difficult to draw the line between religion and other cultural activities; the impact of religion is ubiquitous. This fact becomes particularly evident when one considers how religion has affected not only specific societies but also the conduct of world affairs.

This section considers some of the many ways in which religion overlaps with and impinges on the broader culture. While the articles chosen for inclusion here are by no means exhaustive, they should give a sense of the variety of ways in which religion can (and frequently does) shape human thought and action.

Paul Marshall, in his article "Keeping the Faith: Religion, Freedom, and International Affairs," looks at the importance of religion in societies around the world. Writing roughly a year and a half before September 11, Marshall accuses the West—and the U.S. in particular—of "secular myopia," of focusing almost exclusively on secular issues while ignoring powerful and disturbing manifestations of religious belief. He points to the many parts of the world, including China, the Balkans, Sudan, Latin America, Nigeria, and Indonesia, where religion is playing a significant role in the struggle for freedom, or where human rights are regularly violated in the name of religious principles.

While many in the West are slow to recognize the significance of religious beliefs in world societies, there are signs in academic circles of a growing awareness of what religion might contribute to the social sciences. As Mark Clayton explains in "Scholars Get Religion," historians, sociologists, political scientists, and even some economists have very pragmatic reasons for taking a second look at religion. In a theme similar to Marshall's, Clayton asserts that world events in the past three decades have called into question the so-called "secularization thesis," which held that, with the spread of modernity, religion was headed for the proverbial dustbin of history. At the same time, Clayton suggests, the new interest in religion is in some cases decidedly personal. According to Dr. Kathleen Mahoney, co-author of a book on religion in higher education, "scholars are realizing there is no such thing as value-free inquiry."

Academicians are not the only group of professionals to reconsider the role of faith in human life, as is evident in William R. Breakey's "Psychiatry, Spirituality and Religion." While he acknowledges the mutual distrust that has

3

always existed between the scientific and religious communities, Breakey also reminds his fellow psychiatrists that many of their patients are as likely to seek religious counsel as they are to hire mental-health professionals in times of crisis. Given the fact that so many people find peace of mind through religion, Breakey suggests that "psychiatry and religion have much to gain from collaborating and developing better understanding of each other's concepts and methods."

The rest of the articles in this section examine specific religions, religious figures, and one particular site that is deemed "holy" by the world's three major religions. That site is Jerusalem, significant to Jews, Christians, and Muslims. In "A City That Echoes Eternity," Kenneth L. Woodward explains the history of the city, the role it has played in the development of each religion, and why it has been at the center of political conflict for so many years.

Next is a profile of Pope John Paul II, one of the most famous, well-traveled, and influential religious figures in the world. Scott Appleby looks at a number of significant aspects of John Paul's pontificate, including the role he and the Catholic Church played in the downfall of communism in the Soviet Union and Eastern Europe, his views on western style capitalism and Latin American liberation theology, and his positions on birth control and the role of women in the Church. Appleby concludes by examining the legacy John Paul will leave to his successor and speculating on who that successor might be.

The fall of communism that Pope John Paul II helped to bring about led to drastic changes in the cultural landscape of those countries that were part of the former Soviet Union. With the ban on religious worship removed, individuals in the region were free to practice their faiths in churches and synagogues that were no longer considered useless remnants of the past. In "Russian Renewal," Michael Bourdeaux examines the state of religious worship in Russia and considers how churches have struggled to carve a place for themselves in the political and spiritual life of the country. While freedom of worship was at first granted to numerous indigenous faiths—including Orthodox, Jewish, Buddhist, and Muslim—it was denied to others until recently, when missionary groups representing Roman Catholics, the Salvation Army, and Jehovah's Witnesses, among others, finally began to overcome discrimination. The result, as Bourdeaux explains, is the reopening of many monasteries and religious educational institutions, just some of the "signs of religious revival" appearing throughout the country.

The final article in this section seeks to shed light on one of the most misunderstood religions of the present day, Islam. Since September 11, non-Muslims have tried to reconcile what they have been told are important Muslim values—the fundamental respect for human life, the teaching of peace over violence, and the concern for education—with the oppression of women in many Islamic societies and the perpetration of some of the most horrific terrorist acts in human history in the name of jihad. In "A Faith with Many Faces," David R. Sands attempts to shed light on the various groups who call themselves Muslim, such as the Shiite, Sunni, and Wahhabi, in an effort to explain how such seemingly contradictory values could be drawn from the same sacred text (the Koran).

Keeping the Faith: Religion, Freedom, and International Affairs[1]

By Paul Marshall
USA Today Magazine, January 2000

At the end of 1997, former *New York Times* executive editor A. M. Rosenthal confessed: "I realized that in decades of reporting, writing, or assigning stories on human rights, I rarely touched on one of the most important. Political human rights, legal, civil, and press rights, emphatically often; but the right to worship where and how God or conscience leads, almost never."

The habit of ignoring religious persecution is all too common in the West. On Aug. 22, 1998, for example, seven leaders of underground churches in China released an unprecedented joint statement calling for dialogue with the communist government. The U.S. media virtually ignored the statement, despite the fact that these leaders represent the only nationwide group in China not under government control. Their membership of 15,000,000 is several times larger than the population of Tibet and hundreds of times larger than the number of China's democracy and human rights activists. Nevertheless, the press just wasn't interested.

Nor is it interested in religious persecution in Sudan, the largest country in Africa, which still practices crucifixion. After enduring more than 40 years of civil war, the predominantly Christian population in southern Sudan is subject to torture, rape, and starvation for its refusal to convert to Islam. Christian children routinely are sold into slavery. Muslims who dare to convert to Christianity are faced with the death penalty.

In the last 15 years, Sudan's death toll of more than 1,900,000 is greater than Rwanda's, Bosnia's, and Kosovo's combined. The United Nations' special rapporteur on Sudan, Gaspar Biro, produced five official reports documenting the carnage, declaring that "abuses are past proving . . . these are the facts." He resigned when his reports were consistently ignored.

Not a week goes by that Freedom House's Center for Religious Freedom does not learn of major stories of religious persecution abroad. Christians are usually the victims, but so are many others, such as Buddhists in Vietnam, Baha'is in Iran, and Shiite Muslims in Afghanistan. These stories rarely make headlines or penetrate the consciousness of journalists and foreign policy professionals.

---

1. Article by Paul Marshall from *USA Today Magazine* January 2000. Copyright © Society for the Advancement of Education. Reprinted with permission.

One main cause for this ignorance is what I call "secular myopia"—an introverted, parochial inability even to see, much less understand, the role of religion in human life. It is a condition that mainly afflicts the "chattering classes," which include diplomats, journalists, political commentators, and policy analysts. As strategic theorist Edward Luttwak has observed, the chattering classes are eager to examine economic causes, social differentiations, and political affiliations, but they generally disregard the impact of faith upon the lives of individuals and nations.

Secular myopia can have painful consequences. Remember how little the U.S. knew about the Ayatollah Khomeini and his followers in Iran during the late 1970s? Luttwak notes that there was just one proposal for the CIA to examine "the attitudes and activities of the more prominent religious leaders" and that this proposal was vetoed as an irrelevant exercise in sociology.

As the Shah's regime was collapsing, U.S. political analysts kept insisting that everything was fine. True to their training, they focused on economic variables, class structure, and the military, and they concluded that, since businessmen, the upper classes, and the military supported the Shah, he was safe. There were, of course, many mullahs (religious teachers and leaders) arousing Islamic sentiment, but the analysts believed that religious movements drew merely on folk memories, were destined to disappear with "modernization," and were irrelevant to the real forces and institutions of political power.

Consequently, the U.S. did not clear its embassy of important documents or staff. When Khomeini seized power, his followers captured both. They used the former to attack American personnel throughout the Middle East and the latter to precipitate a hostage crisis that paralyzed America for two years.

According to Luttwak, during the Vietnam War, "every demographic, economic, ethnic, social, and, of course, military aspect of the conflict was subject to detailed scrutiny, but the deep religious cleavages that afflicted South Vietnam were hardly noticed." Moreover, the "tensions between the dominant Catholic minority [and] a resentful Buddhist majority . . . were largely ignored until Buddhist monks finally had to resort to flaming self-immolations in public squares, precisely to attract the attention of Americans so greatly attentive to everything else in Vietnam that was impeccably secular." Similar tales can be told of Washington's myopic view of conflicts in Bosnia, Nicaragua, Israel, Lebanon, India, the Philippines, and Indonesia.

Misunderstanding Religion

Religion as Ethnicity. In 1997, when Malaysian Prime Minister Mahathir Mohamed railed against speculators with the outrageous claim, "We are Muslims, and the Jews are not happy to see the Muslims progress," the *Los Angeles Times* described him as "race-obsessed." Perhaps the *Times* took its cue from media descriptions of former Yugoslavia. In this tortured land, the war raging among the Orthodox, Catholics, and Muslims always is referred to as "ethnic," and attacks on Bosnian and Kosovar Muslims always are referred to as "ethnic cleansing."

There are many such instances of media misunderstanding. The *Economist* headlined a 1997 story about attacks on 25 churches and a temple in eastern Java that were prompted by a Muslim heresy trial as "Race Riots." A 1998 *New York Times* editorial on rampant violence in Indonesia cited "tensions between Indonesia's Muslim majority and Chinese minority" as if there were no Chinese Muslims and no non-Muslims except for the Chinese.

Religion as Irrationality. Western opinionmakers and policymakers consider themselves the heirs of the Enlightenment, an 18th-century intellectual movement that stressed rationalism and science over faith and other forms of "superstition." To them, all contemporary peoples, events, and issues fall into Enlightenment categories, which are most often political or ideological.

Muslims are identified as "right-wing" even when they advocate leftist economic controls. Hindus who propose to build a temple on the site of the Babri mosque in India and Jews who propose to build a Third Temple on the site of the Dome of the Rock in Jerusalem are also labeled "left-wing" or "right-wing" without any regard to religious context.

When the vocabulary of "left" and "right" has run its tired course, what remains is the old standby, "fundamentalist"—a word that is dredged up from the American past, despite dubious provenance. What "fundamentalist" means when applied to Christians, Buddhists, Hindus, or Muslims is hard to understand. Using the term is a sign of intellectual laziness. If what worshippers believe does not easily fall into an Enlightenment category, it is assumed that they must be "irrational." Thus, "fundamentalist" now is merely shorthand for "religious fanatic"—for someone who is to be categorized rather than heard, observed rather than comprehended, and dismissed rather than respected.

Religion as Sublimated Anxiety. When ethnicity and psychology fail to subsume religion, the alternative is to treat it, in quasi-Marxist fashion, as the sublimation of drives that supposedly can be explained by poverty, economic changes, or the stresses of modernity. Of course, these factors do play a role, but, all too often, what one encounters is an a priori methodological commitment to treating religion as secondary—as a mildly interesting phenomenon that can be explained, but is never an explanation in and of itself.

So great is this bias that, when the *Journal of International Affairs* devoted its 1996 edition to studies of religious influences, it apologized in part for even mentioning faith with the admission,

"Religion may seem an unusual topic for an international affairs journal." The editors added that "it is hardly surprising that scholars . . . have, for the most part, ignored [religion]."

Religion and War. If people do start to take religion seriously in international affairs, they will learn a great deal about war, democracy, and freedom of all kinds. It was pointed out by religion scholars long before political scientist Samuel Huntington's book, *The Clash of Civilizations and the Remaking of the World Order*, that chronic armed conflict is concentrated on the margins of the traditional religions, especially along the boundaries of the Islamic world. The Middle East, the southern Sahara, the Balkans, the Caucasus, Central Asia, and Southern Asia are where Islam, Christianity, Judaism, Buddhism, and Hinduism intersect. It is also where most wars have broken out in the last 50 years.

These are not explicitly religious wars, but since religion shapes cultures, people in these regions have different histories and differ-

---

If people do start to take religion seriously in international affairs, they will learn a great deal about war, democracy, and freedom of all kinds.

---

ent views of human life. Regardless of the triggers for conflict, they are living in unstable areas where conflict is likely to occur—in religious fault zones that are prone to political earthquakes.

Religion and Democracy. Religion shapes governments as well. In Eastern Europe, authoritarian governments are finding it easier to hold on in the areas where the Orthodox church, with its long history of association with the state, has had special influence. The new boundaries of Eastern and Western Europe are tending to fall along the old divide between Orthodox and Catholic/Protestant.

Huntington makes a strong case that, in the 1970s and 1980s, a "third wave of democracy" swept over Portugal, Spain, Eastern Europe, Latin America, and the Philippines, in part because of important changes in the dominant nongovernment institution—the Catholic church. He concludes that changes made after the Second Vatican Council inspired a major movement toward democracy and human rights.

The role of the church in the fall of communism may not be clear to Western observers afflicted with secular myopia, but it is all too clear to Chinese government officials. As brutal practitioners of communism, they are perversely aware of the power of human spirituality, and so they regard religion with deadly seriousness. In 1992, the Chinese press noted that "the church played an important role in the change" in Eastern Europe and the former Soviet Union and warned, "If China does not want such a scene to be repeated in its land, it must strangle the baby while it is still in the manger."

Underground church or "house church" leaders consistently report that the current government crackdown is due to fears which are prompted by religious events in the former Soviet bloc. Even Chinese government documents actually implementing the crackdown state that one of their purposes is to prevent "the changes that occurred in the former Soviet Union and Eastern Europe."

Each year, Freedom House conducts a comparative survey of political rights and civil liberties around the world. The 1998–99 survey found that, of the 88 countries rated as "free," 79 "are majority Christian by tradition or belief." Clearly, correlations are not causalities, so this does not imply any direct link between Christianity and democracy. (The survey also finds a connection between Hinduism and democracy.) However, the existence of such

---

> *The church ... always had to acknowledge that there were forms of political power which it could and should not exercise.*

---

a relationship is significant, not least because it is far greater than material factors such as economic growth, on which theorists and analysts lavish attention.

Politics and the Nature of the Church. One reason for the modern correlation between Christianity and political freedom lies in the nature of the church. From the beginning, Christians, while usually loyal citizens, necessarily have an attachment to "another king" and a loyalty to a divine order that is apart from and beyond the political order.

In the Latin churches of the West, the two realms of sacerdotium (church) and regnum (state) emerged. Henceforth, there were two centers of authority in society. As political philosopher George Sabine points out, the Christian church became a distinct institution, independent of the state, entitled to shape the spiritual concerns of mankind. This, he adds, "may not unreasonably be described as the most revolutionary event in the history of Western Europe, in respect both to politics and to political thought."

It is not that the church or state directly advocated religious or any other freedom—they did not, and inquisitions often were defended. People in both realms, though, always believed that there should be boundaries, and they struggled over centuries to define them. This meant that the church, whatever its lust for civil control, always had to acknowledge that there were forms of political power which it could and should not exercise. Meanwhile, the state, whatever its drive to dominate, had to acknowledge that there were areas of human life that were beyond its reach.

The very existence of the modern church denies that the state is the all-encompassing or ultimate arbiter of human life. Regardless of how the relationship between God and Caesar has been confused, it now at least means that, contrary to the Romans and modern totalitarians, Caesar is not God. This confession, however mute, sticks in the craw of every authoritarian regime and draws an angry and bloody response.

Faith and Freedom. This confession suggests that people interested in democracy should heed religion. For example, attention to China's courageous pro-democracy activists is certainly deserved, but it must be remembered that their following is quite small. Therefore, more attention should be paid to China's dissident churches, which, at a conservative estimate, number about 25,000,000 members (apart from 15,000,000 in official churches) and are growing at a rate of 10–15% a year.

In a 1997 cover story, "God Is Back," the *Far East Economic Review* quoted the words of one Beijing official: "If God had the face of a 70-year-old man, we wouldn't care if he was back. But he has the face of millions of 20-year-olds, so we are worried." Clearly, the rapid growth of the only nationwide movement in China not under government control merits political attention.

International Relations

Apart from some of the horrific situations already described in Sudan, the Balkans, and elsewhere, the following religious trends merit political reflection as well:

- The rise of large, militant religious parties such as the Welfare Party in Turkey and the Bharatiya Janata Party in India and the spread of radical Islam all over the world.

- The rapid growth of charismatic Protestantism and Catholicism in Latin America. As Cambridge University sociologist David Martin has shown, these indigenous developments represent one of the largest religious changes of the century. Moreover, they produce personal reform and provide a major impetus toward entrepreneurial activity.

- The pattern of violence and warfare along the sub-Saharan boundary from Nigeria to Ethiopia. This constitutes a huge Christian/Muslim breach that must be addressed before peace is possible.

- Massive rates of Christian conversions in South Korea (currently 25% of the population), China (a minimum of 40,000,000, up from 1,000,000 in 1980), Taiwan, and Indonesia.

- Increasing religious tensions in trouble spots such as Nigeria and Indonesia. There is widespread religious violence in the northern and central regions of Nigeria, with thousands dead in recent years, that could lead to all-out religious war. In Indonesia, escalating religious strife precedes and has some separate dynamics from recent anti-Chinese violence. Two hundred churches were destroyed in Java alone in a recent 15-month period, and most of them were not attended by ethnic Chinese. Such incidents threaten to undermine what has been one of the world's best examples of interreligious toleration and cooperation. In both of these regions, there is the possibility that instability and violence will spread far beyond the religious communities themselves.

- The exodus of Christians from the Middle East—about 2,000,000 in the last five years. Currently, around three percent of Palestinians are Christians, compared to an estimated 25% 50 years ago. Similar mass flight from Egypt, Syria, Lebanon, Turkey, and Iraq has occurred.

- The emergence of the Orthodox church as a unifying symbol in Russia, the Balkans, and other parts of the former Soviet Union.

- The increasing prominence of religion in the conflicts between India and Pakistan, which now possess nuclear weapons.

I am not making the absurd suggestion that religion—apart from other cultural, ethnic, economic, political, or strategic elements—is the sole or the key factor in international affairs. Societies are complex. What I am saying is that it is absurd to examine any political order without attending to the role of religion. Religion consistently needs to be dealt with as an important independent factor. Analyses that ignore religion should be inherently suspect.

In the West, there are hopeful signs of a new awareness of the importance of religion and religious freedom. On Oct. 9, 1998, the U.S. Senate passed the landmark International Religious Freedom Act. The following day, the House of Representatives did the same. On Oct. 27, Pres. Clinton—a strong opponent—cut his losses and signed the act, which establishes a commission appointed by Congress and the White House to monitor global religious persecution and recommend responses to it. This is a small step, but it is a step in a vital area where few have trod. It is vital that concerned citizens take similar steps.

Policies, programs, and organizations that promote and defend religious freedom must be supported and religious freedom must be made a core element of human rights. This is not a parochial matter. Historically, it is the first freedom in the growth of human rights, as well as in the First Amendment to the U.S. Constitution.

While all human rights pressures make "geopolitical realists" nervous, religion carries the additional burdens of touching on deeply felt commitments, facing confused domestic claims about separation of church and state, and feeding fears that the U.S. is an imperial Christian power. This is no reason to hesitate. Religious rights must be at the forefront of any sound human rights policy. Unless this is understood, the ability to fight for any freedom at all is compromised.

Scholars Get Religion[2]

BY MARK CLAYTON
CHRISTIAN SCIENCE MONITOR, FEBRUARY 26, 2002

When it comes to academic scholarship, blue sky and dollars are often the only limits on research.

But Luis Lugo discovered another obstacle early in his scholarly career. All it took was for the doctoral candidate in political science to suggest a project that would delve deeply into religion.

The response, at best, was cool. "In my own discipline, political science, the Emily Post rule applied," recalls Dr. Lugo, who took his PhD at the University of Chicago in the 1970s. "Religion was simply not something one discussed in polite company."

Lugo, who persevered and went on to examine religion's impact on early United States foreign policy, chuckles about the incident. But that's not the only thing that makes him smile. In the years since he started his studies, U.S. higher education has done a sharp about-face. American scholarship, Lugo says, has gotten religion.

The ivory tower has gone from keeping a rigid distance between religion and social-science scholarship to a still-modest, but growing, embrace of it, says Lugo, director of the religion program at the Pew Charitable Trusts in Philadelphia.

He's not alone in his assessment of the shift. "Since the early 1990s, there has been a broad increase in the amount of interest in religion in the academy as a research topic," says Kathleen Mahoney, coauthor of a forthcoming book on religion's role within higher education. "We are seeing religion-and-fill-in-the-blank research: religion and economics, religion and political science, religion and history."

For most of the 20th century, scholarship and religion were at opposite poles when it came to research—with religion confined to its own department. Religion's ingrained values were seen as antithetical to a search for answers based on a scientific line of reasoning.

Now, however, a broader range of academics are beginning to see the "religion factor" as a key to understanding historical, political, social, and even economic forces.

"Increasingly, scholars are realizing there is no such thing as value-free inquiry," Dr. Mahoney says. "Why can't Christians bring their values into inquiry—and have that perspective inform their research?"

Among scores of research projects, books, and monographs, examples of scholarship branching out are easier to find than ever.

A Santa Clara University economist is using economic tools to study religious extremism. An Emory University interdisciplinary institute is conducting a research project on marriage, sex, and family issues as they relate to Christianity, Judaism, and Islam. A Harvard University history professor is authoring a book about the rise of evangelical political power and the Christian right in Orange County, Calif. And such research is trickling into the classroom, observers say, through courses with words like "God" or "religion" in their titles, many of them offered outside the religion department.

Caution Still Prevails

Mahoney, Lugo, and others note that some disciplines have warmed to religion research, while others remain in the deep freeze.

Political science and sociology were relatively early and growing adopters over the past two decades. History, too. But go to the economics department, and the idea of focusing on religion may still get a skeptical reception.

Robert Barro is helping to change that. A leading conservative economist at Harvard, he is examining the impact of religions on the economies of nations. It's still a small shock to some of Dr. Barro's colleagues.

When Barro began his research, there really wasn't a department on Harvard's campus where it fit well, he says. So he and Rachel McCleary, a religion and philosophy expert, formed the Religion, Political Economy and Society Project. Now, the idea is to branch out beyond economics and involve other disciplines in basic religion and social-science research.

"I started by thinking about why some countries grow faster than others over a long time," Barro says. "At first I was thinking about political institutions and property rights, but I've expanded to think about the impact of religion and culture on economies."

Up Against the Scientific Method

Such innovation, however, is still a fairly recent development.

After World War II, American higher education became captivated by advances in the hard sciences. Social-science research veered sharply in favor of strictly quantitative methods that mimicked research in the natural sciences. Religion was hard to measure and didn't fit the new mold.

Another factor was the scholarly embrace of the "secularization thesis." As society became more advanced, it would naturally becomes less religious—or so the thesis held. Religion, therefore, would soon be as relevant as a buggy whip, so why try to study its effects on society?

Then real life intervened. Even as church attendance was dropping, Jimmy Carter became America's first "born again" president in 1976. Ronald Reagan enjoyed Christian-right support—as did Pat Buchanan later. George W. Bush may be president today because he appealed more to Christian-right voters. Add to that the Iranian revolution, the Branch Davidian battle with the FBI in 1993, and most recently, the Sept. 11 attacks, and it's clear that understanding religion's impact on society has never been more important.

> *It's clear that under-standing religion's impact on society has never been more important.*

Such events have driven scholars to adopt a pragmatic view, says Alan Wolfe, a political scientist and sociologist who directs the Boisi Center for Religion and American Public Life at Boston College.

"I'm not a religious person," he says, "But I and others are interested in understanding religion's role in society. One thing after another has led me to realize if you want to understand American politics or Sept. 11, you really need to know more about American history and the role religion has played in it."

Even onetime proponents of the secularization thesis, like Boston University sociologist Peter Berger, have reversed course.

"I started out my career believing with almost everyone else that modernity goes hand in hand with a decline in religion," says Dr. Berger, who wrote *The Desecularization of the World: Resurgent Religion and World Politics* in 1999. "Well, I was wrong. . . . There are secularized regions—Western Europe, for example. But it doesn't go hand in hand with modernity. So there has to be something else going on."

Growing numbers of political scientists and historians have also found religion to be a critical element in their work.

"I think we [in the academy] are finally figuring out that the importance of religion is self-evident," says Ted Jelen, a political scientist at the University of Nevada at Las Vegas. "Social scientists have been constantly predicting the secularization of the world. That simply has not happened. Religion is remarkably resilient."

While not yet ubiquitous by any means, this shift in attitudes is scattered across the academy. Mahoney ticks off a list that includes growing enrollments in academic organizations with a

Christian orientation—the Society of Christian Philosophers, for instance. More faculty are attending conferences on the place of religion in the academy and the role of spirituality in teaching.

Evidence of the upsurge can also be seen in more and better submissions to scholarly journals, which are coming from a greater variety of disciplines. "We're starting to crack the mainstream journals in all fields," exults Dr. Jelen, who edits the *Journal for the Scientific Study of Religion*.

Still, political scientists are "pretty recent converts," he says. Just a few hardy adventurers dissected religion and American politics in the early 1980s. Now, however, mainstream academic organizations have subgroups catering to religion research, like the American Political Science Association's religion section, which has about 500 members.

The trend seems unlikely to abate anytime soon. Islamic fundamentalism, for example, is the subject of new scholarship at many institutions.

Follow the Money

There's another reason multidisciplinary religious scholarship is picking up speed: money. Several well-known endowments have funded religion research projects across disciplines, including the Pew Charitable Trusts, the Lilly Endowment, the Ford Foundation, and, most recently, the John Templeton Foundation.

"These large organizations want to study religion in a social-science context, so now there is money for scholars who might not otherwise study religion," says Philip Goff, director of the Center for the Study of Religion and American Culture at Indiana University-Purdue University at Indianapolis.

The 1990s stock market certainly helped make these goals a reality. Share prices of Eli Lilly & Co. shot skyward, propelled by sales of popular drugs like Prozac. The Lilly Endowment holds much of that company's stock. The result is a well-funded endowment (about $15 billion) giving generously to research, Dr. Goff says.

"I know professors who say, 'I got a 'Prozac grant' to study religion," he says. "The mutual-fund boom has been great. Studies being funded by Lilly and Pew have attracted many scholars."

Even with a sagging stock market, though, religion-research funding looks to be more than a flash in the pan. Pew, under Lugo's direction, is starting up 10 cross-disciplinary research institutes on university campuses. The institutes must be located in the center of campus—to woo faculty from many disciplines, he says.

"We're trying to enrich the academy," Lugo says, "to get academics to think more broadly about issues important to the public. The long-term result, we hope, will be students who graduate with a better understanding of religion's impact on society because their professors understand it better."

A Magnet for Budding Scholars

If that happens, then it may be easier to attract young scholars to carry on the research. When Harvard's Barro needed help gathering data, he recruited Brian Boyle, a junior majoring in sociology, and Jeremy Galen, a sophomore religion major.

Both young men are excited by the prospects—and open to incorporating religion into their own future scholarship.

"I've read the last 15 years of literature in this field," Mr. Galen says. "What interests me is that the study of religion goes hand in hand with these other questions about society. I would have no hesitancy whatsoever about doing research in this area. There's enough scholarship support for it to be well received."

Psychiatry, Spirituality and Religion[3]

By William R. Breakey
International Review of Psychiatry (2001)

Training programs in psychiatry are increasingly offering structured curricula on the interface of religion and psychiatry . . . . After decades of neglecting spirituality and religion in psychiatric discourse, research programs are delineating the relationships between spirituality and health and casting light upon the processes by which spirituality may have positive effects. . . .

Most medical specialties are distinguished by their narrow focus on a particular organ system: the heart, the lungs, the skin, the gut, and so forth. In contrast, Psychiatrists broaden the focus. Their area of interest not only includes all organ systems, but also extends to many areas of human experience whose relationship even to the brain, as an organ, is partially understood at best. On a daily basis we help our patients with aspects of their lives that include self-worth, enjoyment, motivation, life goals, achievement, personal fulfillment, and family relationships. Our field of expertise is the disorders of mental life, and psychiatrists use a variety of perspectives to conceptualize these disorders (McHugh & Slavney, 1998). It is surprising, then, that in psychiatric discourse we tend to skirt around spirituality and religion (Neeleman & Persaud, 1995), all the more so in light of evidence that, for most of our patients, religion and spirituality are important motivating and supportive factors (Koenig & Larson . . .). We consider personal identity, family relationships, guilt, sexuality, work and ambition to be legitimate areas of interest for psychiatry, and appropriate issues for psychotherapy, but spirituality is avoided.

For the majority of people in every culture, belief in divine or transcendent reality is an important fact of daily life. This belief determines values and motivations, gives meaning to life and molds behavior. Psychiatrists understand that people do not live in a vacuum—patients and their psychopathology must be understood in terms of the culture in which they live. Social and community psychiatrists, in particular, understand the need for cultural competence if they are to appreciate fully and communicate adequately with patients whose culture differs from their own (Gaw, 1993). But we perhaps do not reflect sufficiently on the extent to which the culture of a group is shaped by the spiritual beliefs and values of its

---

members. We should make efforts to be knowledgeable about the origins of our patients' culture if we hope to understand their heritage in any depth. Frank & Frank (1991) stress the importance of understanding the *assumptive world* of a patient in psychotherapy: that set of ideas, beliefs and principles used consciously or unconsciously by the person to provide meaning to the events of his or her life. Religious ideas are important in the formation of many people's assumptive world.

Mutual Suspicion

Psychiatry and religion have so much in common that it is perhaps not surprising that they have often viewed each other as rivals. Psychiatry, until relatively recently, had little empirical data to support its theories. Its trainees not so long ago entered a period of apprenticeship and indoctrination which relied more on coming to accept psychiatric dogma than on acquiring a body of scientific knowledge or learning the methods of critical and objective study. In the era when psychiatry was dominated by psychodynamic approaches the interactions that took place in psychiatrists' offices often had more in common with the confessional than with the clinic. From the other side, some religious people have adopted a ministry of counseling people with emotional or behavioral problems, moving into territory that psychologists and psychiatrists have considered exclusively their own. In some cases, these are well trained and certified pastoral counselors who are indistinguishable from many "mental health professionals" in terms of their methods and level of competence.

> *Psychiatry and religion have so much in common that it is perhaps not surprising that they have often viewed each other as rivals.*

Some strands of psychiatric and psychological thought have been frankly hostile to religion. Freud is most often quoted as being dismissive of religion. In *Obsessional Acts and Religious Practices* (1907), he draws parallels between the rituals of obsessional patients and those of very religious people and comments that religion might be considered "a universal obsessional neurosis," an interpretation that now seems absurd in light of present day thinking on obsessive-compulsive disorders. In another brief paper he explains the religious convictions of a young physician in terms of an oedipal conflict, using the arguments developed in *Totem and Taboo* to explain the primitive development of religion (Freud, 1928). Because of his once powerful influence on psychiatric thought, particularly in the U.S., Freud's criticism of religion and his own lack of religious faith had a disproportionate influence in prejudicing psychiatrists against religion. However, it is worth noting that although he himself had no religious belief, he returned to the topic again and again in his writings, indicating that he realized that religious ideas were of great importance in the mental life of his patients. What is more, as Küng (1990) points out, Freud's speculations as to the oedipal mechanisms involved in the development of religious ideas may or may not be correct, but have little bearing on the validity of the ideas or their value to the person.

The psychologist Albert Ellis has also been a prominent critic of religion. In a brief paper in 1980 he presented a summation of his position, including that "Devout, orthodox or dogmatic religion (or what might be called religiosity) is significantly correlated with emotional disturbance," and "The less religious (people) are, the more emotionally healthy they will tend to be." These statements flow from his own atheistic convictions and from his experience as a psychotherapist. They fly in the face of the accumulating empirical evidence of the positive influence of religiosity on health as described by Koenig & Larson . . . .

More often than being frankly hostile to religion, psychiatrists have simply ignored it. Standard textbooks of psychiatry pay scant attention to this aspect of human life. They do not mention religion as a factor in personality development or identity, much less as a

---

More often than being frankly hostile to religion, psychiatrists have simply ignored it.

---

potential source of support for a healthy personality or sustenance during times of illness or trouble. Where religion is mentioned, it is pathologized: textbooks describe symptoms with religious coloration, such as guilt-ridden obsessional ruminations, delusions of religious grandeur or spirit possession, hallucinations with religious content, or a delusional preoccupation with having a divine mission. What Neeleman & Persand (1995) describe as "medical materialism" was manifested by one of the fathers of English psychiatry, Henry Mandsley, when he wrote that, "The corporeal or the material is the fundamental fact—the mental or the spiritual only its effect." This emphasis on the physical basis for mental disorders has been another contributor to the trend in twentieth century psychiatry to devalue the importance of spirituality.

The American Psychiatric Association has given some recognition to the importance of religion and spirituality for many patients by incorporating "Religious or Spiritual Problem" among the "Additional Conditions That May Be a Focus of Clinical Attention" in its *Diagnostic and Statistical Manual* (DSM-IV) (American Psychiatric Association, 1994). Of course DSM-IV is a cataloguing of disorders; little attention has been given in mainstream psychiatry to religious faith as a source of strength, religious affiliation as an important source of social support or belief in transcendent reality as something that provides meaning and motivation in a person's life.

As psychiatrists have often treated religion with disdain or neglect, religious people have often treated psychiatry with caution or distrust. They accuse psychiatrists of materialistic or reductionistic approaches to understanding the human condition. Some perceive psychiatry to be anti-religious and fear that a psychiatric therapist may try to undermine the beliefs that are precious to them. Religious people sometimes resist what they perceive to be a system that tries to explain away spiritual truth in psychological terms, or that tries to cover up a spiritual problem by "drugging" the patient. In instances where they believe that people's problems are more spiritual than psychological or medical, spiritual interventions rather than psychological or medical approaches to solving them are believed to be appropriate. In some extreme cases psychiatry has been branded as actually being oppressive and anti-religious. In this sense, some religious groups have been part of the anti-psychiatry movement which has increased the stigma associated with psychiatry and impeded scientific progress in understanding mental disorders.

To some extent the religious distrust of psychiatry is based on ignorance. Psychiatry has not been good at explaining itself to the public, whose perceptions are largely based on fictional portrayals and aging stereotypes. To some extent, however, the distrust is justified: psychiatrists have in general been ill informed about the importance of spirituality in their patients' lives. The level of distrust may also be exacerbated by psychiatry's increasing scientific base. As knowledge of the brain mechanisms underlying mental diseases accrues, psychiatrists enjoy a more "scientific" image. Public media emphasize this aspect of their work, and the successes of psychopharmacology, leaving the impression that psychiatrists nowadays are only interested in neurotransmitters. As psychiatrists assume a more scientific stance, the old issues of the science versus religion debate become attached to the psychiatry versus religion debate and "medical materialism" seems an apt description of our current posture.

In fact, psychiatry and religious institutions have very similar objectives. They promote healthy lives and supportive relationships, quality of life, strong families, trust, integrity, personal growth and freedom from anxiety. Hope and optimism are valued, as are mutual support and the peaceful resolution of conflicts. A great deal of psychiatrists' work in treating patients with anxiety and depression, what Frank & Frank (1991) describe as demoralization, involves helping them deal with issues arising from their values and motivations. They struggle with questions such as Why do I feel a failure? How do I relate to my spouse in a way that leads to a healthier relationship? Why am I bored with my life? Why am I always struggling? Why do people treat me the way they do? These are questions for which people often seek answers from religion also.

Practitioners of scientific medicine would do well to reflect that from ancient times, caring for the sick and healing disease has been an important religious function. In Europe and America many of the health care institutions that are most prestigious today were founded originally by religious groups or by individuals as an expression of their religious faith. In many societies even today, spiritual approaches to healing are predominant. What is more, data from the Epidemiologic Catchment Area study demonstrate that today many Americans with diagnosable psychiatric disorders seek help from clergy as well as, or instead of, getting treatment from a mental health professional (Larson *et al.*, 1988). Unfortunately in most cases there is little communication between these care-providing professionals. Clearly psychiatry and religion have much to gain from collaborating and developing better understanding of each other's concepts and methods.

Spirituality and Religion

We have a limited vocabulary in psychiatry to discuss spirituality and religion. They are not synonymous. The Merriam-Webster dictionary defines spirit as an "Animating or vital principle held to give life to physical organisms." Thomason & Brody (1999) reflect a broader and deeper understanding in writing that spirituality may be thought of as "that which gives meaning to life and draws one to transcendence, to whatever is larger than or goes beyond the limits of the individual human lifetime." People who do not espouse any religion may nonetheless have a spiritual dimension to their lives. They may believe that there are spiritual realities underlying the material world, without accepting any particular system of religious beliefs. Many people who consider themselves spiritual have a sense of transcendent reality or ultimate purpose that they would not necessarily call "God." Alcoholics Anonymous and related "12-step" groups refer to a "Higher Power," without being explicit as to what that actually means. People may find all sorts of things sacred: the natural environment, the bonds of matrimony and friendship, or human life itself. Many people agree that there is more to human experience than physiology and psychology can comprehend, and reject materialistic values, but do not turn to theology for explanations. Some of these, seeking a way to understand and express their spirituality, turn to ancient belief systems, others turn to "New Religious Movements" (Barker, 1997). At the most fundamental level, spirituality gives an individual a sense of ultimate meaning and trust—what Küng . . . refers to as a *Standpunkt*. For some people this is barely articulated and is assumed, almost from birth—"I am a Muslim," or "I am a Sikh," or "I am a Jehovah's Witness,"—with all that this simple statement implies in terms of behavior, motivations and values. For others this sense of meaning and purpose is attained through some type of conversion. For some it comes easily, for others it requires struggle.

Religion aims to lead people to higher levels of spirituality through individual and communal participation in worship and practice. Religion might be defined in terms of adherence to a system of spiritual beliefs and/or participation in a community of faith and practice. A person derives his or her religious viewpoint from family and community influences, teaching of doctrines by family or religious institutions, personal reactions to these teachings, participation in rituals and ultimately in some form of personal commitment to divine reality and to a structured religious community.

Religion is significant for a variety of reasons in many people's lives. At one level, the social support dimension of religious practice is of great importance to most religious people. Participation in the worship and other activities of a church or temple can contribute to a sense of community, can provide both instrumental and emotional support in times of trouble and can add to a sense of personal security and self-confidence. Many churches or other religious bodies understand the need of sick people for comfort and support and make it a practice to visit them and provide material help. As Harrison *et al.*, discuss . . . an extensive literature exists on the variety of ways in which religion aids in coping with adversity. At another level, the benefits of specific religious practices such as prayer and meditation in enhancing health have been documented in a growing body of empirical studies. There is increasing evidence that people who pray are healthier and recover from illness better than those who do not pray. The mechanisms involved are not clear. Whether the benefit comes from enhanced coping mechanisms or in some other way remains to be determined. Ritual is also an element whose importance in religion and in many aspects of life including medical practice, should not be underestimated. Sociologists since Durkheim (1912) have documented the importance of ritual in religion and healing. Rituals set the stage for something important to occur; they create a connection with a long tradition and provide a sense of confidence and expectation. Some of the ritual aspects of the doctor—patient relationship have been eliminated from some modern medical practice in the interests of efficiency, but physicians and patients alike often deplore the resulting "assembly line"as being less conducive to healing.

> *There is increasing evidence that people who pray are healthier and recover from illness better than those who do not pray.*

In practice, psychiatrists often take a very superficial approach to a patient's spirituality and religion. A history is likely to include information about a person's religious affiliation, but less likely to reflect the meaning or strength of the person's faith or practice. Clearly different people who profess membership of the same religious group may have very different degrees of religious commitment. Allport (1950) first distinguished two aspects of religious life, the *intrinsic* or experiential aspect and the *extrinsic*, or institutional aspect. Its intrinsic aspect provides an inner sense of meaning, purpose and values, a relationship with a transcendent being, a sense of the sacred. It constitutes one of the major motivating forces in the believer's decisions and behavior (Koenig *et al.*, 1998).

Its extrinsic dimension encompasses a defined set of doctrines and practice and participation in a faith community. It includes prayer, study of scriptures, congregate worship, ceremony, ritual, observance of holy days and commitment of one's resources to support the activities of the religious community. Extrinsic religiosity may or may not reflect depth of intrinsic spirituality.

Waldfogel & Wolpe (1993), basing their work on that of Glock (1962), identify six dimensions of religious faith and practice: The *ideological* dimension encompasses belief in spiritual realities, personal faith and identity as a believer. The *intellectual* dimension covers the knowledge, doctrines, and theology. The *ritualistic* dimension includes participation in private or public worship, observances of holidays and special dietary or other customs. The *experiential* dimension extends beyond knowledge and ritual to a personal experience of transcendent reality. Two other dimensions deal with the impact of religion on the person's life: The *consequential* dimension includes the influence of religion on other aspects of the person's life, such as the stability of marriages or the frequency of substance abuse; and the *social* dimension incorporates the influence of the religious community, either positive or negative, on the person's well being and social adjustment.

Implications for Practice

There are a number of practical implications for psychiatrists. Many psychiatrists are not religious themselves (Neeleman & King, 1993; Shafranske, 2000) and thus do not perhaps identify with the religious or spiritual values or concerns of their patients; it therefore requires deliberate effort to be informed about the religion of their patients—an important aspect of cultural competence. Psychiatrists who are well informed about their own system of religious beliefs need to be informed also about other religions. For psychotherapists in particular, acquiring this knowledge is one step towards understanding the patient's assumptive world. The therapist can not necessarily be an expert on details of the particular system of beliefs and practice often it will be useful to allow the patient to educate the clinician.

A clinical examination should include a history of the patient's spiritual or religious faith and practice. In many cases this may be quite brief if it is not relevant to the problem that is being addressed in treatment. In other cases a more detailed history is appropriate, inquiring about religious background, current religious affiliations, practices, beliefs and the importance of these beliefs in supporting the person and in determining the person's motivations.

Therapists should be aware that patients may have spiritual or religious concerns and be open to these concerns or conflicts being expressed. A therapist may attempt to help the patient with these problems or may encourage him or her to seek advice from a religious advisor. Therapists should also be aware that while in most instances goals established for treatment will be supportive of the patient's ethical and spiritual values, very occasionally a situation may arise where traditional therapeutic goals may conflict with the values of the person's religious community. Issues of dominance in the marital relationship, or assertiveness in relationships generally, are examples of where the values of the therapist may conflict with the values of the patient's specific religious group. The therapist may need to help the patient consider to what extent these values are fundamental aspects of his or her spirituality and have the patient establish appropriate goals for therapy in light of this.

> *Psychiatrists must be careful not to intrude into a person's private spiritual world uninvited.*

However, psychiatrists must be careful not to intrude into a person's private spiritual world uninvited. They must respect patients' sincerely held views even if they are in contradiction to their own belief or lack of belief. For psychiatrists who come from evangelistic or proselytizing religious backgrounds themselves, and who may sincerely believe that a religious conversion may be the best possible outcome for their patient, the impulse to press the patient in this direction and to incorporate prayer and exhortation into their therapy may be very strong. The American Psychiatric Association issued guidelines in 1990, making clear their view that practices of this sort are unacceptable (American Psychiatric Association, 1990).

Because of the evidence that participation in religious activities is associated with better health, generally religious people should be encouraged to be active in the practice of their religion. In some cases the history may indicate that a particular person's participation may have been traumatic, anxiety-provoking or destructive in some way, in which case they may be helped in finding a more positive and supportive way of meeting their spiritual needs.

Clinicians should take advantage of the supports provided by religious communities. Pastors, priests, rabbis, pastoral counselors and others can be of great assistance to individuals in need of help; religious groups or congregations can provide both emotional and material support as well as opportunity for social interaction that is otherwise lacking in many patients' lives. In the health care context, hospital chaplains are appointed specifically to provide this type of support. Not only can chaplains contribute to patient care themselves, they can also act as a link between the patient and his or her religious community. Foskett . . . describes the chaplain's work as collaborative with the other members of the health care team in providing "soul care."

Expanding the Knowledge Base

Efforts to add to our knowledge of the interface between religion and psychiatry and how spiritual resources can be used productively and therapeutically are to be encouraged. Theoretical models have been proposed of the ways in which religion and spirituality may affect health and mental health (Levin & Chatters, 1998). These need to be tested and elaborated. Work on defining and describing spirituality needs to continue, so that colleagues in the field can converse using agreed upon concepts and a common vocabulary. This will enable better data to be gathered on the ways in which spirituality may increase resilience, aid recovery and enhance rehabilitation of people with psychiatric disorders. Models for collaboration between religious organizations and mental health services should be evaluated, particularly in the area of community care and rehabilitation (Fallot . . .). Dialogue between mental health professionals and theologians should be encouraged at several levels. At the most practical level, to help both groups: so that religious people can understand the concepts and methods of psychiatry and so that mental health professionals can learn how to work more effectively with churches and other religious organizations. At a deeper level, dialogue can explore topics such as guilt and hope which are of great interest in both spheres—as spiritual states considered important by religious people and phenomena which may become the focus of treatment in psychiatry. Promoting such dialogue can only be of benefit to both.

References

Allport, G.W. (1950). *The individual and his religion*. New York: Macmillan.

American Psychiatric Association (1990). Guidelines regarding possible conflict between psychiatrists' religious commitments and psychiatric practice. *American Journal of Psychiatry, 147,* 542.

American Psychiatric Association (1994). *Diagnostic and statistical manual of mental disorders*, 4th edition. Washington, DC: American Psychiatric Association.

Barker, E. (1997). New religions and mental health. In: D. Bhugra (Ed.), *Psychiatry and religion: context, consens and controversies*. London: Routledge.

Durkheim, E. (1912). *The elementary forms of religious life* (republished 1995). New York: Free Press.

Ellis, A. (1980). Psychotherapy and atheistic values: a response to A.E. Bergin's "Psychotherapy and religious values." *Journal of Consulting and Clinical Psychology, 48,* 635–639.

Frank, J.D. & Frank, J.B. (1991). *Persuasion and healing: a comparative study of psychotherapy*, 3rd edition. Baltimore, MD: Johns Hopkins University Press.

Freud, S. (1907). Obsessive acts and religious practices, reprinted in *Sigmund Freud: Collected Papers* (Vol. 2, pp. 25–5). New York: Basic Books, 1959.

Freud, S. (1928). A religious experience, reprinted in *Sigmund Freud: Collected*

Papers (Vol. 5, pp. 243–46). New York: Basic Books, 1959.

Gaw, A.C. (Ed.) (1993). *Culture, ethnicity and mental illness.* Washington, DC: American Psychiatric Press.

Glock, C.Y. (1962). On the study of religious commitment. *Religious Education, 57,* 898-S109.

Koenig, H.G., George, L.K. & Peterson, B.L. (1998). Religiosity and remission from depression in medically ill older patients. *American Journal of Psychiatry, 155,* 536-542.

Kong, H. (1990). *Freud and the problem of God,* enlarged edition. New Haven, CT: Yale University Press.

Larson, D.B., Hohmann, A.A., Kessler, L.G., Meador, K.G., Boyd, J.H. & McSherry, E. (1988).The couch and the cloth: the need for linkage. *Hospital and Community Psychiatry, 39,* 1064–1069.

Levin, J.S. & Chatters, L.M. (1998). Research on religion and mental health: an overview of empirical findings and theoretical issues. In: H. Koenig (Ed.), *Handbook of Religion and Mental Health.* New York: Academic Press.

McHugh, P.R. & Slavney, P.R. (1998). *The perspectives of psychiatry,* 2nd edition. Baltimore, MD: Johns Hopkins University Press.

Neeleman, J. & King, M.B. (1993). Psychiatrists' religious attitudes in relation to their clinical practice. *Acta Psychiatric Scandinavica, 88,* 420–424.

Neeleman, J. & Persaud, R. (1995).Why do psychiatrists neglect religion? *British Journal of Medical Psychology, 68,* 169–178.

Shafranske, E.P. (2000). Religious involvement and professional practices of psychiatrists and other mental health professionals. *Psychiatric Annals, 30,* 525–532.

Thomason, C.L. & Brody, H. (1999). Inclusive spirituality. *Journal of Family Practice, 48,* 96–97.

Waldfogel, S. & Wolpe, P.R. (1993). Using awareness of religious factors to enhance interventions in consultation-liaison psychiatry. *Hospital and Community Psychiatry, 44,* 473–477.

A City That Echoes Eternity[4]

BY KENNETH L. WOODWARD
NEWSWEEK, JULY 24, 2000

One man, Jesus warned, cannot serve two masters. Yet Jerusalem is sacred stone and soil to Jew and Christian and Muslim alike. A place on the map like any other city, Jerusalem exists more vividly, more powerfully, more dangerously within the longitude and latitude of the religious imagination. In that fertile region of the mind, what has already occurred in time past—the building of Solomon's temple, the crucifixion of Christ, the ascension of the Prophet Muhammad—is also promise of what is to come, "when time shall be no more." Among all the cities of the earth, only Jerusalem is seen as the locus of redemption and final judgment. For that reason alone, it inspires the fanatic. It is a burden no merely civil administration should ever have to bear. But short of that eschatological moment, Jerusalem seems to be always searching for respite from political tension, that it might live up to the meaning of its name: City of Peace.

To know what Jerusalem means to the three great monotheisms is to realize that politics alone can bring only a provisional kind of peace. Jews have the oldest identification with the city—and the Bible, which mentions Jerusalem 667 times, for their witness. In the background is God's promise of land and progeny to Abraham, His obedient servant. In the Book of Exodus, that promise takes the specific form of Canaan—the Holy Land—for the wandering tribes of Israel. King David made Jerusalem his capital and there, some 30 centuries ago, Solomon built the first temple. The exile of the Jews to Babylon only made the yearning for Jerusalem more intense. "If I forget you, O Jerusalem," wrote the Psalmist, "let my right hand wither." A second temple was built by King Herod, only to be destroyed in A.D. 70 by the Romans. What remains of the Western wall is now Judaism's holiest shrine. Jerusalem, wrote Abraham Joshua Heschel right after the Israeli occupation of the city in 1967, is "a city of witness, an echo of eternity." It is also a city of waiting, the place where the messiah, when he comes, will rebuild the temple. To die in Jerusalem, pious Jews believe, is to be assured of atonement.

For Christians, the messiah has already come and atonement has been accomplished in the person of Jesus. Jerusalem is where he suffered, died and rose again in glory—and where he will return to judge the living and the dead. It is also the city where the Last Supper was celebrated and where, at Pentecost, the church itself was born. As a place of Christian pilgrimage, Jerusalem has no equal. Medieval maps place it at the center of the universe (as did Dante), and paintings show medieval Jerusalem descending as the heavenly city to come. Today pilgrims can touch the rock where Jesus was crucified and, under the same church roof, the tomb where he was buried. The cross is gone, but in the Christian iconography, it continues to be the axis mundi connecting earth with heaven in the sacred drama of redemption.

Map No. 3854
UNITED NATIONS
October 1994

Department of Public
Information
Cartographic Section

For Muslims, Jerusalem is the third holiest place, after Mecca and Medina. To Muhammad, it was the city of the holy prophets who had preceded him. And so, before Mecca became the center of the Islamic universe, Muhammad directed all Muslims to bow for prayer toward Jerusalem. According to later interpretations of a passage in the Qur'an, Muhammad himself made a mystical "night flight" to Jerusalem aided by the angel Gabriel. From there, on the very rock where Abraham had offered his son as a sacrifice (now the shrine of the Dome of the Rock, atop the Temple Mount), Muhammad ascended a ladder to the throne of Allah. This ascension confirmed the continuity between Muhammad and all previous prophets and messengers of God, including Jesus, in a lineage going back to Adam. It also established a divine connection between Mecca and Jerusalem.

Thus, for billions of believers who may never see it, Jerusalem remains a city central to their sacred geography. This is why the future of the city is not just another Middle Eastern conflict between Arabs and Jews. From a purely secular perspective, of course, the shrines dear to Jews, Christians and Muslims are precious tourist attractions, and as such important sources of revenue. But Jerusalem is not some kind of Disneyland of the spirit. Both Israel and the Palestinians have real roots in the Holy Land, and both want to claim Jerusalem as their capital. The United Nations, supported by the Vatican, would have the city internationalized and under its jurisdiction. The issue, however, is not merely one of geopolitics. There will be no enduring solution to the question of Jerusalem that does not respect the attachments to the city formed by each faith. Whoever controls Jerusalem will always be constrained by the meaning the city has acquired over three millenniums of wars, conquest and prophetic utterance. Blessed or cursed, Jerusalem is built with the bricks of the religious imagination. Were this not so, Jerusalem would be what it has never been: just another city on a hill.

Pope John Paul II[5]

By R. Scott Appleby
Foreign Policy, Summer 2000

Is Pope John Paul II a progressive champion of human freedoms or an authoritarian throwback to an antiquated Christianity? Although the pontiff's profound influence on international geopolitics has captured headlines, John Paul's enduring legacy may be his reshaping of the Roman Catholic Church's global presence through cultural politicking and unprecedented outreach to other faiths.

The Pope Was a Central Player in the Defeat of Communism

Indisputable. By the late 1970s, the conditions necessary for a popular revolt against the Soviet-sponsored regime in Poland were in place: economic stagnation, state persecution of intellectual and religious leaders, and a series of workers' strikes and student protests. However, the catalyst—the "sufficient cause"—that led to the actual revolution was none other than the charismatic former actor, poet, philosopher, mystic, and social activist Karol Wojtyla, who, as Pope John Paul II, helped inspire the formation of Solidarity—the first independent trade union in the communist world. Solidarity was central to the downfall of Polish communism and propelled a domino effect throughout the East bloc. Even former Soviet Premier Mikhail Gorbachev acknowledged in 1992 that "everything that happened in Eastern Europe in these last few years would have been impossible without this pope."

Wojtyla had prepared for this role throughout much of his life. During the German occupation of Poland, he belonged to a clandestine cultural resistance movement that sought to protect Polish Jews from Nazi persecution. He also directed and acted in patriotic, revolutionary plays as part of an underground theater group, while studying theology in secret. Thirty-two years after his ordination as a Roman Catholic priest, Karol Wojtyla returned to his homeland in 1979 as Pope John Paul II. During open-air masses and other events, millions of Poles saw or heard their native son challenge the moral premise of the totalitarian system, demand freedom for the church, and affirm the right of workers to organize. In subsequent visits, John Paul chided the Polish premier for his

5. Reproduced in entirety with permission from *Foreign Policy* # 119 (Summer 2000). Copyright © 2000 by the Carnegie Endowment for International Peace.

regime's human rights abuses and reminded workers that "solidarity" means that burdens are carried together, in community—not through the class struggle promoted by Marxists.

Such direct appeals broke with traditional Vatican policy, which in the past had emphasized official dealings with sovereign powers, either through concordars or confrontations [see box on page 33]. However, John Paul recognized that in the emerging milieu of global communications, the church would have a greater impact by operating in civil society rather than solely in alliance with or in opposition to nation-states. The pope carried his message directly to the masses—not only in Poland but in Hungary and the former Czechoslovakia as well. Beyond Eastern Europe, John Paul reached out to peoples struggling under oppressive regimes in Latin America, Asia, and Africa.

Of course, the pope must rely on the cardinals, bishops, priests, and laity to implement Catholic social teaching after his galvanizing but brief appearances. In Poland, as elsewhere in Eastern Europe, revolutionary euphoria soon gave way to partisan rancor as religious and political leaders jockeyed for position in the postcommunist state. Ironically, the Polish church—a source of unity and moral leadership during the resistance—later seemed to revert to more sectarian and authoritarian behavior.

John Paul II Supports Western Capitalism

Not really. The pope's abhorrence of communism does not translate into an uncritical embrace of the free market. A champion of labor and the traditional nuclear family, John Paul II has been highly critical of capitalism. His major statement on this theme came in 1991, in the encyclical *Centesimus Annus* ("In the Hundredth Year"). Guided by the belief that culture is prior to politics and economics, the pope has argued time and again that democratic politics and market economies must be disciplined if humanity is to flourish. John Paul II endorses a form of capitalism that is unfamiliar (and anathema) to most Wall Street denizens—one that places the economy "at the service of human freedom . . . and which sees it as a particular aspect of that freedom, the core of which is ethical and religious." Although the pope has explicitly rejected the notion of a Catholic "Third Way," some observers argue that John Paul II has outpaced British Prime Minister Tony Blair and U.S. President Bill Clinton in blazing an alternative path to a more humane global economic condition.

The hoarding of wealth by the West and the inequality between the developed North and the underdeveloped South have been constant themes of John Paul's pontificate. The pope believes that unregulated capitalism—crippled by its obsession with material wealth—is prone to the same social ills that plagued atheistic communist societies: divorce, alcoholism, crime, and a general disregard

The Vatican's Cold Warriors

Excerpts from "Papal Foreign Policy" (*Foreign Policy*, Spring 1990), by J. Bryan Hehir, chair of the executive committee of Harvard Divinity School:

Pius XII (1939–1958) was profoundly impressed by the danger of communist doctrine and policies . . . . [He] placed the full weight of Catholic teaching and policy against the USSR and its allied governments . . . . While careful reading of Pius XII's teaching reveals a desire not to be simply a voice of the West, the church's de facto posture translated into religious and moral support for the Western alliance in its struggle with the East . . . .

John XXIII (1958–1963) changed the atmosphere of Vatican-Soviet relations by moving from containment to limited engagement. During the Cuban missile crisis, he responded to signals from both sides that intervention by the pope could help legitimate de-escalation of the confrontation without severe loss of face. His messages to both President John Kennedy and Soviet leader Nikita Khrushchev were credited with doing just that. He received Khrushchev's son-in-law, despite much internal opposition in the church bureaucracy, and he accepted the Balzan peace prize from Khrushchev . . . .

Paul VI (1963–1978) had spent virtually his entire priesthood in the diplomatic service; like John XXIII, he had become convinced in the 1950s of the need for an opening to the East . . . . [He] held several visits during his pontificate with then Soviet Foreign Minister Andrei Gromyko . . . . By the 1970s Paul VI was taking positions that were critical of the policies of both superpowers. Without announcing major departures from previous policies, he moved the Catholic Church in a series of small steps to a position of having contacts with both major powers, formal relationships with neither, and a record of critical commentary about both . . . .

John Paul II (1978–) demonstrates both continuity and change in papal policy. His teaching on human rights, economic justice, and international order develops ideas from the eras of Pius XII through Paul VI. But his historical experience, his philosophical convictions, and his personal style of pastoral leadership and diplomacy have all set John Paul II's pontificate apart from his predecessors . . . . [T]his pope engages world leaders with a more explicitly geopolitical analysis than his predecessors; he speaks more openly about power and how it should be directed and contained . . . .

for human life. The self-absorption of Western consumerism, he asserts, weakens the traditional family no less than communism's denial of the family's right to private property. In his 1995 encyclical *Evangelium Vitae* ("The Gospel of Life"), John Paul decried this fundamental moral failure to recognize and protect human dignity as symptomatic of a "culture of death" infecting modem developed societies.

The Church Has Shrunk Under John Paul II

No. The Catholic Church is growing significantly in Africa and Asia and more than holding its own in North America [see chart on page 34]. The recent losses in Latin America are reversible and not nearly as apocalyptic as some evangelical Protestant missionaries like to claim. However, the church faces a severe crisis of ministry that eventually may lead to overall declines in Catholic ranks.

Even as Catholics increased in number from 660 million in 1977 to more than 1 billion in 1997, the number of clergy dropped over the same period [see chart on page 35]. Worldwide, the number of priests per 100,000 Catholics declined from 74 in 1965 to 40 in 1995. In particular, the number of priests and nuns has plummeted in Europe and declined in North America—historically the sources of most Catholic vocations. These developments have led many theologians and some bishops to propose an official theology of lay ministry, reinforced by adequate financial planning to support full-time, professionally trained lay ministers. However, rather than heed these calls, John Paul II has bet the church's future on the recruitment of new priests.

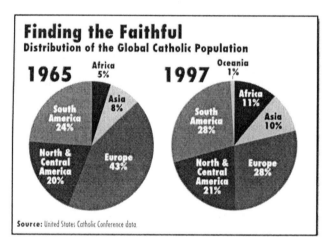

Finding the Faithful
Distribution of the Global Catholic Population

1965 Africa 5%
South America 24%
Asia 8%
North & Central America 20%
Europe 43%

1997 Oceania 1%
Africa 11%
South America 28%
Asia 10%
North & Central America 21%
Europe 28%

Source: United States Catholic Conference data.

This gamble has paid off in South America, Africa, and Asia, where the number of seminarians has grown significantly during the last quarter century. Even so, the far more accelerated growth of the laity foretells a "full pews, empty altars" scenario worldwide. The church's effectiveness as a force for social justice operating in civil society will diminish if its educational and formative mission wanes. Latin America's experience serves as a cautionary tale; the losses there will be duplicated elsewhere if the imbalance persists between an elite but understaffed clergy and eager but inadequately trained and underpaid lay ministers. The future may reveal a new face for the global Catholic Church, with African and Asian missionary priests seeking to evangelize the masses throughout Europe and the Americas.

The Pope Squashed Liberation Theology

He tried. The liberation theology movement emerged in the 1960s and 1970s and sought to reinterpret the Christian faith from the perspective of the poor struggling to overcome oppression. Led by Latin American theologians such as Peru's Gustavo Gutiérrez and El Salvador's Jon Sobrino, proponents of liberation theology employed "Christian-Marxist" analysis and a liberationist reading of the Bible to highlight the ideologies they saw as perpetuating unjust economic and social systems in the developing world.

Many bishops, as well as the pope, acknowledged the failures of the church in Latin America to protect the material, social, and political interests of the poor; indeed, in ministering to the landowning elite, the church had often positioned itself on the wrong side of this struggle. Nonetheless, the pope's lifelong animus toward communism and his rejection of the Marxist call for class conflict shaped his evaluation of liberation theology. During a trip to Central America in 1983, John Paul explicitly rejected the notion of a partisan and "popular" class-based church as exclusive and narrow (i.e., unsuitably catholic), as well as divisive and potentially insubordinate to the hierarchy (i.e., unsuitably Roman Catholic).

Over time, the Vatican gave more qualified support to the concerns—though not the prescriptions—of liberation theologians. In 1984, the Vatican issued the *Instruction on Certain Aspects of the Theology of Liberation*. Although this document acknowledged that the liberation of the poor is at the heart of the church's mission, it stated that the eradication of political arid economic injustice could never proceed apart from the conversion of the human heart—a religious, not political, task. And in *Instruction on Christian Free-*

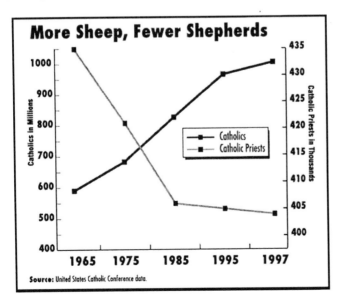

More Sheep, Fewer Shepherds

Catholics in Millions

Catholic Priests in Thousands

Legend: Catholics; Catholic Priests

1965   1975   1985   1995   1997

Source: United States Catholic Conference data.

dom and Liberation, issued in 1986, the Vatican endorsed the non-violent struggle for human freedom, accomplished in "solidarity" with the poor. It acknowledged the systematic abuse of human rights by totalitarian states and affirmed the liberationist goal of replacing dictatorships and oligarchies with democratic governments.

Despite these pronouncements, John Paul's critics on the left continue to view him as an opponent of liberation theology. They point to the pope's support of Opus Dei, a traditionalist religious community and church-reform movement originating in Spain. Impressed with Opus Dei's goal of fostering rigorous lay discipleship, the pope elevated the group to the status of a personal prelature in 1982, enabling it to circumvent the authority of local bishops and govern itself. Critics charge that Opus Dei has encouraged or pursued alliances with right-wing political figures or governments, such as the Franco regime in Spain. Journalist Penny Lernoux noted that after Francisco Franco's death in 1975, Opus Dei "expanded to other countries in Europe, and to the United States and Latin America, gaining political influence in the latter, particularly in Pinochet's Chile . . . . Opus Dei members and sympathizers supported the CIA-backed coup that overthrew Chilean President Salvador Allende, and one of them, Hernán Cubillos, became General Pinochet's foreign minister."

The Vatican Is More Interested in Blocking Birth Control than Stopping Genocide

It's not so simple. John Paul II has befuddled many secular observers with his seemingly confused mix of socially progressive and socially regressive attitudes. Some wonder how a pope who champions human rights and personal dignity could have inaugurated a global Catholic campaign against the 1994 U.N. Conference on Population and Development in Cairo, opposing measures designed to curb the developing world's population crisis—a crisis that heaps untold suffering upon the very people the pope claims to defend. Indeed, John Paul sent a letter of protest to every head of state and the United Nations secretary general and instructed the Vatican's representatives in Cairo to mobilize support against the conference's program of action. Detractors contrast this zeal with Catholicism's historical failure to prevent terrible crimes against humanity, including instances of genocide, some of which were committed in the deluded conviction that they were expressions of the will of God or the church.

Yet there is an internal logic to the church's position on the sanctity of life. John Paul II sees artificial birth control as an expression of radical Western individualism run amok, threatening to detach men and women from the family, and the family from the church. The pope believes that in order to promote openness to and respect for life in all its phases, the church must protect life where it is most vulnerable: at conception. "Free choice" removed from moral grounding becomes a recipe for the widespread violation of human life—be it through abortion, euthanasia, war, or genocide. On a fundamental level, therefore, the church believes it is addressing a whole range of human rights issues when it seeks to preserve life in the womb.

In practice, however, the church's focus on birth control can sometimes obscure other important moral considerations. There is no getting around the moral failures of Catholic leaders who were silent during the Holocaust and complicit in the eruption of genocidal fury in Rwanda in 1994—to name only two of the major catastrophes of the century now past. John Paul II has been publicly apologetic for these failures [see sidebar on page 38]. In particular, he has apologized on many occasions for Catholic expressions of anti-Semitism, some of which, he has acknowledged, were rooted in distorted interpretations of Christian doctrine propagated by Catholics in positions of authority.

> *On a fundamental level, . . . the church believes it is addressing a whole range of human rights issues when it seeks to preserve life in the womb.*

Roman Catholic structures have also failed the church at crucial junctures. The Vatican bureaucracy in Rome—known as the Curia—coordinates Roman Catholic policy by drawing upon intelligence reports from bishops, papal nuncios, and other apostolic delegates around the world. While these networks often serve Catholicism extremely well, at times the system breaks down or fails to respond quickly to warning signs emanating from troubled churches or regions. Bickering and outright intraecclesial conflict can and does occur, especially in regions beset by severe ethnic, tribal, or class divisions. In Rwanda, many priests and other Catholic religious leaders, when faced with life-or-death choices, chose their Tutsi or Hutu tribe over their "universalist" Roman Catholic identity. Or, what is more likely and more depressing, they conflated the two.

The Pope's Holy Land Pilgrimage Was a Calculated Political Statement

Yes and no. Predictably, media accounts of John Paul's pilgrimage to the Holy Land in March 2000 highlighted the region's volatile political environment, as analysts looked for any misstep that might reveal the pope's personal leanings. John Paul's remarks

---

Not Quite Mea Culpa

Recognizing that Catholicism has been at times a force for ill as well as for good, Pope John Paul II has engaged in a series of dramatic and unprecedented acts of public repentance. Either the pope himself or church agencies under his direction have apologized for fostering discrimination against women, promoting and practicing anti-Semitism, and resorting to violence—in cases like the Crusades and the Inquisition—to propagate or "defend" the faith. But how can a pope apologize for the sins of a church that proclaims itself infallible? Three considerations may illuminate John Paul's reasoning and motivations.

First, the Catholic Church has clearly changed its self-understanding since Cardinal Bellarmine—a key 16th-century Catholic leader—described it as "an eternal, perfect, society," spotless and free of sin. By contrast, the Second Vatican Council (1962–65) depicted the church as "at one and the same time holy and ever in need of purification," acknowledging the presence of both sin and grace throughout church history. In this respect, John Paul II is simply emphasizing that the church is human as well as divine and is therefore vulnerable to temptations and pitfalls.

Second, the pope is careful to distinguish between a "perfect society" and its imperfect citizens. He will not apologize for the papacy or the church per se, but only for the actions of individual Catholics—including particular priests, nuns, and bishops-who sinned egregiously at certain times in the church's history. In recent statements on the Holocaust, for example, the Vatican underscores the errors of the Catholic Church's "sons and daughters"—not of the church itself or of Pope Pius XII.

Furthermore, popes may invoke infallibility only when they address matters of religious doctrine, such as the divinity of Christ or the Immaculate Conception of Mary. Since John Paul's recent apologies do not address such issues, they fail to contradict the dogma of infallibility.

Ultimately, John Paul II sees the millennium as a turning point in the history of the world and of the church—and as a time for change in the human heart. His statements seeking forgiveness are made by a person who is himself a forgiver, a person who actively seeks reconciliation, as he did with his own would-be assassin Mehmet Ali Agca.

---

and itinerary certainly were politically calculated: He "kissed the soil" of the Palestinian West Bank as well as that of Jewish Galilee and visited Jewish, Muslim, and Christian sacred sites in Jerusalem; he identified with the human suffering and religious and spiritual aspirations on every side of the conflict—the Palestinians as well as the Israelis, the Muslims as well as the Christians. On specific political issues, however, John Paul did little more than endorse the facts in the field as accepted by the major players prior to his arrival. His few overt political references—such as to the Palestinian right to a "homeland" (he disappointed those who wanted him to use the word "state")—were notably cautious.

Indeed, John Paul was not focused primarily on politics. He was hunting bigger game: cross-cultural and interreligious dialogue. His pilgrimage was the dramatic capstone to a series of bold gestures and policy reversals undertaken over the course of his pontificate, seeking to reconcile Christianity with Judaism and—perhaps to a lesser extent—with Islam.

John Paul has signaled his desire to repair relations with the Jewish people in many ways. He was the first pope to set foot in the Synagogue of Rome, where on April 13, 1986, he affirmed that the church condemned anti-Semitism "by anyone—I repeat: by anyone." He spoke of the "common heritage" of Jews and Christians and closed the meeting by reciting Psalm 118 in Hebrew. The pope established diplomatic relations with Israel in 1993; five years later, the Vatican issued the historic document *We Remember: A Reflection on the Shoah*. Although the document stopped short of mentioning Christian "coresponsibility" for the tragedy of the Holocaust as some had hoped, it acknowledged that Nazi persecution of the Jews was facilitated by the anti-Jewish prejudices of some Christians.

These initiatives notwithstanding, Catholic-Jewish relations have been tense at times during John Paul's tenure, especially in the highly charged arena of religious symbolism. For example, the pope's 1998 canonization of Edith Stein (a Jewish convert to Catholicism who was killed by the Nazis) was interpreted by some in the Jewish community as an offensive attempt to "Christianize" the Holocaust. Similarly, John Paul's audience with right-wing Austrian leader Jorg Haider—scheduled for late 2000—will likely spur much controversy, as did the pope's meeting with former Austrian President Kurt Waldheim in 1987.

The Pope Has Made It More Difficult for Women to Join the Priesthood

In the short term, yes. John Paul II has not apologized for continuing to exclude women from the priesthood. His views stem from his reading of the New Testament and the apostolic tradition, from which he concludes that Jesus chose not to include his female disciples among the inner core of apostles. The pope claims that this functional inequality does not undermine the personal equality of men and women, and that dignity of women is not violated by their exclusion from the ordained priesthood. The church is not a democracy, and the priesthood is not a matter of personal advancement or basic right; it is a call to service and sacrifice. The pope believes women have a different calling. Although "the specific spousal relationship of marriage" is not the source of the woman's special dignity, "God entrusts the human being to her in a special way," the pope observes, through childbirth and the nurturing of children.

Other Christian denominations allow women to become priests; for example, the Church of England reversed its ban on female clergy in 1992, and five years later had ordained nearly 2,000 women. Indeed, many Catholics—both men and women—reject the pope's teachings on this matter, finding more than a trace of condescension in his arguments. Ironically, however, John Paul may have done more to further the cause of female ordination than he ever intended. In his 1995 *Letter to Women*, the pope apologized for recurrent sexism in the church, and for systematic discrimination against women both in the church and in the larger patriarchal society whose attitudes the church has helped shape. He also lamented the church's consistent failure to honor women's critical roles in building up the church through their witness to the faith and through the founding, administering, and staffing of countless Catholic schools, hospitals, orphanages, and religious orders. John Paul holds aloft the Virgin Mary as the model for all women and men, emphasizing not only her "maternal love" but her thirst for justice and the liberation of the poor. In fact, John Paul has often called for Roman Catholicism to become a "Marian" church. Although his refusal to ordain women undermines the force of these statements, a future pope may well quote reams of John Paul's own writings—in support of a reversal of the ban on women priests.

The Next Pope Will Be Radically Different from John Paul II

Unlikely. Speculation on papal succession is invariably a doomed exercise. Few predicted the election of Wojtyla in 1978, much less the stunning accession of Angelo Roncalli, the little-known Patriarch of Venice, who in 1958 became John XXIII and proceeded to revolutionize the Catholic Church by convoking the Second Vatican Council. Nonetheless, the next pope will more than likely continue and extend some of John Paul's key policies. By his 20th anniversary as pope in 1998, John Paul had named 101 of the 115 cardinals eligible to vote in a conclave, as well as more than half of the Catholic Church's 4,200 bishops. These princes and bishops of the church are intensely loyal to their patron and are cut along the same authoritarian and traditional lines. (Support for the ban on artificial birth control, for instance, has often been said to be a litmus test for bishops appointed on John Paul's watch.) And in 1996, John Paul changed the procedure for electing a pope, so that the next pontiff will be chosen by a simple majority rather than a two-thirds majority. This change makes it much less likely that a deadlocked conclave will turn to a surprise choice, as occurred with Roncalli.

Italians no longer dominate the College of Cardinals, increasing the chances that the next pope will be drawn from the developing world—quite possibly Africa. Experience in interreligious and crosscultural dialogue is also a likely characteristic of any successor. Whoever follows John Paul II will probably be concerned with defending religious freedom and pluralism, as well as engaging new ideological and intellectual issues that challenge the Christian worldview, such as the complex moral questions raised by advances in biotechnology and genetic engineering.

Russian Renewal[6]

By Michael Bourdeaux
Christian Century, April 4, 2001

When he became president of Russia last year, Vladimir Putin disclosed that "when I was serving in the KGB in Germany, I always wore a cross under my shirt." Whether or not one believes this astonishing claim, there is no doubt that Putin embraces the Russian Orthodox Church as a partner in his blueprint for a strong new Russia. On his first Easter Sunday in office he declared, "The widespread celebration of Easter is visible proof of the rebirth of the spiritual foundations of our society. I believe that together with the church we will achieve the spiritual revival of a strong, prospering Russia in the 21st century."

A democratic mandate brought Putin into office, though there were accusations of vote-rigging. He rode a wave of popular support for his "solution" to the problem of Chechnya's attempted secession, a solution that might well have earned him the title—not in current usage—of the "butcher of Grozny." In that conflict, the Moscow Patriarchate stressed the duty of all young Russian males to serve in the army—thus not falling far short of implicitly condoning genocide.

The Orthodox Church's long history of validating state policy goes back to the Czarist period. Though the church consistently backed the state under communism, it clearly did so under duress and the threat of increased persecution. The accession of Mikhail Gorbachev 16 years ago freed the church from coercion. Its current alliance with Putin is voluntary.

This chorus of church and state now has new words. The Czarist national anthem proclaimed, "Powerful and sovereign, reign for glory, reign for terror to enemies, Orthodox Czar, God save the Czar!" The new Russian national anthem (to the old Soviet tune) goes, "You are unique in the world, inimitable, native land protected by God!" The author of the new words is the same Sergei Mikhalkov, now 87, who 60 years ago to the same tune wrote the words glorifying Stalin, words later adapted again as, "O Party of Lenin, the strength of the people, o communism's triumph lead us on!"

How did the new harmony between church and state come about? No one could have predicted this development when believers first threw off their shackles during Gorbachev's *perestroika*. In April

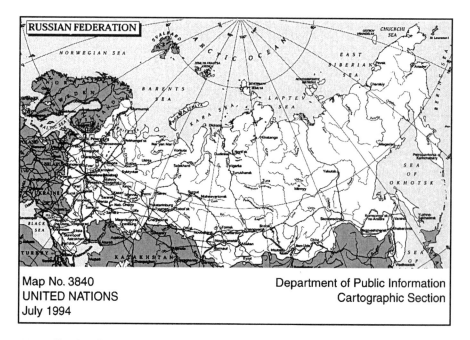

Map No. 3840
UNITED NATIONS
July 1994

Department of Public Information
Cartographic Section

1988 Gorbachev summoned the senior bishops of the Orthodox Church to the Kremlin to discuss their role in his reconstruction policy. As an inducement, he offered them the opportunity more fully to celebrate the millennium of the 988 baptism of Prince Vladimir.

The ensuing June days were intoxicating. The news media vied with each other to laud the achievements of Russian Christianity. But church leaders were unprepared for these new opportunities. There were neither books, buildings nor teachers to take advantage of the situation.

Gorbachev's second promise to the church leadership was to prepare a new law on religion. Experts outside as well as inside the Soviet Union were consulted. The new law, passed in September 1990, represented a total reversal of fortunes not only for the Russian Orthodox Church but for all other religious creeds. It gave believers virtually complete religious liberty. Stalin's nefarious 1929 law, which had completely subjugated the churches, was abolished, along with the dreaded Council for Religious Affairs, the arm of the KGB which had "supervised" the lives of believers. The U.S. had provided Russia with the model for a true separation of church and state, such as Russia had never known. And the Orthodox Church was given all the freedom it needed to rebuild its shattered institutions.

But it was not long before sentiments and policies changed. The Soviet Union was inundated with foreign evangelists and missionaries commanding technological resources unimaginable to a church just emerging from captivity. People began to blame the liberality of the 1990 law for the onslaught of foreign missionaries. The Moscow patriarch lobbied behind the scenes for the reintroduction of controls. During the ensuing debate, the old communists sensed an opportunity to reverse Gorbachev's policy and regain lost jobs in the offices which monitored religious activities. President Bill Clinton and Pope John Paul II both intervened with President Boris Yeltsin in 1997 when they saw drafts of a new law which threatened to negate the freedoms of the non-Orthodox and move toward reestablishing Orthodoxy as the state religion.

Eventually Yeltsin signed a new law which, while maintaining a theoretical separation of church and state, protected the Russian Orthodox Church and, surprisingly, the other "traditional" religions of Russia—Islam, Judaism and Buddhism—from the supposedly foreign incursions of the Protestant and Catholic churches. The fact that there have been Protestants in Russia since the 17th century and Catholics for even longer made for confusion and the probability of bureaucratic intrusion. The law did not provide grounds for banning the incursion of foreign missionaries, though that had obviously been one of its key intentions. The hated provision of mandatory registration was reestablished, with advantage conferred on those bodies which had legally existed during the Brezhnev period. This discriminates not only against such groups as the Salvation Army and the Jehovah's Witnesses but even against the Catholics, whose only official presence at that time had been one church in Moscow. While all this was going on, Yeltsin was appearing in church at major festival times and inviting Patriarch Alexsy II to bless the great occasions of state.

Putin has no interest in revising this law. A move to repeal it will arise only if enforcement becomes brutal. Until then, we can expect messy and confused local wrangles about registration, about the return of former church property and about the presence of foreign missionaries.

The Orthodox Church's willingness to enlist the state on its behalf, and in turn to offer sacral endorsement of the state's policies, has deep psychological and historical roots. It is impossible for the outsider to understand the depth of the humiliation endured by the church during the 70 years of its captivity under communism. After exerting influence on state affairs under Czarist rule, the church found itself overnight banished from public life, its property confiscated, its worship repressed, and its role in the educational system ended. Most of its hierarchy, as well as thousands of parish clergy, monks and nuns lost their liberty, and many lost their lives. Only those willing to submit to the state survived.

The KGB archives, opened fleetingly after the collapse of the Soviet Union, proved what many Russians had known but few in the West had believed: that the leaders of the Russian Orthodox Church were often forced to carry out the specific instructions of the more nefarious organs of state. Only those who toed the line were appointed to positions of authority. Many of the best priests could not even secure places in the three theological seminaries. "Spiritual formation," therefore, included being malleable enough to become, if not a KGB agent, someone ready to do the state's bidding. When the reversal of fortune came in 1997, the urge to recapture the privileges of an established church was overwhelming.

Putin needs the church to legitimate his policies. Yeltsin had struggled at personal cost to free himself from his communist past, and he fought on the front line of democracy. Putin has no such record. Therefore his embrace of the church in general and of its hierarchy in particular is part of a self-protective policy to accord himself added legitimacy.

The character of the present patriarch of Moscow, Alexsy II, reflects this convoluted church history. He was born in free Estonia in 1929, the son of a Russian mother and an aristocratic Estonian father. He saw his country suffer successively under the Red Army, the Germans and then the Soviets again. After the war the only way he could enter a theological seminary was by suppressing his nationality and any anticommunist tendencies which his experiences might have bred. When he was in his 30s the authorities recognized that his political compliance made him an ideal candidate for bishop in an area where nationalism could (and one day would) cause unrest. His reward for helping to pacify Estonia was the license to travel extensively abroad to further ecumenical contacts (Soviet style), and his elevation to metropolitan of Leningrad and eventually patriarch in 1990, the next-to-last year of Soviet power.

KGB material in the Estonian archives leaves no doubt about the patriarch's connections with the KGB. It even gives a specific date for his recruitment: February 28, 1958. He received the code name "Drozdov." The Estonian document, signed by a Colonel I. P. Karpov, head of the KGB in the republic, states: "During the period of collaboration with the organs of the KGB 'Drozdov' positively recommended himself: During secret rendezvous he was punctilious, energetic and convivial. He is well-orientated in theoretical questions of theology and the international situation. He has a willing attitude to the fulfillment of our tasks and has already provided materials deserving attention."

Other aspects of the Orthodox hierarchy are also a cause for concern. The church has always been extremely reluctant to accord any legitimacy to the views of its most forward-looking theologian, Alexander Men, known as the "apostle of church *perestroika*." Men was murdered in 1990, before his books were widely available in Russia. After his death the bishop in Yekaterinburg ordered the burning of his books, along with those of the American theologians Alexander Schmemann and John Meyendorff. (A hopeful sign that the church is changing, however, is that a group of clergy petitioned successfully for the bishop's removal, and the new bishop welcomes contact with the West.)

The late Metropolitan Ioann of St. Petersburg was an ultranationalist whose writings were explicitly anti-Semitic. Alexsy never censured him beyond saying that he did not share his views. In Moscow, Father Georgi Kochetkov was removed from his parish for attempting to introduce a translation of the Slavonic liturgy into modern Russian. Another Moscow priest lost his parish for making it a center for the city's most disadvantaged people.

Yet the Moscow Patriarchate is not the whole of the church, nor is it even typical. I was reminded of this last year when I visited Smolensk, one of the most ancient Russian cities. Smolensk embraced Christianity

> *Not one of [Moscow's] ancient chuches was left unscathed by the long years of official atheism.*

in the 11th century, while Moscow was still a village. As a guardian of Russia's western flank, the city has witnessed the passage of many armies. Napoleon was defeated here in 1812, and Germany ravaged it in 1941. In its indomitable spirit it encapsulates the essence of Russia, and it is now being extensively restored and rebuilt.

Not one of the city's ancient chuches was left unscathed by the long years of official atheism. Nothing that one would recognize as normal religious life remained. In the huge area covered by the Smolensk diocese, only 25 churches maintained some semblance of a regular pattern of worship.

But now almost all of Smolensk's churches are being restored. More than 100 have reopened, including some in Kaliningrad, in the section of the Smolensk diocese lying beyond Belarus and Lithuania—a region cut off from the rest of Russia. In the Soviet period, Kaliningrad's communists prided themselves on having established a model atheist city. Now it is full of new churches—Orthodox, Catholic and Lutheran.

The rebuilding visible everywhere in Smolensk is typical of Russia's provincial cities. Despite economic deprivation, civic pride is driving reconstruction, and the Russian Orthodox Church is playing a large part in the rebuilding. Smolensk is untypical of the provinces only insofar as it provides the most direct link between them and the Moscow Patriarchate. Its bishop, Metropolitan Kirill, is the second most influential figure in the church hierarchy. He divides his time between Smolensk and Moscow, and his responsibility as head of the Department of Foreign Relations of the Moscow Patriarchate frequently takes him abroad. Though ecumenical relations have suffered a severe blow under his leadership, he is superbly successful as a diocesan bishop.

Starting in the Gorbachev period, Kirill established close relations with the Smolensk civic authorities, which gave him a head start in his rebuilding program. He was the first bishop to receive back a substantial swathe of ecclesiastical buildings, including the episcopal palace and administrative buildings adjacent to the cathedral.

Kirill has also established a theological seminary for catechists, nurses and choir trainers in part of the administrative complex. All except one or two students are female, and they are all developing extraordinary talents under the energetic guidance of a nun, Mother Ioanna, from whom goodness and efficiency flow in equally generous measure. This is happening in a church which is not exactly known for the contribution it has made to the feminist cause—and under the watchful eye of a bishop whose conservatism has caused much disappointment on the international front.

A mile away, visible on top of a hill, is the seminary for training priests. Some 100 young men live in cramped conditions while their building is gradually being restored. Their library may be among the best of any Russian seminary—though it would pale beside its equivalent in, say, a deprived African country.

Metropolitan Kirill invited the BBC to do a broadcast from Smolensk on the Sunday before Christmas 1999, and I was asked to take part. Though there was, of course, a measure of self-promotion in

---

Many . . . martyrs had opposed the patriarchate's policy of accommodation with the Soviet regime. Thousands gave their lives for their stand.

Kirill's invitation, the reception we received was not only warm but professional and cooperative. No one asked to see our script or to listen to any of the taped material before transmission. The radio broadcast, a worship service, demonstrated the authenticity and energy of the religious life in the provincial diocese most closely under the protection of the central authorities. One has to encounter the religious energies in Smolensk as well as the political concerns in Moscow to begin to grasp today's Russian Orthodox Church.

Given the links that the church's current leaders had with the KGB, one can understand why the patriarchate's policymakers are finding it difficult to come to terms with the church's activities during the Soviet period. The worst injustice has been the church's inability to recognize the sacrifice of the martyrs under Lenin, Stalin, Khrushchev and even Brezhnev. Many of these martyrs had opposed the patriarchate's policy of accommodation with the Soviet regime. Thousands gave their lives for their stand.

The most notable center of opposition was the Solovki monastery-prison on an archipelago in the Arctic Ocean which had become virtually a death camp for the clergy and intellectuals of Czarist Russia. It prompted Alexander Solzhenitsyn's title, *The Gulag Archipelago*, for his history of the Soviet prison-camp system, which was dispersed around the U.S.S.R. like a land-bound archipelago. The most significant opposition to the church's compromise with the state in the Stalin years were the letters signed in 1927 by 17 bishops incarcerated in the Solovki prison. These letters called on the government to renounce its systematic persecution of believers, and denounced the collaborationists who claimed that the state's goals and interests were identical with those of the church.

To this day the Moscow Patriarchate (which did not exist at the time of the declaration) has never acknowledged the text or even printed it for study. Lawrence Uzzell, the director of Oxford's Keston Institute, which specializes in the study of religion in Russia, recently called on the Orthodox Church to undertake a study of the document. The possibility that his words may be heeded was suggested by the church's decision in 2000 to canonize six men who had signed the letters.

The church building is probably more essential in the Orthodox than in any other Christian tradition. This fact makes the extensive rebuilding of churches and the opening of new theological seminaries in the Russian provinces especially notable. Two thirds of the 68 dioceses of the Russian Orthodox Church, many themselves newly created or reestablished after a gap of 80 years, now have their own theological schools, and in every region churches devastated in the Soviet period are being rebuilt.

At one end of the spectrum is the Cathedral of Christ the Savior in Moscow, criticized by many for its grandiosity and expense; visible from inside the Kremlin, it replaces its predecessor, destroyed by Stalin in the 1930s. At the other end is a church in the village of Gridino, about 90 miles southeast of Moscow. Here a 70-year-old woman saw a vision of "three angels, as pretty as princesses, shining in their white raiment and lighting up my kitchen. They told me to build a church." As she trekked through the offices of administrative officialdom, Olga Fedorovna was often called mad. But she persisted, finally received permission to build the church, and then had another vision in which the angels told her where to build it. She collected donations for the bricks and mortar, but the breakthrough came when "three newly rich businessmen donated the bricks that had been destined to build their second homes in the country." The church now stands in modest splendor.

In 1995 I had an unforgettable vision of the new life of the Orthodox Church. I was in the Russian Arctic, sailing across the White Sea through a dense fog. When the fog cleared, a magnificent sight appeared on the skyline: the Solovki Monastery seemed to rise from the depths of the waters, like the Invisible City of Kitezh of Russian legend, sunk by God to escape destruction by the Tatars. According to the legend, it arises to the surface once a year, its packed churches offering songs of praise to the savior.

The vision dispelled when we arrived at the quayside. Many of the horrors of the former prison were still visible, though the reconstruction of the monastery had begun. This ruin housing the bare and fractured bones of once magnificent churches could never again become the place of pilgrimage, inspiration and learning it once had been, I thought. But the restoration has steadily progressed and may yet return it to its former glory.

Last summer I visited the Tolga Convent, on the Volga near Yaroslavl in Central Russia. Here the rebuilding of another former prison (a boys' reformatory) is proceeding at an amazing pace. Every vista is magnificent, every encounter with the nuns a torrent of warm words explaining how the convent is re vitalizing the whole countryside—not only providing work, but also spreading Christian enlightenment and education. I remembered that the great Danilov Monastery in Moscow, formerly also a juvenile prison, was restored just in time to host the Millennium of the Baptism of Russia in June 1988.

Before the end of the Gorbachev years, many bishops began to make plans for the daunting task of rebuilding seminary life. The strides they have made over the past ten years have been impressive. A useful benchmark is the remarkable ecumenical venture by the Roman Catholic agency, Aid to the Church in Need. In 1992 its founder, the Dutch Norbertine monk Werenfried van Straaten, already 79 years old, had a vision which challenged him to support the Russian Orthodox Church. His advisers settled on helping Russian Orthodox theological education as the most effective focus for this new outreach. Of the 46 theological academies, seminaries and schools in Russia, Aid to the Church in Need is now helping 26 financially.

In the Crimean city of Yalta I visited an Orthodox junior school taking pupils up to the age of ten. Here they receive a grounding in the faith from dedicated teachers. The parents want their children's Christian education prolonged through the equivalent of their high school years, which at present is financially impossible. Similar initiatives exist in Russia.

Clergy introducing innovative programs have been heavily scrutinized by the patriarchate, especially in Moscow. But even here some clergy who are daring to be more innovative are retaining their posts. Last July, in the central Moscow church of St. Cosmas and Damian, I helped organize a unique event: a tour of Russia by an English Episcopal cathedral choir. Georgi Chistyakov, one of the remarkable clergy associated with this church, invited the Exeter Cathedral Choir (boys and men, clad in scarlet cassocks) to sing a concert. The occasion was informal but also deeply spiritual. Benches to seat the audience appeared (no Orthodox churches in Russia have seats). Georgi gave a short theological reflection about the words of each selection the choir sang. A Russian radio broadcast of the concert described the choir as made up of "small English gentlemen or cardinals."

Some—perhaps most—of the graduates from the new theological seminaries are as conservative as the bishops or rectors who selected them for training, but theirs is not the only mind-set in the provincial dioceses. In 2000 I had only two opportunities for protracted conversations with young clergy, in places far distant and different from each other. Both of the men wished to see urgent reforms in the life of the church, one in its theology, the other in its order, which lays down an unbridgeable divide between married (parochial) and celibate (monastic) clergy. Individuals must decide this issue for all time before ordination; it can never be reconsidered (except in cases where the wife dies).

The far north of European Russia is showing strong signs of a religious revival in which the laity are playing a leading role, according to two researchers at Keston Institute, Sergei Filatov and Roman Lunkin. The regions they name are Karelia (formerly part of Finland), Arkhangelsk (on the White Sea, the southern extremity of the Arctic Ocean), the Komi Republic (the next area to the east) and Novgorod (further south, adjacent to St. Petersburg). This is especially remarkable because church life here was even more devastated by communism than it was in central Russia. When I toured Petrozavodsk (capital of Karelia) in the company of Father Nikolai Ozolin a few years ago, he told me that in that whole vast region only four of the formerly 400 churches, mostly wooden, had survived for worship by the beginning of the Gorbachev period.

Generalizing about the region, Filatov and Lunkin write of a rare phenomenon in the Orthodox Church: its "cooperation with the intelligentsia, university teachers, writers, artists and museum staff and widespread involvement of teachers in the work of Sunday schools. The atmosphere in these regions, where culture and education have always enjoyed pride of place, and also the attitude of the diocesan leadership help to reduce the barrier between the intelligentsia and the church."

A building firm run by a believer, Yevgeni Kuzkin, supports a religious and educational center in Petrozavodsk, where he participates in the selection of teaching staff. The courses themselves are run by the church, with significant participation by the diocesan bishop. Would-be catechists can study for three years, during which time they can explore their vocation for the priesthood. There is a lively interchange with secular institutes of higher education.

Ozolin, who was born and studied in Paris, brings his knowledge of the rest of Europe to Russia's far north. He has set up an educational project in conjunction with the directors of the Kizhi museum, a remarkable collection of ancient wooden churches on an island accessible from Petrozavodsk. He also works with Aid to the Church in Need, advising the charity on the distribution of its aid over this huge and deprived region. Ozolin and others also receive help from neighboring Finland, where the Lutherans (as well as the small Orthodox community) care intensely about Karelia. It may be the most ecumenical region in the whole of Russia.

In Arkhangelsk a businessman, Dmitri Zenchenko, supports the church-sponsored Children's Aid Foundation and the Medicines for Children program. A mathematician in Syktyvkar (capital of the Komi Republic), Yuri Yekishev, has revived the Boy Scout movement with the help of the church.

The rebirth of monastic life is of special significance throughout these northern regions. A new generation of monks is involving itself widely in educational and social projects, as well as spiritual counseling for the many visiting pilgrims, just as monks did in medieval Russia. As monastic communities pushed further north, partly to avoid the press of the crowds they attracted, they opened up the economy of new regions. People flocked to follow them, creating new work in field and forest to support both themselves and the monastic communities.

Despite the problems confronting the Russian Orthodox Church today, and the issues that cloud its past, many positive things are happening. Perhaps, through them, it will find the confidence to embark on a new era, in which it engages with society at all levels and cooperates with its friends around the world.

A Faith with Many Faces[7]

BY DAVID R. SANDS
INSIGHT, NOVEMBER 19, 2001

President George W. Bush and British Prime Minister Tony Blair repeatedly stress that the military campaign against global terrorism is not a "war on Islam." But military planners and policymakers acknowledge that understanding Islam's internal dynamics—the ideas that unite and the controversies that divide the world's 1.2 billion Muslims—will be critical to solidify a coalition to contain and defeat Islamic militants.

"There are core things that every Muslim believes, but beyond those things you can find an exception to virtually every generalization you hear," says Ali Reza Abootalebi, a professor at the University of Wisconsin at Eau Claire who specializes in social development in the Middle East.

No short survey can do justice to the vast diversity of modern Islam, a 1,400-year-old faith that stretches from sub-Saharan Africa to Indonesia. Muslim culture claims figures as diverse as Saudi militant Osama bin Laden and Indian-born novelist Salman Rushdie to U.S. boxing great Muhammad Ali and Libyan strongman Muammar Qaddafi. Theological disputes as old as the faith itself are compounded by ethnic divisions, historical variations and accommodations to local political realities.

Despite the identifcation of Islam with its Middle Eastern roots, less than one-quarter of all Muslims are Arabs. India, among the most vocal critics of extremist Islamic militancy, boasts the world's second-largest Muslim population, trailing only Indonesia, yet Muslims make up just 14 percent of its population. An estimated 6 million followers of Islam reside in the United States.

"Islam is by no means a monolith" says Thomas Lippman, author of *Understanding Islam*. "The differences in social practices, political thought, the feel of everyday life can be vast. Fly from Tripoli, Libya, to Dubai in the United Arab Emirates—two prominent Muslim capitals—and you get a totally different impression."

But Islamic scholars say a grasp of the basic divisions within the faith is critical to an understanding of the larger challenge facing the Muslim world and the United States in the months and years ahead. It matters, they say, that Shiite (pronounced "she-ite") Muslims are vastly outnumbered by Sunni Muslims but that Shiites are the dominant faith in Iran, Iraq, Lebanon and among some of the rebels fighting Afghanistan's ruling Taliban militia. It mat-

---

ters that Saudi Arabia, a longtime U.S. ally and home to Islam's two most sacred cities, Mecca and Medina, practices a strict offshoot of the Sunni faith—Wahhabism—that strongly influenced Osama bin Laden, suspected mastermind of the Sept. 11 attacks, and his followers in Afghanistan and Pakistan (see sidebar). It matters that Central Asian states such as Uzbekistan and Tajikistan, potentially critical allies in the military strikes against neighboring Afghanistan, are themselves moderate Islamic regimes confronting the same kind of radical Islamic elements that dominate the Taliban.

Complicating matters for a Westerner trying to understand Islam's various strains is the fact that "Islam has no Vatican," adds Lippman. While all Muslims read Islam's holy book, the Koran, "there's no one central authority Muslims can look to. There are theologians, but no sacraments and, strictly speaking, no clergy."

The most basic division in the Islamic world is between the Sunni majority and the Shia minority, a split as profound and enduring as the schisms among the Roman Catholics, Protestants and Eastern

---

What about Wahhabism?

Wahhabism, a strict form of Muslim orthodoxy backed by Saudi Arabia's wealth and its members' missionary zeal, may be overshadowing alternative strands of Islam in the United States. Said to be the strictest of four legal schools of Islam, it is more likely to claim itself as "true Islam" and expect other Muslims to conform.

The strand was revived by a religious leader named Muhammad Abd al-Wahhab, who joined forces with the military founder of the Saudi dynasty. "The royals, in alliance with the United States, used Wahhabism in the Middle East to drum up support against secular socialism," says Sulayman Nyang, a professor of Islam at Howard University, who notes that the sect was backed by the Saudi royal family during the Cold War. "What we see today is some leaders demanding a rigidity that is really not Islamic. They want to show off as being more pious.

Muslims abroad use the Wahhabi term negatively "to mean fundamentalist, fascist," says Nyang. In Western countries, its adherents can be divisive in their missionary zeal. But Azizah al-Hibri, a law professor at the University of Richmond, thinks Wahhabism is merely part of religious diversity working itself out in America, not a major split among the faithful.

"The problem is that some ideas have more funding than others," says al-Hibri, referring to Saudi funding of Wahhabi schools, literature and religious teachers. But its influence in the United States, imported with immigration, has softened over the years. "It has a strong presence, and that makes it an issue for people who are not Wahhabi," she says. "But it's not a split in Islam. It is part of the marketplace of ideas."

Wahhabism also has been characterized as an ardent political critic of Muslim regimes that secularize. It hopes to enforce a more literal interpretation of the Koran, Islam's holy book, in social custom and criminal law, says Khalid Duran, a Muslim scholar who is of the Sufi, or more mystical, persuasion.

One Sufi leader, Sheik Hisham Kabbani, who founded the Islamic Supreme Council of America as an alternative to Wahhabi influence, stirred an explosive debate on the issue in 1999. In a State Department hearing, he said that 80 percent of the nation's mosques had been taken over by imams with Wahhabilike loyalties. Estimates of the number of mosques, or prayer centers, in the United States range from 1,200 to 3,000.

Orthodox faiths in Christianity. Sunni, or "traditionalist" Muslims make up the vast majority of the Islamic faithful, with estimates as high as 90 percent. Most Muslim nations feature a majority Sunni population and a significant Shiite minority. (In the United States, Sunnis make up more than 72 percent of the Muslim population, and Shiites account for 11 percent, with the remainder from other branches.)

Sunnis trace their faith to the tradition established by the first successors to the prophet Mohammed after his death in 632, in particular the line of caliphs beginning with his father-in-law, Abu Bakr, and ending with the prophet's son-in-law, Ali. Sunni adherents see their faith as a straightforward continuation of the revelations given by Allah to Mohammed. While broadly seen as the "establishment" religion in most Muslim-majority countries, Sunni Islam also contains fundamentalist elements that resist Western cultural and economic models and seek a return to a purer understanding of Islam and the Koran.

Notable among these strains is the Wahhabi movement that was born in and still dominates heavily Sunni Saudi Arabia. Bin Laden himself was raised in the Wahhabi tradition. Based on the teachings of 18th-century Islamic scholar Mohammed ibn Abd Wahhab, the movement was a reaction to what its founder considered polytheistic corruptions of Muslim theology and lax observance of Islamic law. Allied with the powerful southern Arabian Saud clan, Wahhabism eventually became the reigning theology and political philosophy of modern Saudi Arabia, whose constitution includes the Koran. Wahhabism inspired similar reform movements from India to the Sudan and, crucially, it dominates the Saudi-funded religious schools in Pakistan where many of Afghanistan's Taliban rulers were educated.

The Taliban's destruction of ancient Buddhist statues earlier this year—a move that brought global condemnation on the regime—was a direct historical echo of the idol-smashing early days of Wahhabism, when ancient shrines, tombs and minarets deemed incompatible with Islam were razed. "There is a great affinity between the Taliban and Wahhabism," says the University of Wisconsin's Abootalebi. "They supported the Taliban ideologically and financially."

The connection is of vital importance to many of the Central Asian front-line states critical to the U.S.-led military campaign now under way against Afghanistan. With heavily Muslim populations, leaders in states such as Uzbekistan and Turkmenistan are anxious to keep the stricter Taliban interpretation of Islam from undermining their rule. Alexei Malashenko, a scholar at the Institute of Oriental Studies in Moscow, has noted that both Uzbekistan and Turkmenistan deported Iranian and Saudi Muslim clerics in the mid-1990s. "The growing influence of Islamic views from abroad is causing concern both to the local elites and to the clergy in Central Asia," Malashenko wrote in a selection from a new collection of essays on Central Asian security, published before the Sept. 11 attacks.

Shiites constitute the second-largest branch of Islam, with an estimated 10 to 15 percent of the world's Muslims. The name comes from the Arabic *shiat Ali* (the party of Ali) and points to the key doctrinal difference between Sunni and Shia Islam. Shiites reject the legitimacy of the first three caliphs in the line after the prophet. They place primary authority instead in a line of spiritual leaders (imams) who followed Ali, the fourth caliph and husband of Mohammed's only surviving daughter, Fatima.

Shiites have their own interpretation of Koranic law and their own books and texts explaining Koranic tradition. Imams tend to have more power and authority in Shiite communities than their Sunni equivalents, although the focus on a single leader has produced some bitter divisions and power struggles within the Shia tradition.

Islamic fundamentalism covers a broad, even mutually incompatible range of movements and ideas

The central political fact of modern Shiite Islam is its dominance in Iran and the tensions that it has created with neighboring Arab/Sunni states. Iran's Shiite leadership had bitter disputes with the Wahhabi-influenced Taliban long before the terrorist attacks, for example, culminating in the 1998 murder of 10 Iranian diplomats in the provincial Afghan city of Mazar-e-Sharif. In fact, Tehran has been internally divided by its distaste for both Washington and the regime in Kabul, loudly criticizing the U.S. military campaign against the Taliban but stopping far short of actively working to prevent it from going ahead.

But Iran's tense relations with the Taliban have as much to do with Afghanistan's booming drug trade, the press of Afghan refugees and the fear of rising influence by regional rival Pakistan as with theological disputes. In Malaysia, Prime Minister Mahathir Mohamad is seen as a big political winner because of the terrorist attacks. He has made political gains at the expense of the opposition Islamic Party of Malaysia by linking his rivals to international Islamic extremist elements.

As in other religious traditions, Islamic fundamentalism covers a broad, even mutually incompatible range of movements and ideas that claim to be returning the faith to its original, uncorrupted form. Bin Laden, for instance, sees the strictly Sunni regime in Saudi Arabia as a betrayal of the true faith. His biggest complaint is that the government allows "infidel" U.S. troops to be stationed in what he considers inviolable Muslim holy lands.

In postwar times, the first eruption of Islamic fundamentalism originated in Shia Iran with Ayatollah Ruhollah Khomeini's successful drive to overthrow the U.S.-allied shah of Iran in the late 1970s. Iranian-sponsored Middle Eastern terror groups, including Hezbollah in Lebanon and Hamas on the West Bank, strengthened

Wine, Women and Other Worldly Pleasures

A sensuous heaven, replete with all manner of delights, is a little-known but important part of the mentality that seems to inspire Muslim terrorists. Passages from the Koran and attendant commentaries, known as the Hadith, describe a paradise with rivers, trees and cool breezes, perfect for a religion originating in the desert. Only Arabic will be spoken there, and the blessed will be clothed in green and gold robes, showered with jewels and imbibe and consume copious food and drink.

"It's where the payoff comes," says Barbara Stowasser, an Islamics professor at Georgetown University. "Every deed, good or bad, will come out in a balance sheet in the end and that balance sheet will decide on whether one is admitted to the garden or thrown into the fire. It's a cool and green and delightful place. What makes it so dear is that believers know they are in the presence of God."

The conception of an Islamic heaven is part of the popular culture of the East. When Sheik Ismail Aal Ghadwan recently spoke about a martyr's reward on Palestinian TV, he described a widely perceived belief. "The martyr, if he meets Allah, is forgiven with the first drop of blood," he said. "He is saved from the torments of the grave; he sees his place in paradise; he is saved from the great horror [of the day of judgment], he is given 72 black-eyed women, he vouches for 70 of his family to be accepted to paradise; he is crowned with the crown of glory, whose precious stone is better than all of this world and what is in it."

The Koran teaches paradise automatically awaits someone who dies defending Islam. While suicide is wrong, the bombers are considered martyrs, not suicides. In a well-publicized terrorist-training-camp video aired by several news organizations, Osama bin Laden speaks of the benefits of an early death. "The love of this world is wrong," he says. "You should love the other world; you should not be afraid to die, because to die in the right cause and go to the other world, that's praiseworthy."

The "other world," according to the Koran, has the virtuous reclining on thrones, green cushions or carpets, attended by "companions" with "beautiful, big and lustrous eyes," according to Sura (Chapter) 52. These buxom companions do not sleep, get pregnant, menstruate, spit, blow their noses or defecate. Seventy of them are promised as a reward to the faithful Muslim, who also gets to keep all of his earthly wives.

Stowasser questions whether the Koran promises unlimited sex, noting theologians debate the matter, as "there is an emphasis on families being reunited." Women will get their due too, she adds, as Sura 52 mentions "youths handsome as pearls," who will serve the righteous.

Muslims have not specifically addressed what happens to women and children after they die, although the women apparently are promised a place in paradise with their husbands, according to Yvonne Haddad and Jane Smith, coauthors of the 1981 book *The Islamic Understanding of Death and Resurrection*. However, when the prophet Mohammed received a vision of hell, most of the inhabitants were women. The chief reason: ungratefulness to their husbands.

Taha Jaber Alalwani, president of the Graduate School of Islamic and Social Sciences in Leesburg, Va., says carnal delights are more appealing to Muslims than a Christian heaven, where Jesus specifically said believers would not marry. "The concept of the hereafter is very different," explains Alalwani. "We will stay human beings. You will never lose anything from what you have now. You will find everything you like there, and everything you want, you'll have immediately."

Christian doctrine holds believers will receive a glorified physical body in heaven. But the hereafter is used in all religions to motivate the individual to deeds of self-sacrifice, says Carol Zaleski, a Smith College professor who coauthored *The Book of Heaven*. "Sensual language is used when more abstract terms fall dead," she says. "The latter does not reach the imagination and inspire hope."

—Julia Duin

the image, both in the West and in the region, of the dangers of Shiite fundamentalism. But several scholars, including Georgetown University's John Esposito, say the Taliban-bin Laden nexus could mean the next phase of Islamic militancy will come out of the majority Sunni tradition. Afghanistan serves as the logistical base and political symbol for Sunni fundamentalism worldwide.

Still, Islam experts caution that religion can't be used to explain everything, even a faith as all-embracing as Islam. As Abootalebi notes, the regime of Wahhabi-dominated Saudi Arabia has been a source of political stability in the region, while the secular regime of Saddam Hussein's Iraq has warred continually with fellow Muslim states as well as with the West.

Many Muslims say they are frustrated that fundamentalists—Sunni or Shia—have become the public face of their religion in the West. But the lack of political diversity and freedom of expression in leading Islamic states only has compounded the problem.

There is one unifying force across the Muslim world: an attempt to come to terms with the cultural, material and political achievements of the secular, non-Muslim West, embodied, perhaps, in the World Trade Center and the Pentagon. With powerful memories of a medieval Islamic civilization that far surpassed Europe in arts and learning, Muslims virtually since the Industrial Revolution have struggled to understand how they became, in the blunt words of Middle East scholar Milton Viorst, "something of an underclass among the civilizations of the world."

Says Viorst, "For whatever reason, we benefited from the Golden Age of Islam and Muslims by and large have failed to do so. It is that frustration that the bin Ladens tap into."

II. Religion and Political Violence

Editor's Introduction

While the September 11 terrorist attacks on the United States brought the subject to the forefront of public consciousness, religiously motivated violence is nothing new. In fact, much of the language used to describe extremists of one sort or another can be traced to ancient religious contexts: "fanatic" comes from the Latin *fanaticus*, meaning "inspired by a deity"; "assassin" is derived from the Arabic name for a Muslim order that attacked Christians during the Crusades; and "zealot" originally referred to a militant Jewish sect that opposed the Roman occupation of Palestine in the first century A.D. Even before September 11, modern instances of religiously motivated violence were not uncommon in the news. One recalls, for example, the 1995 chemical attack on a Tokyo subway by members of the Aum Shinrikyo cult, or the Catholic/Protestant killings in Northern Ireland.

In the first article in this section, "Occidentalism," Avishai Margalit and Ian Buruma argue that religious extremism of the sort that brought down the World Trade Center is in no way a characteristically Islamic phenomenon; rather, it is the latest incarnation of an anti-Western, antiliberal ideology that is not confined to any particular locale. In fact, "Occidentalism," as the authors term this ideology, provided many of the philosophical underpinnings for German Nazism and Japanese nationalism during World War II. Occidentalism can be broadly defined in relation to those things it opposes: urban power and pluralism, bourgeois "weakness" and "depravity," secular rationalism, and feminism. In its more extreme versions, the authors observe, Occidentalism can become a form of heroic death-worship and, as such, exhibits an undeniable religious dimension.

When President Bush referred to an "axis of evil" that Americans must combat, he was adding a religious dimension to the war on terror that began after September 11. As Harvey Cox explains in "Religion and the War Against Evil," the representation of Osama bin Laden, the Taliban, and alleged weapons suppliers Iran and Iraq as satanic figures of Biblical proportions reflected the renewed interest in religious worship that Americans experienced in response to the terrorist attacks. According to Cox, however, the devout who cling to the idea of an American "war against evil" should look critically at the role religion has played in this crisis. So too, he suggests, should critics of religion refrain from condemning believers in the name of "modernity," itself a problematic concept throughout the world. Cox calls for an "alternative paradigm" that accommodates both modern thinking *and* religious faith, since neither on its own is responsible for the current conflict.

Many individuals who seek to place blame for the September 11 attacks point to *fundamentalist* Muslims, as opposed to all Muslims, as if the word "fundamentalist" were synonymous with "violence." In their article "Fundamentalism," R. Scott Appleby and Martin E. Marty take a closer look at religious fundamentalism and identify several misconceptions about the phenomenon. First, fundamentalists are not necessarily monotheistic, and they are heavily invested in interpretations of religious texts, rather than in "literal" readings. Fundamentalism also appeals more to the educated unemployed or underemployed than to the uneducated, and it does not necessarily lead to violence. Finally, fundamentalism is dedicated to social change and differs from religious cults in its appeal to the authority of a religious tradition, rather than to that of a charismatic leader.

The final two articles in this section present examples of religious militancy by examining long-standing conflicts in which religious affiliation is closely linked with nationalism and ethnicity. The first, "Separated at Birth" from *ABCNews.com*, concerns the 50-year-old hostilities between Muslim-dominated Pakistan and Hindu-controlled India. As the article explains, their battle over the region of Kashmir that separates their two countries has escalated to the point where each has aimed nuclear weapons at the other. While this conflict is primarily a 20th-century phenomenon, shaped by the partitioning of the subcontinent when the British withdrew in 1947, the war that has ravaged the Balkans goes back centuries. In "Religious Wars?: A Short History of the Balkans," Paul Mojzes tries to untangle the complex web of religious and ethnic affiliations that has prompted Nazi-style atrocities in the name of "ethnic cleansing," raised the specter of World War III, and provoked an international response. By focusing on the way religion has helped define the identities of and shaped alliances among those living in the region, Mojzes attempts to explain why no amount of bombs from outsiders can "settle intractable ethnoreligious conflicts."

Occidentalism[1]

By Avishai Margalit and Ian Buruma
New York Review of Books, January 7, 2002

1.

In 1942, not long after the attack on Pearl Harbor, a group of Japanese philosophers got together in Kyoto to discuss Japan's role in the world. The project of this ultra-nationalist gathering was, as they put it, to find a way to "overcome modern civilization." Since modern civilization was another term for Western civilization, the conference might just as well have been entitled "Overcoming the West." In a complete reversal of the late-nineteenth-century goal of "leaving Asia and joining the West," Japan was now fighting a "holy war" to liberate Asia from the West and purify Asian minds of Western ideas. Part of the holy war was, as it were, an exercise in philosophical cleansing.

The cleansing agent was a mystical mishmash of German-inspired ethnic nationalism and Zen- and Shinto-based nativism. The Japanese were a "world-historical race" descended from the gods, whose divine task it was to lead all Asians into a new age of Great Harmony, and so on. But what was "the West" which had to be purged? What needed to be "overcome"? The question has gained currency, since the chief characteristics of this Western enemy would have sounded familiar to Osama bin Laden, and other Islamic extremists. They are, not in any particular order, materialism, liberalism, capitalism, individualism, humanism, rationalism, socialism, decadence, and moral laxity. These ills would be overcome by a show of Japanese force, not just military force, but force of will, of spirit, of soul. The key characteristics of the Japanese or "Asian" spirit were self-sacrifice, discipline, austerity, individual submission to the collective good, worship of divine leadership, and a deep faith in the superiority of instinct over reason.

There was of course more at stake in Japan's war with the West, but these were the philosophical underpinnings of Japanese wartime propaganda. The central document of Japan's claim to national divinity was entitled *Cardinal Principles of the National Polity (Kokutai no Hongi)*. Issued in 1937 by the ministry of education, this document claimed that the Japanese were "intrinsically quite different from so-called citizens of Western nations," because the divine imperial bloodlines had remained unbroken, and "we

---

always seek in the emperor the source of our lives and activities." The Japanese spirit was "pure" and "unclouded," whereas the influence of Western culture led to mental confusion and spiritual corruption.

> *War against the West is partly a war against a particular concept of citizenship and community.*

Western, especially German, ideas inspired some of this. A famous right-wing professor, Dr. Uesugi Shinkichi, began his spiritual life as a Christian, studied statecraft in Wilhelminian Germany, and returned home to write (in 1919): "Subjects have no mind apart from the will of the Emperor. Their individual selves are merged with the Emperor. If they act according to the mind of the Emperor, they can realize their true nature and attain the moral ideal."[1] Of such stuff are holy warriors made.

Similar language—though without the neo-Shintoist associations—was used by German National Socialists and other European fascists. They, too, fought against that list of "soulless" characteristics commonly associated with liberal societies. One of the early critical books about Nazi thinking, by Aurel Kolnai, a Hungarian refugee, was actually entitled *The War Against the West*.[2] Nazi ideologues and Japanese militarist propagandists were fighting the same Western ideas. The West they loathed was a multinational, multicultural place, but the main symbols of hate were republican France, capitalist America, liberal England, and, in Germany more than Japan, the rootless cosmopolitan Jews. Japanese propaganda focused on the "Anglo-American beasts," represented in cartoons of Roosevelt and Churchill wearing plutocratic top hats. To the Nazis "the eternal Jew" represented everything that was hateful about liberalism.

War against the West is partly a war against a particular concept of citizenship and community. Decades before the coming of Hitler, the spiritual godfather of Nazism, Houston Stewart Chamberlain, described France, Britain, and America as hopelessly "Jewified" countries. Citizenship in these places had degenerated into a "purely political concept."[3] In England, he said, "every Basuto nigger" could get a passport. Later he complained that the country had "fallen utterly into the hands of Jews and Americans."[4] Germany in his view, and that of his friend Kaiser Wilhelm II, was the only nation with enough national spirit and racial solidarity to save the West from going under in a sea of decadence and corruption. His "West" was not based on citizenship but on blood and soil.

Oswald Spengler warned in 1933 (of all years) that the main threats to the Occident came from "colored peoples" (*Farbigen*).[5] He prophesied, not entirely without reason, huge uprisings of enraged peoples in the European colonies. He also claimed that after 1918 the Russians had become "Asiatic" again, and that the Japanese Yellow Peril was about to engulf the civilized world. More interesting, however, was Spengler's view that the ruling white races (*Herrenvölker*) were losing their position in Europe. Soon, he said, true Frenchmen would no longer rule France, which was already awash with black soldiers, Polish businessmen, and Spanish farmers. The West, he concluded, would go under because white people had become soft, decadent, addicted to safety and comfort. As he put it: "Jazz music and nigger dances are the death march of a great civilization."

If criticism of the West was influenced by half-baked ideas from Germany, more positive views of the West were also influenced by German ideas. The Slavophiles and the Westernizers, who offered opposing views of the West in nineteenth-century Russia, were both equally inspired by German intellectual currents. Ideas for or against the West are in fact to be found everywhere. The East does not begin at the river Elbe, as Konrad Adenauer believed, nor does the West start in Prague, as Milan Kundera once suggested. East and West are not necessarily geographical territories. Rather, Occidentalism, which played such a large part in the attacks of September 11, is a cluster of images and ideas of the West in the minds of its haters. Four features of Occidentalism can be seen in most versions of it; we can call them the City, the Bourgeois, Reason, and Feminism. Each contains a set of attributes, such as arrogance, feebleness, greed, depravity, and decadence, which are invoked as typically Western, or even American, characteristics.

The things Occidentalists hate about the West are not always the ones that inspire hatred of the U.S. The two issues should not be conflated. A friend once asked in astonishment: "Why does he hate me? I didn't even help him." Some people hate the U.S. because they were helped by the U.S., and some because they were not. Some resent the way the U.S. helped their own hateful governments gain or stay in power. Some feel humiliated by the very existence of the U.S., and some by U.S. foreign policy. With some on the left, hatred of the U.S. is all that remains of their leftism; anti-Americanism is part of their identity. The same goes for right-wing cultural Gaullists. Anti-Americanism is an important political issue, related to Occidentalism but not quite the same thing.

2.

Anti-liberal revolts almost invariably contain a deep hatred of the City, that is to say, everything represented by urban civilization: commerce, mixed populations, artistic freedom, sexual license, scientific pursuits, leisure, personal safety, wealth, and its usual concomitant, power. Mao Zedong, Pol Pot, Hitler, Japanese agrarian fascists, and of course Islamists all extolled the simple life of the pious peasant, pure at heart, uncorrupted by city pleasures, used to hard work and self-denial, tied to the soil, and obedient to authority. Behind the idyll of rural simplicity lies the desire to control masses of people, but also an old religious rage, which goes back at least as far as the ancient superpower Babylon.

The "holy men" of the three monotheistic religions—Christianity, Judaism, and Islam—denounced Babylon as the sinful city-state whose politics, military might, and very urban civilization posed an arrogant challenge to God. The fabled tower of Babylon was a symbol of hubris and idolatry: "Let us build a city and a tower, whose top may reach unto heaven; and let us make us a name" (Genesis 11:4). Indeed, God took it as a challenge to Himself: "And now nothing will be restrained from them, which they imagined to do" (Genesis 11:6). That is, the citizens of this urban superpower will act out their fantasies to become God.

"He loveth not the arrogant," the Koran (16:23) tells us, and goes on to say: "Allah took their structures from their foundation, and the roof fell down on them from above; and the Wrath seized them from directions they did not perceive" (16:26). The prophet Isaiah already prophesied that Babylon, "the glory of all kingdoms," would end up as "Sodom and Gomorrah" (Isaiah 13:19), and that the arrogant would be overthrown so that even an "Arabian pitch tent" would not inhabit the place (13:20). The Book of Revelation goes on to say about Babylon the great, "the mother of harlots and of the abominations of the earth" (17:5), that it "is fallen, is fallen" (18:2).

There is a recurring theme in movies from poor countries in which a young person from a remote village goes to the big city, forced by circumstances or eager to seek a new life in a wider, more affluent world. Things quickly go wrong. The young man or woman is lonely, adrift, and falls into poverty, crime, or prostitution. Usually, the story ends in a gesture of terrible violence, a vengeful attempt to bring down the pillars of the arrogant, indifferent, alien city. There are echoes of this story in Hitler's life in Vienna, Pol Pot's in Paris, Mao's in Beijing, or indeed of many a Muslim youth in Cairo, Haifa, Manchester, or Hamburg.

In our world you don't even have to move to the city to feel its constant presence, through advertising, television, pop music, and videos. The modern city, representing all that shimmers just out of our reach, all the glittering arrogance and harlotry of the West, has found its icon in the Manhattan skyline, reproduced in millions of posters, photographs, and images, plastered all over the world. You cannot escape it. You find it on dusty jukeboxes in Burma, in discothèques in Urumqi, in student dorms in Addis Ababa. It excites longing, envy, and sometimes blinding rage. The Taliban, like the Nazi provincials horrified by "nigger dancing," like Pol Pot, like Mao, have tried to create a world of purity where visions of Babylon can no longer disturb them.

The Taliban, to be sure, have very little idea what the fleshpots of the West are really like. For them even Kabul sparkled with Occidental sinfulness, exemplified by girls in school and women with uncovered faces populating and defiling the public domain. But the

Taliban, like other purists, are much concerned with the private domain too. In big, anonymous cities, separation between the private and the public makes hypocrisy possible. Indeed, in Occidentalist eyes, the image of the West, populated by city-dwellers, is marked by artificiality and hypocrisy, in contrast to the honesty and purity of a Bedouin shepherd's life. Riyadh, and its grandiose Arabian palaces, is the epitome of hypocrisy. Its typical denizens behave like puritanical Wahhabites in public and greedy Westerners at home. To an Islamic radical, then, urban hypocrisy is like keeping the West inside one like a worm rotting the apple from within.

Most great cities are also great marketplaces. Voltaire saw much of what he admired about England in the Royal Exchange, "where the Jew, the Mahometan, and the Christian transact together as tho' they all profess'd the same religion, and give the name of Infidel to none but bankrupts."[6] Those who hate what Voltaire respected, who see the marketplace as the source of greed, selfishness, and foreign corruption, also hate those who are thought to benefit from it most: immigrants and minorities who can only better their fortunes by trade. When purity must be restored, and foreign blood removed from the native soil, it is these people who must be purged: the Chinese from Pol Pot's Phnom Penh, the Indians from Rangoon or Kampala, and the Jews from everywhere.

Sometimes such impurities can extend to nations, or even great powers. In their professed aim to bring back true Asian values to the East, Japanese wartime leaders promised to kick out the white imperialists as one way to "overcome unrestrained market competition."[7] Whatever Israel does, it will remain the alien grit in the eyes of Muslim purists. And the U.S. will always be intolerable to its enemies. In bin Laden's terms, "the crusader-Jewish alliance, led by the U.S. and Israel," cannot do right. The hatred is unconditional. As he observed in a 1998 interview for al-Jazeera TV: "Every grown-up Muslim hates Americans, Jews, and Christians. It is our belief and religion. Since I was a boy I have been at war with and harboring hatred towards the Americans." The September angels of vengeance picked their target carefully. Since the Manhattan skyline is seen as a provocation, its Babylonian towers had to come down.

3.

What did Hitler mean by "Jewish science"? For that matter, what explains the deep loathing of Darwin among Christian fundamentalists? Nazi propagandists argued that scientific truth could not be established by such "Jewish" methods as empirical inquiry or subjecting hypotheses to the experimental test; natural science had to be "spiritual," rooted in the natural spirit of the *Volk*. Jews, it was proposed, approached the natural world through reason, but true Germans reached a higher understanding through creative instinct and a love of nature.

Chairman Mao coined the slogan "Science is simply acting daringly." He purged trained scientists in the 1950s and encouraged Party zealots to embark on crazy experiments, inspired by the equally zany theories of Stalin's pseudoscientist T. D. Lysenko. "There is nothing special," Mao said, "about making nuclear reactors, cyclotrons or rockets. . . . You need to have spirit to feel superior to everyone, as if there was no one beside you."[8] All the sense of envious inferiority that Mao and his fellow Party provincials felt toward people of higher education is contained in these words. Instinct, spirit, daring . . . In 1942, a Japanese professor at Tokyo University argued that a Japanese victory over Anglo-American materialism was assured because the former embodied the "spiritual culture" of the East.

Like those towers of Babel in New York, the "Jewish" idea that "science is international" and human reason, regardless of bloodlines, is the best instrument for scientific inquiry is regarded by ene-

---

It is a fairly common belief among all peoples that "others" don't have the same feelings that we do.

---

mies of liberal, urban civilization as a form of hubris. Science, like everything else, must be infused with a higher ideal: the German *Volk*, God, Allah, or whatnot. But there may also be something else, something even more primitive, behind this. Worshipers of tribal gods, or even of allegedly universal ones, including Christians, Muslims, and Orthodox Jews, sometimes have a tendency to believe that infidels either have corrupt souls or have no souls at all. It is not for nothing that Christian missionaries speak of saving souls. In extreme cases, this can furnish enough justification to kill unbelievers with impunity.

Soul is a recurring theme of Occidentalism. The nineteenth-century Slavophiles pitted the "big" Russian soul against the mechanical, soulless West. They claimed to stand for deep feelings and profound understanding of suffering. Westerners, on the other hand, were deemed to be mechanically efficient, and to have nothing but an uncanny sense for calculating what is useful. The skeptical intellect, to promoters of soul, is always viewed with suspicion. Occidentalists extol soul or spirit but despise intellectuals and intellectual life. They regard the intellectual life as fragmented, indeed as a higher form of idiocy, with no sense of "totality," the "absolute," and what is truly important in life.

It is a fairly common belief among all peoples that "others" don't have the same feelings that we do. The notion that life is cheap in the Orient, or that coolies feel no pain, is a variation of this, but so is the idea we have heard expressed many times in China, India, Japan, and Egypt that Westerners are dry, rational, cold, and lacking in warm human feelings. It is a mark of parochial ignorance, of course, but it also reflects a way of ordering society. The post-Enlightenment Anglo-Franco-Judeo-American West sees itself as governed by secular political institutions and the behavior of all citizens as bound by secular laws. Religious belief and other matters of the spirit are private. Our politics are not totally divorced from shared values or moral assumptions, and some of our current leaders would like to see more religion brought into our public life; but still the West is not governed by spiritual leaders who seek to mediate between us and the divine world above. Our laws do not come from divine revelation, but are drawn up by jurists.

Societies in which Caesars are also high priests, or act as idols of worship, whether they be Stalinist, monarchical, or Islamist, use a different political language. Again, an example from World War II might be useful. Whereas the Allies, led by the U.S., fought the Japanese in the name of freedom, the Japanese holy war in Asia was fought in the name of divine justice and peace. "The basic aim of Japan's national policy lies in the firm establishment of world peace in accordance with the lofty spirit of All the World Under One Roof, in which the country was founded." Thus spoke Prime Minister Konoe in 1940. Islamists, too, aim to unite the world under one peaceful roof, once the infidels and their towers have been destroyed.

When politics and religion merge, collective aims, often promoted in the name of love and justice, tend to encompass the whole world, or at least large chunks of it. The state is a secular construct. The Brotherhood of Islam, the Church of Rome, All the World Under One Japanese Roof, world communism, all in their different ways have had religious or millenarian goals. Such goals are not unknown in the supposedly secular states of the West either. Especially in the U.S., right-wing Christian organizations and other religious pressure groups have sought to inject their religious values and agendas into national politics in ways that would have shocked the Founding Fathers. That Reverend Jerry Falwell described the terrorist attacks on New York and Washington as a kind of punishment for our worldly sins showed that his thinking was not so far removed from that of the Islamists.

But ideally, the U.S. and other Western democracies are examples of what Ferdinand Toennies termed a *Gesellschaft*, whose members are bound by a social contract. The other kind of community, the *Gemeinschaft*, is based on a common faith, or racial kinship, or on deep feelings of one kind or another. Typically, one German thinker, Edgar Jung, described World War I as a clash between the Intellect (the West) and the Soul (Germany).

4.

Enemies of the West usually aspire to be heroes. As Mussolini exhorted his new Romans: "Never cease to be daring!" Islamism, Nazism, fascism, communism are all heroic creeds. Mao's ideal of permanent revolution was a blueprint for continually stirring things up, for a society invigorated by constant heroic violence. The common enemy of revolutionary heroes is the settled bourgeois, the city dweller, the petty clerk, the plump stockbroker, going about his business, the kind of person, in short, who might have been working in an office in the World Trade Center. It is a peculiar trait of the bourgeoisie, perhaps the most successful class in history, at least so far, according to Karl Marx, to be hated so intensely by some of its most formidable sons and daughters, including Marx himself. Lack of heroism in the bourgeois ethos, of committing great deeds, has a great deal to do with this peculiarity. The hero courts death. The bourgeois is addicted to personal safety. The hero counts death tolls, the bourgeois counts money. Bin Laden was asked by his interviewer in 1998 whether he ever feared betrayal from within his own entourage. He replied: "These men left worldly affairs, and came here for jihad."

Intellectuals, themselves only rarely heroic, have often displayed a hatred of the bourgeois and an infatuation with heroism—heroic leaders, heroic creeds. Artists in Mussolini's Italy celebrated speed, youth, energy, instinct, and death-defying derring-do. German social scientists before World War II were fascinated by the juxtaposition of the hero and the bourgeois: Werner Sombart's *Händler und Helden* (*Merchants and Heroes*) and Bogislav von Selchow's *Der bürgerliche und der heldische Mensch* (*The Civil and the Heroic Man*) are but two examples of the genre. Von Selchow was one, among many others, by no means all German, who argued that bourgeois liberal society had become cold, fragmented, decadent, mediocre, lifeless. The bourgeois, he wrote, is forever hiding himself in a life without peril. The bourgeois, he said, is anxious to eliminate "fighting against Life, as he lacks the strength necessary to master it in its very nakedness and hardness in a manly fashion."[9]

To the likes of von Selchow or Ernst Jünger, World War I showed a different, more heroic side of man. That is why the Battle of Langemarck, a particularly horrific episode in 1914, in which Jünger himself took part, became such a subject for hero worship. Some 145,000 men died in a sequence of utterly futile attacks. But the young heroes, many of them from elite universities like the Japanese kamikaze pilots thirty years later, were supposed to have rushed to their early graves singing the *Deutschlandlied*. The famous words of Theodor Körner, written a century before, were often evoked in remembrance: "Happiness lies only in sacrificial death." In the first week of the current war in Afghanistan, a young Afghan warrior was quoted in a British newspaper. "The Americans," he said, "love Pepsi Cola, but we love death." The sentiments of the Langemarck cult exactly.

Even those who sympathize with the democratic West, such as Alexis de Tocqueville, have pointed out the lack of grandeur, the intellectual conformity, and the cultural mediocrity that is supposed to be inherent in our systems of government. Democracy, Tocqueville warned, could easily become the tyranny of the majority. He noted that there were no great writers in America, or indeed anything that might be described as great. It is a common but somewhat questionable complaint. For it is not at all clear that art and culture in New York is any more mediocre than it is in Damascus or Beijing.

Much in our affluent, market-driven societies is indeed mediocre, and there is nothing admirable about luxury per se, but when contempt for bourgeois creature comforts becomes contempt for life you know the West is under attack. This contempt can come from many sources, but it appeals to those who feel impotent, marginalized, excluded, or denigrated: the intellectual who feels unrecognized, the talentless art student in a city filled with brilliance, the time-serving everyman who disappears into any crowd, the young man from a third-world country who feels mocked by the indifference of a superior West; the list of possible recruits to a cult of death is potentially endless.

Liberalism, wrote an early Nazi theorist, A. Moeller v.d. Bruck, is the "liberty for everybody to be a mediocre man." The way out of mediocrity, say the sirens of the death cult, is to submerge one's petty ego into a mass movement, whose awesome energies will be unleashed to create greatness in the name of the Führer, the Emperor, God, or Allah. The Leader personifies all one's yearnings for grandeur. What is the mere life of one, two, or a thousand men, if higher things are at stake? This is a license for great violence against others: Jews, infidels, bourgeois liberals, Sikhs, Muslims, or whoever must be purged to make way for a greater, grander world. An American chaplain named Francis P. Scott tried to explain to the Tokyo War Crimes Tribunal the extraordinary brutality of Japanese soldiers during the war. After many interviews with former combatants, he concluded that "they had a belief that any enemy of the emperor could not be right, so the more brutally they treated their prisoners, the more loyal to the emperor they were being."[10]

The truest holy warrior, however, is not the torturer but the kamikaze pilot. Self-sacrifice is the highest honor in the war against the West. It is the absolute opposite of the bourgeois fear for his life. And youth is the most capable of sacrificial acts. Most kamikazes were barely out of high school. As bin Laden has said, "The sector between fifteen and twenty-five is the one with ability for jihad and sacrifice."

5.

Aurel Kolnai argued in 1938 in his *War Against the West* that "the trend towards the emancipation of women [is] keenly distinctive of the West." This somewhat sweeping claim seems to be born out by the sentiments of Kolnai's enemies. Here is Alfred Rosenberg, the Nazi propagandist: "Emancipation of woman from the women's emancipation movement is the first demand of a generation of women which would like to save the Volk and the race, the Eternal-Unconscious, the foundation of all culture, from decline and fall."[11] Leaving aside what this woolly-headed thinker could have meant by the Eternal-Unconscious, the meaning is clear enough. Female emancipation leads to bourgeois decadence. The proper role for women is to be breeders of heroic men. One reason the Germans imported such huge numbers of workers from Poland and other countries under Nazi occupation was the dogmatic insistence that German women should stay at home.

Bin Laden is equally obsessed with manliness and women. It is indeed one of his most cherished Occidentalist creeds. "The rulers of that region [the Gulf States] have been deprived of their manhood," he said in 1998. "And they think the people are women. By God, Muslim women refuse to be defended by these American and Jewish prostitutes." The West, in his account, is determined "to deprive us of our manhood. We believe we are men."

Few modern societies were as dominated by males as wartime Japan, and the brutal policy of forcing Korean, Chinese, and Filipina, as well as Japanese, girls to serve in military brothels was a sign of the low status of women in the Japanese empire. And yet, the war itself had the peculiar effect of emancipating Japanese women to a degree that cannot possibly have been intended. Because most able-bodied men were needed on the battlefronts, women had to take care of their families, trade in the black markets, and work in the factories. Unlike the men, who experienced defeat as a deep humiliation, many Japanese women regarded the Allied victory as a step toward their liberation. One of the most important changes in postwar Japan was that women got the right to vote. They did so in large numbers as early as 1946. A new constitution was drawn up mostly by American jurists, but the articles concerning women's rights were largely the work of a remarkable person called Beate Sirota, who represented most things enemies of the West would have loathed. She was European, educated, a woman, and a Jew.

To all those who see military discipline, self-sacrifice, austerity, and worship of the Leader as the highest social ideals, the power of female sexuality will be seen as a dire threat. From ancient times women are the givers and the guardians of life. Women's freedom is incompatible with a death cult. Indeed, open displays of female sexuality are a provocation, not only to holy men, but to all repressed people whose only way to exaltation is death for a higher cause. Pictures of partly naked Western women advertising Hollywood movies, or soft drinks, or whatever, by suggesting sexual acts, are as ubiquitous in the world as those images of the Manhattan skyline. They are just as frustrating, confusing, and sometimes enraging. For again they promise a sinful, libidinous world of infinite pleasure beyond most people's reach.

6.

There is no clash of civilizations. Most religions, especially monotheistic ones, have the capacity to harbor the anti-Western poison. And varieties of secular fascism can occur in all cultures. The current conflict, therefore, is not between East and West, Anglo-America and the rest, or Judeo-Christianity and Islam. The death cult is a deadly virus which now thrives, for all manner of historical and political reasons, in extreme forms of Islam.

Most religions, especially monotheistic ones, have the capacity to harbor the anti-Western poison.

Occidentalism is the creed of Islamist revolutionaries. Their aim is to create one Islamic world guided by the *sharia* (Islamic law), as interpreted by trusted scholars who have proved themselves in jihad (read "revolution"). This is a call to purify the Islamic world of the idolatrous West, exemplified by America. The aim is to strike at American heathen shrines, and show, in the most spectacular fashion, that the U.S. is vulnerable, a "paper tiger" in revolutionary jargon. Through such "propaganda by action" against the arrogant U.S., the forces of jihad will unite and then impose their revolution on the Islamic world.

Ayatollah Khomeini was a "Stalinist" in the sense that he wanted to stage a revolution in one significant country, Iran, before worrying about exporting it. Bin Laden, by contrast, is a "Trotskyite," who views Afghanistan as a base from which to export revolution right away. There is a tension between the "Stalinists" and the "Trotskyites" within the Islamist movement. September 11 gave the "Trotskyites" an advantage.

Al-Qaeda is making a serious bid to stage an Islamist revolution that would bring down governments from Indonesia to Tunisia. It has not succeeded yet. We can expect more "propaganda by action" against the U.S. and U.S. installations, accompanied by crude Occidentalist propaganda. The West, and not just the geographical West, should counter this intelligently with the full force of calculating bourgeois anti-heroism. Accountants mulling over shady bank accounts and undercover agents bribing their way will be more useful in the long-term struggle than special macho units blasting their way into the caves of Afghanistan. But if one thing is clear in this murky war, it is that we should not counter Occidentalism with a nasty form of Orientalism. Once we fall for that temptation, the virus has infected us too.

Notes

1. D.C. Holtom, *Modern Japan and Shinto Nationalism* (University of Chicago, 1943), p. 10.
2. Viking, 1938.
3. *Briefe 1882–1924* (Munich: Bruckmann, 1928).
4. *England und Deutschland* (Munich: Bruckmann, 1915).
5. *Jahr der Entscheidung* (Munich: C.H. Beck, 1933).
6. *Letters Concerning the English Nation* (Oxford University Press, 1994), p. 30.
7. Akira Iriye, *Power and Culture: The Japanese-American War 1941–1945* (Harvard University Press, 1981).
8. Jasper Becker, *Hungry Ghosts: Mao's Secret Famine* (Free Press, 1996), p. 62.
9. Quoted in Kolnai, *The War Against the West*, p. 215.
10. Arnold C. Brackman, *The Other Nuremberg: The Untold Story of the Tokyo War Crimes Tribunals* (Morrow, 1987), p. 251.
11. Quoted in George L. Mosse, *Nazi Culture: Intellectual, Cultural and Social Life in the Third Reich* (Grosset and Dunlap, 1966), p. 40.

Religion and the War Against Evil[2]

By Harvey Cox
The Nation, December 24, 2001

> Proclaim this among the nations: Prepare for war, stir up the
> mighty men, Let all the men of war draw near, let them come
> up.
>   Beat your plowshares into swords, and your pruning hooks
> into spears; Let the weak say, "I am a warrior."
>
> *Joel 3:9–10*

No, this is not an ironic misquotation of the well-known words
from the prophet Isaiah about beating swords into plowshares,
which are inscribed on the wall of the UN. This one comes from a
later biblical prophet. I have never seen it inscribed on any church
or synagogue wall. Little wonder. It is a call to arms, something of
an embarrassment to those who would like to claim that although
someone else's religion might inspire them to violence, ours certainly does not. And it is not an isolated text. Both the Old and
New Testament are replete with similar, if even less widely
quoted, ones. According to the Gospel of Matthew, even the Prince
of Peace tells his disciples, "I have come not to bring peace, but a
sword" (Matthew 10:34).

In the aftermath of September 11, we all learned a lot about religion and the American psyche. Droves of people crowded into
prayer and memorial services, lit candles, sang hymns many of
them scarcely knew and listened, sometimes in near desperation,
to readings from ancient scriptures. Of course, they were looking
for sympathy and consolation. But they were also looking for something more, perhaps some intangible frame of reference that might
bring a bit of meaning to their rage, fear and bewilderment. It is
notable that in a society that is so famously dependent on thera-
pies of all kinds, the therapists were not much in evidence. When
the cataclysm came, what the historian Sidney Mead once called
"the nation with the soul of a church" groped for something deeper
but more elusive. The sheer enormity of the horror visited upon us
in Manhattan suddenly made our various feel-good remedies look a
bit thin. Neither New Age nostrums nor channeling can help when
it comes to such an eruption of primal malice.

In his 1995 book *The Death of Satan*, subtitled *How Americans
Have Lost the Sense of Evil*, Andrew Delbanco posed what has suddenly become an achingly pertinent question. Now that the classi-

---

2. "Religion and the War Against Evil" by Harvey Cox. Reprinted with permission from the
December 24, 2001, issue of *The Nation*.

cal symbols of radical evil—Satan, apocalypse, etc.—seem to have evaporated, how, he asked, would Americans respond if we ever again experienced radical evil? "I believe our culture is now in crisis," he wrote, "because evil remains an inescapable experience for all of us, while we no longer have a symbolic language for describing it." Some years earlier Susan Sontag, in her book *Illness as Metaphor*, asked how we could possibly regain our moral bearings

> *Religion can be at least as much a part of the problem as part of the solution.*

"when we have a sense of evil; but no longer the religious or philosophical language to talk intelligently about evil." These are stubborn questions, and I am not sure the classical religious traditions, already so compromised by their quest for a share of the booming spirituality market, will provide the needed help. But I can understand why so many people are foraging around in them. Did Job or Augustine or Dante know something we don't know? I am quite sure, however, that President Bush's response to this symbolic vacuum—namely, that we are now waging a war against evil, and that one day there will be a clear victory—will not satisfy many people for very long.

But Americans also quickly learned something else about religion. The same people who groped for some half-forgotten religious framing for September 11 also quickly discovered that religion can be at least as much a part of the problem as part of the solution. They learned to exercise what scholars call a "hermeneutic of suspicion." First, two celebrity TV evangelists, Jerry Falwell and Pat Robertson, assured them that because of what gays and abortion clinics and the ACLU are up to, God removed his shield and let this happen. The Rev. Franklin Graham made his own contribution to comparative religious studies by stating that the God of Islam is "a different God, and I believed it is a very evil and wicked religion." Then we all read those verses from the Koran the hijackers were advised to meditate on in the minutes before they snuffed out the lives of thousands of people. Meanwhile, Hindu nationalists continued to look around for the next mosque they could pulverize, Christian fans of the *Left Behind* series smugly assured us that the Last Days were upon us and Jewish settlers on the West Bank and in Gaza pointed again to verses from the book of Joshua that say "conquer" and "settle" is their divine mandate.

Nor should the radical secularists take much "we told you so" comfort from all this. Terrorism has a long and complex genealogy. When I watched the twin towers implode on TV, the scene that flashed into my memory was some footage I had once seen of the Bolsheviks dynamiting the main cathedral of Moscow, at that time the largest church in the Orthodox world. They went on to imprison, exile and murder millions of people in the name of one of the most powerful antireligious ideologies ever concocted. During the Spanish Civil War we saw how Catholics and atheists could massacre each other with equal relish. Religion, it seems, can indeed inspire terrorist horror. But so can nonreligious and antireligious zealotries. We have now reached a point at which mutual recriminations about who has piled up the most corpses begin to sound repetitious and indecent. We are going to have religion, for blessing or for bane, and

> *I have met both religious and secular fundamentalists, and they bear an uncanny resemblance to each other.*

antireligion, for better or for worse, with us for the foreseeable future. We are also going to have evil with us—for a very long time indeed—and we all know that no war is going to vanquish it. So it may be time to tone down the polemics and try to understand why—after all the faith we so touchingly placed in science or human rationality or God—we keep rehearsing the same old arguments.

I have tried for many years to make religious people appreciate how indispensable the secular critics of religion are. Without them religions are tempted to pride, pomposity and power-grabbing. The critics of religion are the allies of the prophets. No one was harder on the religious of their day than Amos and Jeremiah and Jesus. I have also tried to help serious nonreligious people understand why many other serious people are religious, and why faith may be a little something more that what Jesse Ventura calls a crutch for the weak-minded. I have undertaken this effort because I am convinced that when religious traditions and their critics—either ideologies or other religions—interacted with each other openly, remarkable new insights often emerged. But my task has not been an easy one, and it is not helped by the diehards on either side who refuse to entertain any thought of significant conversation. I have met both religious and secular fundamentalists, and they bear an uncanny resemblance to each other.

Both sides now need to reconnoiter. We as religious thinkers must stop simply making nice about this age of ecumenism, interfaith dialogue and fuzzy feelings among priests, imams and rabbis. We need to take a step toward candor. In response to a secularized intelligentsia, at least in the West, we have tried too hard to put a positive face on *religion*, when the truth is we know that all *religions* have their demonic underside. We quote Isaiah, not Joel. We talk about Rabbi Abraham Joshua Heschel, not Rabbi Meir Kahane. We favor St. Francis and his birds, not Torquemada and his racks. Alas, however, they are all part of the story. Telling just the children's version will no longer do.

Some have glumly suggested that the twentieth century was the one in which the nonreligious ideologies—nationalism, fascism, communism—played out their deadly games with lethal consequences, and that now religions (or religiously shaped "civilization") will play out theirs. But his need not be the case. Not if we can transcend the nasty rhetoric—religious and antireligious alike—and tackle the common task of helping one another figure out how we got to this unpromising point and how we can get through it without making things worse. If this is not a war against evil, or against Islam, or "the West against the rest," then where do we start to sort this out?

There is one place we should not start. Recently Salman Rushdie argued in an Op-Ed article in the *New York Times* that this is a war between medieval obscurantism and modernity. Last month the *Washington Post*'s lead editorial complained about the "anti-modern propaganda" emanating from the Arab press. The clear implication is that we in the West should all now lay aside our petty quarrels and rally around the standard of modernity. But is this really the common ground we gratefully share, or the banner we gallantly unfurl? Modernity has undoubtedly brought us some benefits. But do we really believe that its curious amalgam of formal democracy, consumer capitalism, trivialized mass culture, ever-higher-tech communications and American global hegemony is what we should be dispatching the B-52s to defend? Is this to be a war to make the world safe for modernity? Is anyone who finds something amiss about modernity to be lumped with the obscurantists?

I hope not. After all, modernity itself has generated some of its most persuasive critics. The philosophers of the Frankfurt School demonstrated how the Enlightenment soon became its own sacred myth. French humanists eloquently cautioned us about the seductions of a technologism. Poets have warned about the "waste land" and artists have painted their deep misgivings on numberless canvases. Even economists, not always the first to grasp the obvious, are becoming uncertain as they watch market economies, the sine qua non of modernity, drive an ever deeper wedge between the rich and the poor. The atrocity that struck the American homeland in September was already a familiar one to the millions who live every day amid the daily horror of dislocation and destitution.

Religious thinkers have been among the most articulate critics of the myth of a benevolent modernity. One thinks of movements like the Social Gospel or Liberation Theology, or of writers like Reinhold Niebuhr, Paul Tillich and Emmanuel Levinas. But they have hardly carried the torch alone. If fact, the "critique of modernity" has been common enterprise of religious and non-religious thinkers alike. Still, it seems we have not yet quite won the argument. And now we are being advised that because Al Qaeda despises modernity, Western intellectuals should of course defend it down to our last brilliant article and sonorous talk-show contribution.

Again, I hope not. Someday, sooner or later, the movements against which the U.S. coalition is fighting will fall. Maybe then it will become clear not only that we are not the Great Satan of the terrorists' rhetoric but that they are not the incarnation of evil pictured in ours. As we hear President Putin deftly answering questions on American radio and TV, it is easy to forget how recently the Soviet Union was the "evil empire." But when the guns have fallen silent, evil in its many guises—some of then lushly beguiling—will still prowl among us. Remember that the Devil is an angel of light. Meanwhile, we should resist becoming the office of *propaganda fidei* in a spurious metaphysical crusade against evil or in wagon-circling defense of modernity. Rather, our task is to search for a comprehensive alternative to the "modernity" that—though certainly not the Arch Fiend—is arguably the most widely circulated and most destructive myth abroad today, all the more so because it is so alluring, at least to those who benefit from it. Creating an alternative paradigm, however, will be a daunting venture. It will continue to require the best imagination of poets and artists, and the philosophical resources of religious and nonreligious thinkers alike.

Fundamentalism[3]

BY R. SCOTT APPLEBY AND MARTIN E. MARTY
FOREIGN POLICY, JANUARY/FEBRUARY 2002

For all the current focus on fiery Islamic extremists, religious fundamentalists are not confined to any particular faith or country, nor
to the poor and uneducated. Instead, they are likely to spring up
anywhere people perceive the need to fight a godless, secular culture—even if they have to depart from the orthodoxy of their traditions to do it. In fact, what fundamentalists everywhere have in
common is the ability to craft their messages to fit the times.

"All Fundamentalism Is Religious"

Yes. It's true that many sorts of groups share basic characteristics
of religious fundamentalists: They draw lines in the sand, demand
unconditional obedience from the rank and file, expend enormous
energies maintaining boundaries between the pure and impure,
build impenetrable dogmatic fortresses around "the truth," and see
their version of it as absolute, infallible, or inerrant. Indeed, some
may be tempted to seek manifestations of "secular fundamentalism"
in Marxism or Soviet-era state socialism, in the many virulent
strains of nationalism in evidence today, or in the unqualified
extremism of ideologically driven revolutionary or terrorist movements, from Peru's Shining Path to Germany's Baader-Meinhof
gang. In a similar vein, one might speak of "scientific fundamentalism" to connote the assumption, held by many modern scientists,
that empirically based knowledge is the only reliable way of knowing reality.

But we hesitate to call such secular groups "fundamentalist." They
may call upon followers to make the ultimate sacrifice, but unlike
the monotheistic religions, especially Christianity and Islam, they
do not reassure their followers that God or an eternal reward awaits
them. The absence of a truly "ultimate" concern affects how such
secular groups think about and carry out their missions, and the
belief in heaven or paradise serves as a very different kind of framework for and legitimation of self-martyrdom in the monotheistic
religions.

---

3. Article by R. Scott Appleby and Martin F. Marty. Reproduced with permission from *Foreign
Policy* # 128 (January/February 2002). Copyright © 2002 by the Carnegie Endowment for International Peace.

"Fundamentalism Is Limited to Monotheism"

No. Let us put aside for the moment the observation that Hinduism and Buddhism are not religions in the Western sense of the word and that Hindus and Buddhists do not believe in a personal God. Like another major South Asian religion, Sikhism, which has produced its fair share of candidates for the fundamentalist family, these great traditions of belief and practice orient devotees to a reality (or nonreality) that transcends or renders illusory the mundane world. And they have produced powerful modern, antisecular, antimodernist, absolutist, boundary-setting, exclusionary, and often violent movements that bear startling resemblances to fundamentalism within the Jewish, Christian, and Islamic worlds.

Indeed, the Hindutva movement in India has consciously borrowed elements from the theistic Western traditions, including a supernatural patron, the Lord Rama, with his own sacred birthplace, in order to give Hinduism the kind of prickly spine that allows Western theistic fundamentalists to get their backs up when threatened. Sikh radicals exhibit a sense of apocalyptic expectation more natural in non-Asian cultures. And Buddhist "warriors" in Sri Lanka have transformed segments of the *sangha*, or monastic order, into an implacable force for religious and cultural nationalism. These "synthetic" Asian variants of fundamentalism select and canonize sacred epics, poems, and other open-ended genres into the stuff of fundamental, inerrant scripture.

"Fundamentalists Are Literalists"

Not so. Fundamentalists lay claim to preaching and practicing "the unvarnished word of God" as revealed in the Hebrew Bible, the New Testament, or the Koran. This claim undergirds the fundamentalists' larger assertion that their authority comes directly from God and thus their program for reform and transformation is, in principle, beyond criticism. Such claims are patently false. Religious traditions are vast, complex bodies of wisdom built up over generations. Their foundational sources (sacred scriptures, codified oral teachings, and commentaries) express and interpret the experiences of the sacred that led to the formation of their religious communities. Religious traditions are not less than these sources; they are always more. Interpretation is nine tenths of the law— even religious law—and the sources of religious law are often multivalent and contradictory. One verse of the Koran condemns killing while another commands the slaying of infidels. How to choose? The art is called hermeneutics—developing a theory that guides the interpretation.

Fundamentalists claim not to interpret, but they are the narrowest and most ideologically guided interpreters. West Bank settlers of Gush Emunim in Israel, the most prominent fundamentalist movement in Judaism, depend not only on one esoteric way of reading the Torah but on the mystical utterances of two 20th-century rabbis, Rabbi Zvi Yehuda Kook the Elder and his son. The rabbis selected one of the 613 mitzvahs, or Torah duties—to settle "the whole land of Israel"—and elevated it above all others. Similarly, one of American Protestant fundamentalism's main themes, "premillennial dispensationalism," a form of apocalypse that proclaims that the world is deteriorating morally and that Christ will soon return in vengeance, is not "traditional." It was developed in England in the middle of the 19th century.

> *Religious extremists tend to prey upon the young and untutored.*

Fundamentalists are eager to adapt to the exigencies of the moment if it suits the movement's needs. In Lebanon, the militant Hezbollah benefited in the 1980s from Muslim clerics' promotion of the injunction to "be fruitful and multiply": From 1956 to 1975 the Shiite minority population tripled, so that in 20 years the Shiite representation in the population jumped from 19 to 30 percent. In postrevolutionary Iran, by contrast, officials argued that modification of birth control teaching did not violate traditional norms. Ministry of Health officials publicized how unchecked population growth hurt families and lauded the virtues of the small family and its quality of life. Officials then promoted birth control measures, a serious step given what had been interpreted as Islamic injunctions against such measures.

To gain support beyond small cadres of followers, fundamentalist leaders must persuade ordinary believers to suspend existing teachings that condemn violence and promote peacemaking. Believers who are theologically informed and spiritually well formed tend not to be susceptible to such arguments. Unfortunately, ordinary believers are not always sufficiently grounded in the teachings and practices of their traditions to counter fundamentalists' selective reading of sacred texts. Thus religious extremists tend to prey upon the young and untutored.

"Fundamentalism Attracts the Poorest"

A common misperception. Without question, fundamentalist groups often recruit among and appeal to people on the short end of economic development. Often the followers are poor, jobless people, lacking worldly prospects. But they are not the poorest of the poor, who do not have the luxury of becoming disciples—much less leaders of fundamentalist movements—and are more preoccupied with "the fundamentals" of basic survival. More commonly, recruits come from the educated unemployed or underemployed, or from gainfully employed teachers, engineers, medical technicians, and other professionals in the applied sciences, areas of specialization in which modernizing societies are playing catch-up.

In Algeria, "the young men who hold up the walls" swelled the ranks of Islamist cadres in the 1980s and 1990s. The Algerian state had educated a generation of young men but had not developed an economy that could employ novice engineers and technocrats. Un- or underemployed, these young men, entering their sexual prime but frustrated because they could not support brides, hung out on street corners in Algiers and other urban centers, awaiting social salvation. They were thus particularly receptive to the slogan, "Islam is the solution."

Across the Middle East, such desperate but capable men signed on to destroy the corrupt, repressive, ineffective, and nominally Muslim leadership of the Arab world. The daring joined the ranks of the transnational mujahedin—the Islamist "freedom fighters" dispatched to Afghanistan in the 1980s to thwart the godless Soviet invaders. The graduates of that campaign made their way into the ranks of al Qaeda, Islamic Jihad, and other terrorist networks.

The second category, gainfully employed but spiritually unfulfilled, swells the ranks of Jewish, Christian, and Islamic fundamentalist groups. As conservative Christian denominations in the United States split and fundamentalists left them during the 1920s and 1930s, many rural, culturally sheltered, traditionally religious people joined the newly formed independent churches, and fundamentalists got typed and dismissed as redneck, dirt-poor, backwoods people who had nothing to gain on earth and everything to gain by hope of heaven. But identifying Christian fundamentalists with hillbillies and rednecks is a half-truth, at best. Protestant fundamentalist leaders have included Princeton professors and "creationists" boasting Ph.D.'s. Today, Christian fundamentalists live in Dallas suburbs as well as in the Tennessee hill country. They drive BMWs in Nashville and own malls and Bible-based radio stations and cable channels.

The Jewish movements attracted affluent American Jews who made aliyah and upon their return to Israel turned super-Orthodox. The Islamic cadres hail from a variety of backgrounds, including extremely wealthy families, and have advanced degrees from Western universities. Mohammed Atta, the Hamburg-based student who learned to pilot jetliners in preparation for American Airlines Flight 11 (which crashed into the World Trade Center), is typical of the 21st-century fundamentalist—the illiterate or semi-literate peasant is not.

The fact that fundamentalist movements' middle management and rank and file frequently have educational and professional backgrounds in applied sciences, technical, and bureaucratic fields helps explain why fundamentalists tend to read scriptures like engineers read blueprints—as a prosaic set of instructions and specifications. In fundamentalist hands, the complex, multivocal, ambiguous treasury of mysteries is reduced to a storehouse of raw materials to be ransacked as needed for building a political program. Few poets or cosmologists find their way into fundamentalist cadres.

"Fundamentalism Leads to Violence"

Not necessarily. Social context and the local or regional political culture have much to say about the directions that fundamentalism takes. Within the abode of Islam, nation-states are either weak or failing, on the one hand, or dictatorial and repressive, on the other. Both contexts encourage violent variants of fundamentalism bent on replacing the state (as the Taliban did in Afghanistan) or overthrowing it (as the Shiites did in Iran and as radical Islamic groups have hoped to do in Egypt, Algeria, Saudi Arabia, and elsewhere).

American Christian fundamentalists would argue they are and always have been law-abiding citizens. "Why do you compare us to extremist Arabs and gun-toting Jewish settlers?" a fundamentalist

---

What's in a Name?

While the word "fundamentalism" is here to stay, not everyone is at ease with it, and maybe no one ever should be. Clustering movements, for comparative purposes, that share broad "family resemblances" may lead untutored onlookers to wrongly conclude that all believers are fundamentalists, that all fundamentalists are terrorists, and therefore that every form of orthodox religion should be banished from public expression. Phrases like "the rage of Islam" don't help.

For a time, some newspapers chose to avoid the term and referred to fundamentalist movements only as "extremist," "militant," or "fanatic." Readers had a hard time making out just what people were "extremist" about. Militias are militant but not often fundamentalist. Football fans can be fanatic.

Yet many who shunned the word fundamentalist did so with good reason, and what they say gives pause to those who would use it casually. The main argument has been that the term belonged only in the United States, where Protestant fundamentalist Curtis Lee Laws coined the term and where a famous nonfundamentalist minister, Harry Emerson Fosdick, once defined a fundamentalist as "a mad evangelical."

Substitutes have not been satisfying. Call something "neoreformist radical revolutionary Islamism" and you may well point to the features of one movement. But how then may it be compared to others?

Some who attack the use of the word fundamentalism will use "capitalist" or "liberal" without batting an eye, even though both terms were born somewhere in some specific circumstance. Careful scholars and publics will take care to see exactly how various fundamentalist groups invest their movements with meaning and what particular meanings give life to their movements. They will pick their language with care. But to deny use of the term "fundamentalist" because it did not exist in other languages a century ago is not distinctive. It did not exist in English either. A new phenomenon was on the scene, and it needed a name.

friend once demanded. "We do not stockpile arms in the basement of Moody Bible School in Chicago!" Although they may sometimes be associated with abortion-clinic bombers and white supremacist or antigovernment militias—neither of which qualify as fundamentalists because of their tenuous connections to organized Christianity—American Christian fundamentalists do not resort to violence. But that may have more to do with the character of their society—open, pluralist, governed by the rule of law, and tolerant of moderate expressions of fundamentalism—than with their principled rejection of violence.

Many hard-bitten policymakers assume there is no such thing as a moderate fundamentalist—especially in the Islamic cases. Such a view allowed the U.S. government, the putative champion of democracy and free elections, to turn a blind eye to the 1991 invalidation and subsequent cancellation of democratic elections in Algeria, when the

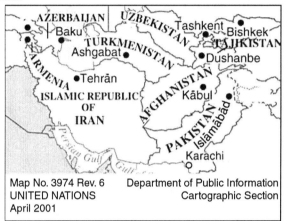

Map No. 3974 Rev. 6   Department of Public Information
UNITED NATIONS   Cartographic Section
April 2001

Islamic Salvation Front won at the ballot box and appeared poised to assume control of the parliament. The Islamic form of democracy, according to the conventional wisdom in the State Department, means "one man, one vote—one time."

There is insufficient evidence to support such a conclusion. Indeed, the majority of fundamentalist Muslims, including Islamists who serve in the parliaments of Jordan, Indonesia, and Malaysia, have consistently refused to identify their movements with the terrorist fringe.

Deadly violence does occur, however, when brands of fundamentalism clash, as in the case of religiously motivated Jewish settlers and Islamic militants fighting for the same territory on the West Bank and Gaza. In Africa, a bitter contest for souls between Christianity and Islam has led to the torture, murder, and, reportedly, the crucifixion of Christians by Islamic extremists. In Pakistan, blasphemy laws putatively based in Islamic law are used to justify the persecution of Christians and other religious minorities.

"Fundamentalists Oppose Change"

Hardly. Fundamentalists are dedicated to changing a world they see as godless, but their remedy is not to preserve or recreate the past. Amish they are not. In an odd way, they are "progressives," not conservatives; most people simply do not agree that the world they envision could be called "progress." They have inhabited the modern material and technical world while attempting to cast off its pernicious, dehumanizing, materialistic philosophy.

How does this profile of the thoroughly modern, change-oriented fundamentalist square with the image of the angry rebel? Fundamentalists are, indeed, reactive: Their independent churches, mosques, and yeshivas and their cadres, networks, and movements originated in heated, defiant opposition to some trend—be it the invasion of Bible criticism and evolutionists into Protestant seminaries and churches, the narrowly secular vision borne out in Israeli policies, or the corruption of "establishment" imams in Cairo and across the Sunni world.

> *Fundamentalists are dedicated to changing a world they see as godless, but their remedy is not to preserve or recreate the past.*

But notice how they reacted. Not by yearning for the return of the golden age of medieval Islam, but by transforming the Prophet into an icon of global jihad who delivers modern nation-states to Islam. Not by hiding out in the ultra-Orthodox enclave of Mea Sharim in Jerusalem, but by forming political parties and playing power politics in the Knesset. Not merely by invoking 16th-century Protestant reformers such as Martin Luther and John Calvin, who defended the supreme authority of the Bible, but by inventing the concept of strict inerrancy.

Likewise, Sayyid Qutb, the major ideologue of the Muslim Brotherhood before his 1966 execution in Egypt, claimed that reputed Muslim societies had descended into a state of *jahiliyya* (pre-Islamic barbarism and ignorance). Under Qutb's teaching, everyone had to pass litmus tests designed to separate the true believer from the infidel, in order to wage jihad against the latter. He thereby displaced the concept of jihad as a believer's internal struggle against his profane passions with jihad as an external war against the unbeliever.

The examples abound: Fundamentalists do not oppose change; they specialize in it.

"Cults of Personality Drive Fundamentalism"

No. It would be comforting to think so. Unfortunately for those who would like to see their influence diminished, fundamentalist movements are not cults. Fundamentalist leaders may be charismatic, as is Sheik Muhammad Hussein Fadlallah, Hezbollah's spiritual guide, or they may not be, but they are always authoritarian. In other words, such leaders' appeal for potential recruits is their continuity with the ancient religious tradition, which they claim to uphold and defend. Thus, fundamentalist leaders, even the fire-brands, must be perceived as acting and interpreting within the bounds of the tradition. And although Osama bin Laden pushes the envelope in this regard, he still argues his case on traditional grounds.

Scholars thus avoid lumping fundamentalists with cult leaders such as Branch Davidian leader David Koresh, Jim Jones in Guy-ana, or Aum Shinrikyo's Shoko Asahara because the cultic leaders have decisively broken with tradition, in rhetoric as well as behav-ior. They claim the ancient prophecies are being fulfilled in their persons; apocalypse is now, and because they say so. Cult leaders have a problem, then, that most fundamentalist movements avoid. When cult leaders die, sometimes at their own beckoning, and the End does not arrive, most of their movements flare out as well. Fundamentalists, by contrast, aspire to be fixed stars in the firma-ment.

Accordingly, Fadlallah may deliver a radical ruling and support it with a fiery homily, but he always genuflects in the direction of Islamic law. And when he departs the scene, the Shiite community will raise up another leader, authoritarian, yes, and charismatic, perhaps. But fundamentalism doesn't require it. Certainly many of the early leaders of U.S. Protestant fundamentalism—Curtis Lee Laws and J. Gresham Machen—lacked charisma.

Most congregations have relied on their local pastors to decree what "the Bible says." Islam, too, is a village religion. It is true that electronic communications make it easier for leaders to reach many congregations. But technology is not the primary impetus for such movements. Fundamentalism appears almost as if by sponta-neous combustion, or as if spread by capillary action, under the guidance of leaders who mumble, stumble, and falter but who are tagged as authorized agents of God because they properly interpret "the word."

Separated at Birth[4]

By Leela Jacinto
ABCNEWS.COM, December 28, 2001

In August 1947, when the British divided the Asian subcontinent into Muslim-dominated Pakistan and Hindu-dominated India, it set off a bloodbath that left around half a million people dead.

Called "Partition" across the subcontinent, it was a bloody baptism for the two newly independent nations from which the region has not recovered.

More than 50 years after independence, the two neighbors have seen three wars, a dangerous arms escalation and the looming threat of a new nuclear war.

At the heart of the seemingly intractable conflict between the two countries is the Himalayan region of Kashmir, famed for its snow-capped mountains and lush green valleys, a region described by travelers, poets and conquerors through centuries as "paradise on earth."

But after a brutal 12-year insurgency that has claimed more than 60,000 lives, according to human rights groups, and almost daily threats of terrorist attacks and military crackdowns, the paradise is for all purposes lost.

Conflicting Claims

While one part of Kashmir lies in Pakistan and a part in India, the two countries have conflicting claims to the whole that are rooted in religion and history.

The Indian position says Kashmir belongs to the Indian republic because of the Instrument of Accession signed in October 1947 by the Kashmiri ruler at the time, Maharajah Hari Singh, which handed over the princely state to India.

But because the maharajah was a Hindu ruler of a majority Muslim kingdom, Pakistan rejected the Instrument of Accession. It maintains numerous U.N. resolutions mean that Kashmiris should be allowed to vote in a plebiscite to decide between India or Pakistan.

For its part, India refers to the Simla Agreement signed by then-Indian Prime Minister Indira Gandhi and Pakistani President Zulfikar Ali Bhutto in 1972, which calls for a bilateral solution to the Kashmir issue.

---

4. Article by Leela Jacinto courtesy of *ABCNEWS.com* December 28, 2001. Copyright © *ABC-NEWS.com*. Reprinted with permission.

The Simla Agreement came at the end of the second war between the two countries, which erupted when the Indian military backed what was then the East Pakistani independence movement.

Separated by the Indian subcontinent from the rest of Pakistan and reeling from human rights atrocities that are still under dispute, East Pakistan emerged from the conflict as the newly independent nation of Bangladesh.

Wars of Words

While the Simla Agreement reaffirmed the Line of Control between Pakistani- and Indian-administered Kashmir that was arrived at after the 1947 war, the violence flared again in 1982 when an insurgency broke out in Indian-administered Kashmir.

India holds Pakistan responsible for sponsoring militant Islamic groups in Indian-controlled Kashmir. It says Pakistani madrassas (religious schools) as well as Pakistani-supported training camps in Afghanistan through the 1980s and 1990s have trained recruits from across the Muslim world to operate in Kashmir.

Pakistan insists it only offers the groups moral support and accuses India of denying Muslim-majority Kashmiris the right to national self-determination.

In the summer of 1998, the conflict reached alarming pro-

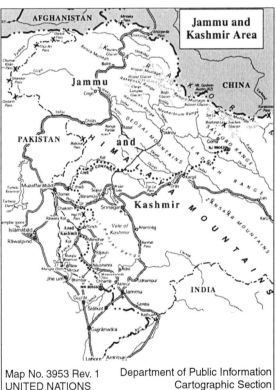

Map No. 3953 Rev. 1   Department of Public Information
UNITED NATIONS   Cartographic Section
July 1999

portions when New Delhi announced it had conducted successful nuclear tests in northwestern India. Weeks later, Pakistan announced that it had conducted five nuclear tests of its own.

Ever since, the international community has watched in dread. A border conflict in 1999 threatened to spill into an all-out war, but wide-scale conflict was averted. Two years later, on Dec. 13, an audacious terrorist attack on the Indian parliament killed 14 people and moved the two countries once again to the brink of war.

India blames two militant Islamic groups, which is says enjoys Pakistani support, for the attack. Pakistan has denied the charge and, following the warming ties between Islamabad and Washington in the post-Sept. 11 war on terrorism, it has announced a crackdown on the two militant Islamic groups.

But India has denounced Pakistan's measures as "cosmetic" and the dangerous animosity between the two South Asian neighbors, once part of a unified entity, continues.

Religious Wars?[5]

A Short History of the Balkans

BY PAUL MOJZES
COMMONWEAL, JUNE 4, 1999

After the commencement of the NATO bombing of Serbia, in April CNN (in my view tendentiously) aired an interview with the notorious Zeljko Raznjatovic-Arkan. As the leader of the paramilitary Serbian "Tigers," Arkan has been indicted by the war crimes tribunal in The Hague for barbarities committed during the Bosnian war. For his "service" in Bosnia, Arkan was elected a deputy in the Yugoslavian parliament as a representative from Kosovo. Christiana Amanpour's report on Arkan's atrocities went on to show him making a cynical display of his alleged Orthodox faith. Before the cameras he pulled out a cross from under his shirt and kissed it, his wedding (his second wife is a Serbian pop star) was officiated at by numerous priests, and he was shown repeatedly crossing himself and in other ways demonstrating his loyalty to the Serbian Orthodox church. His display of religiosity was both a cruel hoax and a window into the nature of the "religious" character of much of the violence that has convulsed the Balkans, Eastern Europe, and the former Soviet Union for the past decade.

After the collapse of communism in 1989, several wars broke out pitting various religious groups against each other. In southwestern Asia, Armenian Christians fought Muslim Azeris for Nagorno-Karabakh. Serbs (who are Orthodox) waged war against Croats (who are Catholics). In Bosnia-Herzegovina the Croats and Serbs continued to fight each other while also fighting Muslim Boshnyaks. Now Orthodox Serbs are fighting or forcibly expelling Muslim Albanians from Kosovo. Everybody seems to be opposed to the Serbs except fellow Orthodox Greeks (including Greek Cypriots) and Russians. All of this may seem like evidence for a theory that links religious attachment to nationalistic efforts to cleanse ethnic "others," but things are somewhat more complicated than they appear.

As in Europe as a whole, powerful forces of secularization, whether in its Marxist atheist or its consumerist "Western" garb, have also been at work in the Balkans. Many of the region's religious leaders vehemently deny that religion (or at least their own religion) plays an important role in these conflicts. They point out how marginalized religion was under communism and how little

---

actual power religious leaders and institutions have. This has a certain plausibility. We mustn't forget how the appeals of many prominent religious leaders—the pope, the patriarchs of Constantinople and Moscow, the World Council of Churches, etc.—have gone unheeded by NATO. Religious pleading usually has little influence in ending wars.

Map No. 3877 Rev. 1   Department of Public Information
UNITED NATIONS   Cartographic Section
June 1999

Still, a nuanced case can be made that religion plays an important, if not decisive, role in many of these conflicts. At the outset, however, we must not confuse these modern nationalistic and ethnic conflicts with the religious wars of old (although even the Crusades and the religious wars of the sixteenth century were not solely or primarily religious). In Bosnia, for instance, religion played a greater role than it does currently in Kosovo, although some of the same religious protagonists are involved. To determine to what degree religion is implicated, each case must be analyzed separately.

Broadly speaking, there are two major ways in which religion comes into play in these modern wars. The first is that religion played a historic role in defining social and individual identities. Consequently, in Eastern Europe ethnic and religious identity are often fused to such a degree that they form an ethnoreligious symbiosis. The volatile interplay of various ethnoreligious allegiances has long worked just below the political surface throughout the region. Like the earth's tectonic plates, these fundamental social realities are little noticed until they shift or collide.

The second important impact of religion is in shaping sympathies (friendships) or antipathies (fears) within and against groups. Three major religious groups, namely the Eastern Orthodox, the Roman (Western) Catholic, and the Muslims are in play in the Balkans. Protestants are seen as pesky evangelizers who tend to deny the authenticity of the religious orientation of the big religions and rob people of their national identity and traditional faith. Anti-Semitism persists, but largely in the absence of any Jews.

Most of the peoples of Eastern Europe were Christianized prior to the Great Schism of 1054, some by missionaries who looked either to Constantinople or to Rome. When the tensions between these two ancient patriarchal sees split "the one, true, apostolic, and universal church," it ripped Christendom apart, creating a visible cultural and political fault line that runs from the Baltic to the Adriatic. Each church feared that reconciliation would mean surrendering dearly held truths and selling out to those whose truth was no longer complete. For the next thousand years the two churches became fierce competitors. The impact on statecraft was enormous, since each side understood itself to be establishing God's rule among an entire people. When necessary, emperors used force to forge a single religious and national identity.

By the thirteenth century, however, Mongol Tartars occupied most of the Russian Orthodox lands while the Ottoman Turks in the fourteenth century captured large portions of the Christian Balkans. Both promoted their Muslim religion among various segments of the population. The Ottoman Empire's hold was longer and more successful, but under both conquerors an imperial Islam laid claim on many lives and all aspects of society. To this day the followers of Islam, very much like medieval Christians, see their religion as a comprehensive way of life. Converts to Islam changed

---

Even under communism . . . there was a distinct cultural and civilizational awareness of religious heritage and identity.

---

not only religious practice but culture and civilization as well. As a consequence, Christian Balkan populations were repressed. Russians were under this "yoke," as they are fond of calling it, for two centuries; the Balkan peoples for five. The Russians gradually threw off the yoke and in the seventeenth and eighteenth centuries became an empire, successfully colonizing millions of non-Christians, most of them Muslims. As the tables turned, the Muslims resented their Russian (Orthodox) colonizers as much as the Russians had resented them. Similarly, when the Islamic colonization of the Balkans ended in the nineteenth and twentieth centuries, an enormous rage, fueled by nascent modern nationalism, erupted. Not only the Turks, but those locals whose ancestors had converted to the religion of the Turks, became the objects of retribution. The "never again" of the Balkan Christians is a "never again" to living under Islam.

In the Balkans the conversion to Islam was most successful among Albanians. About 70 percent of Albanians have an Islamic identity (among the Kosovars the figure is close to 100 percent). Former Orthodox and Catholic Bosnians also converted to Islam, to the tune of a third of the population. In Bulgaria a significant minority of Turks and converted Slavs (Pomaks) complicated the picture. After the collapse of the Ottoman and Hapsburg empires in 1918, most of the newly reestablished nation-states in the Balkans—Greece, Bulgaria, Serbia, Montenegro, Romania (all Orthodox), and Hungary, Czechoslovakia, Poland, Croatia, and Slovenia

(Catholic)—defined themselves in distinctly anti-Islamic ways. Suspicion and discord, however, also continued to run along the fault line of the Great Schism.

This somewhat oversimplified scheme seemed to lose much of its relevance after World War II when all of these countries (except Greece) fell under Communist domination. Ardent efforts were made to suppress all religion. Even under communism, however, there was a distinct cultural and civilizational awareness of religious heritage and identity. There was also a particular resentment by those who were nominally Christian toward the burgeoning Muslim population. Adding to these divisions was the fact that the Eastern Orthodox, and even more so the Muslim population, were less willing to adapt to industrialization and modernization. In many quarters, these groups were seen as obstacles to economic development.

With the collapse of communism in the late 1980s and early 1990s, its leveling of social and ethnic hierarchies dissipated and the underlying resentments and fears rose to the surface where nationalistic leaders like Slobodan Milosevic could exploit them. As the Muslim population started to demand greater rights, including the right to self-determination, Serb resistance hardened. Dark, exaggerated fears of Islamic fundamentalism and a return to a Shariate legal system that would subjugate Christians flourished. As seen in the Bosnian war, inordinate bloodshed, forced migrations, partition, and other calamities quickly followed.

Religion usually nurtures a special feeling for co-religionists. Familial terms such as "brothers" and "sisters" are commonly used not only for co-religionists we know but also in addressing and thinking about the larger religious community. Religion allows disparate peoples to share the same symbols, external signs, and internal values. In times of calm people rejoice when they encounter co-religionists; such meetings are a sign, after all, that our religion is successful, that there are others with values like ours. In times of crisis and threat, these links become even more important. We feel that those who threaten our co-religionists may threaten us. If we do not come to the assistance of our fellow Muslims or Orthodox, who will? From this perspective it is natural that Turks or Iranians will support embattled Bosnian or Albanian Muslims (in Albania, Kosovo, Montenegro, or Macedonia), Greeks support Serbs as do Russians, and that Austrians, Hungarians, Germans, and Italians supported the Catholic Croats and Slovenes. Many Europeans (East and West) have an uneasy feeling that Muslims are making unwanted inroads into Europe, and that their physical presence and high birth rate will be followed by territorial demands. Muslims, undoubtedly, harbor similar fears of "Christians," even when they are motivated by nationalist or capitalist, rather than religious, interests.

Obviously such religious affiliations do not work automatically or universally. Bulgarians are somewhat ambivalent about the Serbs because of their rivalry over Macedonia. A Bulgarian Orthodox spokesperson sharply condemned Milosevic's policies in the Balkans. The Ukrainians do not show the same ardor toward Serbs as do Russians, if for no other reason than their apprehensions about Russian hegemony among Orthodox Slavs. Americans sided with Albanians who are predominantly Muslims, seemingly driven by TV pictures and sensing that something must be done about the flow of refugees. We are also driven, I think, by a delayed sense of remorse over how little was done to stop the Nazi extermination of European Jews.

The religious factor is real enough in the Balkans, and plays a smaller or greater role depending on the specific context. In Kosovo both the Serbs and the Albanians have exploited religious themes. But another factor is also in play. In the Balkans there has been much talk about "living space" and limited resources. Hitler, of course, used precisely these fears to justify his wars, but he was by no means the only modern European politician to do so. As the sometimes sharp increase in population allegedly outstrips the ability of a region to support it, especially in impoverished areas like the Balkans, political conflict increasingly gets cast in the language of life or death. Obviously such extreme rhetoric lends itself to radical or "final" solutions.

American politicians and media are fond of claiming that we are a naive and innocent nation that somehow keeps falling prey to more sinister forces. However, we should not be naive enough to think that by bombing a country into submission or placing an international military force on the ground, we can settle intractable ethnoreligious conflicts. Trying to fix distant conflicts by force before learning how those involved see themselves and their adversaries often compounds the problem.

III. New Religions and
Religious Conversion

Editor's Introduction

I n most surveys of world religion, journalists and scholars begin by identifying five major faiths: Christianity, Judaism, Islam, Hinduism, and Buddhism. Together, these five religions account for the vast majority of believers in the world today. By adding tribal religions and indigenous Chinese traditions such as Confucianism and Taoism to the mix, one can include most within the rest. But aside from the fact that it ignores both minor religions and the extravagant diversity of each of the major traditions, this classification has a significant drawback: it suggests that the genesis of new religions is a phenomenon tidily cordoned off in the distant past. (Islam, by far the youngest of the five major religions, traces its origins to the seventh century.) In fact, new religions continue to appear throughout the world, and the missionary spirit remains alive and well. Practitioners both of established faiths and of new religions work tirelessly to expand their numbers, especially in parts of the world where natural disasters and civil war have created a population hungry for material relief and spiritual guidance.

As Toby Lester argues in his article "Oh, Gods!" the creative impulse that long ago gave birth to today's established religions remains as alive and prolific as ever. Religions, much like biological species, are continually evolving and mutating into new forms. "What is now dismissed as a fundamentalist sect, a fanatical cult, or a mushy New Age fad," writes Lester, "could become the next big thing."

The Falun Gong movement in China is one such religion that began modestly enough but has attracted international attention in recent years because of its persecution by the Chinese government, which chooses to view this increasingly popular religion as a threat to communist authority. "Falun Gong: What's Behind the Movements," by Christopher Wanjek, looks at what the practitioners of Falun Gong actually *do*, rather than at the political controversy surrounding it. Wanjek explains the purpose of the physical motions prescribed by Falun Gong, which have been compared to the Chinese arts of *quigong* and *tai chi*, and presents the conflicting views of experts as to the efficacy of these exercises. While some medical experts find these motions harmless and effective meditation techniques, others see Falun Gong as bordering on quackery, with its claims of healing by touch and other miracles.

The next article in this section, "The Church of the West," looks at the Church of Jesus Christ of Latter-Day Saints, or Mormons, as they are more colloquially known. Mormonism, which traces its roots to upstate New York in the first half of the nineteenth century, is well-established and solidly mainstream compared to the other new religions examined in this section. There are more than 11 million Mormons worldwide, and if current growth rates persist into the next century, Mormonism may well become "the first world religion since Islam." Still, it is a relatively new faith. A little over a century ago, Mormons practiced polygamy (a small minority still do); moreover, church doctrines, such as the "plurality of Gods" and the "eternal progression" of the soul, as well as the practice of posthumous baptism, continue to set Mormonism apart from mainstream Christianity.

Mormons are just one group of missionaries working to convert the people of Latin America, as Rachel Cobb describes in "Guatemala's New Evangelists." Evangelical Christians have stepped up their conversion efforts among the Mayan people of this region, in many places challenging or overcoming the influence of the traditional Catholic ideology. Cobb examines how these Protestant groups have filled a number of voids for the Guatemalan people in the wake of a long and brutal civil war, in many cases providing them not only with spiritual guidance, but also, in many cases, with food and shelter. "This is why I believe that God exists and that he sees us," claims one young Evangelical Protestant who receives food from his church. On the other hand, a Catholic priest describes his parishioners' faith in the crucifix as consistent with their Mayan culture, the primary reason why, as he says, "Some always return" to the Catholic faith after converting to Protestantism.

Another area of the world in which Christian missionaries have been active for over a century is Africa, where Andrew Walls has worked for years among the people of Ghana. In an interview for *Christian Century* entitled "The Expansion of Christianity," he compares the historical spread of Islam, Buddhism, and the Christian faith and speculates as to why Islam has maintained a firmer hold on its converts than Christianity. He then discusses at length the "cultural diversity" that has always informed Christianity, and in comparing the present-day African believers with early Christians, he asserts that the Church's cultural flexibility has enabled it to adapt its message and expand its reach throughout the African continent.

Oh, Gods!¹

BY TOBY LESTER
ATLANTIC MONTHLY, FEBRUARY 2002

In 1851 the French historian and philosopher Ernest Renan announced to the world that Islam was "the last religious creation of humanity." He was more than a bit premature. At about the time he was writing, the Bahai faith, Christian Science, Mormonism, the Seventh-Day Adventists, and a major Japanese religious movement known as Tenrikyo were all just coming to life. Falun Gong and Pentecostalism—both of which now have millions and millions of members—had yet to emerge. Whoops.

Contemporary theories of social and political behavior tend to be almost willfully blind to the constantly evolving role of religion as a force in global affairs. The assumption is that advances in the rational understanding of the world will inevitably diminish the influence of that last, vexing sphere of irrationality in human culture: religion. Inconveniently, however, the world is today as awash in religious novelty, flux, and dynamism as it has ever been—and religious change is, if anything, likely to intensify in the coming decades. The spectacular emergence of militant Islamist movements during the twentieth century is surely only a first indication of how quickly, and with what profound implications, change can occur.

It's tempting to conceive of the religious world—particularly when there is so much talk of clashing civilizations—as being made up primarily of a few well-delineated and static religious blocs: Christians, Jews, Muslims, Buddhists, Hindus, and so on. But that's dangerously simplistic. It assumes a stability in the religious landscape that is completely at odds with reality. New religions are born all the time. Old ones transform themselves dramatically. Schism, evolution, death, and rebirth are the norm. And this doesn't apply only to religious groups that one often hears referred to as cults. Today hundreds of widely divergent forms of Christianity are practiced around the world. Islam is usually talked about in monolithic terms (or, at most, in terms of the Shia-Sunni divide), but one almost never hears about the 50 million or so members of the Naqshabandiya order of Sufi Islam, which is strong in Central Asia and India, or about the more than 20 million members of various schismatic Muslim groups around the world. Think, too, about the strange rise and fall of the Taliban. Buddhism, far from being an all-encompassing glow radiating

---

benignly out of the East, is a vast family of religions made up of more than 200 distinct bodies, many of which don't see eye-to-eye at all. Major strands of Hinduism were profoundly reshaped in the nineteenth century, revealing strong Western and Christian influences.

Religion mutates with Darwinian restlessness.

The fact is that religion mutates with Darwinian restlessness. Take a long enough view, and all talk of "established" or "traditional" faith becomes oxymoronic: there's no reason to think that the religious movements of today are any less subject to change than were the religious movements of hundreds or even thousands of years ago. History bears this out. Early Christianity was deemed pathetic by the religious establishment: Pliny the Younger wrote to the Roman Emperor Trajan that he could get nothing out of Christian captives but "depraved, excessive superstition." Islam, initially the faith of a band of little-known desert Arabs, astonished the whole world with its rapid spread. Protestantism started out as a note of protest nailed to a door. In 1871 Ralph Waldo Emerson dismissed Mormonism as nothing more than an "after-clap of Puritanism." Up until the 1940s Pentecostalists were often dismissed as "holy rollers," but today the *World Christian Encyclopedia* suggests that by 2050 there may be more than a billion people affiliated with the movement. In the period after World War II so many new religious movements came into being in Japan that local scholars of religion were forced to distinguish between *shin-shukyo* ("new religions") and *shin-shin-shukyo* ("new new religions"); one Western writer referred to the time as "the rush hour of the gods." The implication is clear: what is now dismissed as a fundamentalist sect, a fanatical cult, or a mushy New Age fad could become the next big thing.

Anybody who doubts the degree to which the religious world is evolving should have a look at the second edition of the *World Christian Encyclopedia*, published last year by Oxford University Press in two oversized volumes of more than 800 pages each. The encyclopedia's title is misleading: the work is not devoted exclusively to Christianity. It is, in fact, the only serious reference work in existence that attempts both to survey and to analyze the present religious makeup of the entire world. It tracks the birth of new movements, records recent growth patterns, and offers scenarios for future growth. It divides major religions into different denominations and classifies each by country of origin and global reach. It records the dates that movements were founded and the names of their founders. It's the place to turn if you want to know how many Bahais there were in 2000 in the Bahamas (1,241), how many Jews in Yemen (1,087), how many Zoroastrians in Iran (1,903,182), how many Mormons in South Africa (10,200), or how many Buddhists in the United States (2,449,570).

The prime mover and longtime editor of the encyclopedia is a soft-spoken Anglican Charismatic named David B. Barrett. A former missionary in Africa, Barrett began working on the encyclopedia in the 1960s. His idea, which explains the work's title, was to create a reliable and richly informative tool for Christian evangelists around the world. Barrett is now affiliated with the Global Evangelization Movement in Richmond, Virginia, and with Pat Robertson's Regent University, in Virginia Beach, where he is a research professor of "missiometrics"—the science of missions.

I recently asked Barrett what he has learned about religious change in his decades of working on the encyclopedia. "The main thing we've discovered," he said, "is that there is *enormous* religious change going on across the world, all the time. It's massive, it's complex, and it's continual. We have identified nine thousand and nine hundred distinct and separate religions in the world, increasing by two or three new religions every day. What this means is that new religious movements are not just a curiosity, which is what people in the older denominations usually think they are. They are a very serious subject."

The Secularization Myth

Long the subject of ridicule and persecution, derided as cults, alternative religions are finally being taken seriously. The study of new religious movements—NRMs for short—has become a growth industry. NRM scholars come from a variety of backgrounds, but many are sociologists and religious historians. All are sympathetic to the idea that new religious movements should be respected, protected, and studied carefully. They tend to avoid the words "cult" and "sect," because of the polemical connotations; as a result NRM scholars are often caricatured in anti-cult circles as "cult apologists." They examine such matters as how new movements arise; what internal dynamics are at work as the movements evolve; how they spread and grow; how societies react to them; and how and why they move toward the mainstream.

The NRM field is only a few decades old, but already it has made its mark. NRM scholars were pivotal in the de-fanging of the anti-cult movement in the United States, which exercised considerable influence in the 1970s and 1980s and often engaged in the illegal— but frequently tolerated—practice of kidnapping and "deprogramming" members of new religious movements. In the aftermath of Waco, of the Heaven's Gate and Solar Temple suicides, and of the subway poisonings in Tokyo by Aum Shinrikyo, NRM scholars are now regularly consulted by the FBI, Scotland Yard, and other law-enforcement agencies hoping to avoid future tragedies. They are currently battling the major anti-cult legislation—directed explicitly at the "repression of cultic movements which undermine human rights and fundamental freedoms"—that was passed last year in France. (The legislation was implicitly rooted in a blacklist compiled in 1996 by a French parliamentary commission. The blacklist targets 173 movements, including the Center for Gnostic Studies, the Hare Krishnas, some evangelical Protestant groups, practitioners of Transcendental Meditation, Rosicrucians, Scientologists, Wiccans, and the Jehovah's Witnesses.)

NRM scholars have even influenced the Vatican. In 1991, as part of what was then the largest gathering of Catholic cardinals in the history of the Church, an Extraordinary Consistory was held to discuss just two matters: the "threats to life" (that is, contraception, euthanasia, and abortion) and the challenges posed to the Church by neo-religious, quasi-religious and pseudo-religious groups." NRM scholars were involved as advisers, and the result was a surprisingly liberal report, written by Cardinal Arinze, that referred to "New Religious Movements" rather than to "cults" or "sects" and even suggested that these movements have something to teach the Church. "The dynamism of their missionary drive," the report said

---

"Each generation has been confident that within another few decades, or possibly a bit longer, humans will 'outgrow' belief in the supernatural."—sociologist **Rodney Stark**

---

of the NRMs, "the evangelistic responsibility assigned to the new 'converts,' their use of the mass media and their setting of the objectives to be attained, should make us ask ourselves questions as to how to make more dynamic the missionary activity of the Church."

That dynamism also speaks to one of the significant facts of our time: the failure of religion to wither away on schedule. This is a state of affairs that the sociologist Rodney Stark addresses in the book *Acts of Faith* (2000). "For nearly three centuries," he writes, "social scientists and assorted Western intellectuals have been promising the end of religion. Each generation has been confident that within another few decades, or possibly a bit longer, humans will 'outgrow' belief in the supernatural. This proposition soon came to be known as the secularization thesis." Stark goes on to cite a series of failed prophecies about the impending demise of religion, concluding with a statement made by the American sociologist Peter Berger, who in 1968 told *The New York Times* that by "the 21st century, religious believers are likely to be found only in small sects, huddled together to resist a worldwide secular culture."

Secularization of a sort certainly has occurred in the modern world—but religion seems to keep adapting to new social ecosystems, in a process one might refer to as "supernatural selection." It shows no sign of extinction, and "theodiversity" is, if anything, on the rise. How can this be? Three decades ago the British sociologist Colin Campbell suggested an answer. A way to explore the apparently paradoxical relationship between secularization and religion, Campbell felt, might be to examine closely what happens on the religious fringe, where new movements are born. "Ironically enough," he wrote, "it could be that the very processes of secularization which have been responsible for the 'cutting back' of the established form of religion have actually allowed 'hardier varieties' to flourish."

A Theodiversity Sampler

The variety of flourishing new religious movements around the world is astonishing and largely unrecognized in the West. The groups that generally grab all the attention—Moonies, Scientologists, Hare Krishnas, Wiccans—amount to a tiny and not particularly significant proportion of what's out there. Here are just a few representatively diverse examples of new movements from around the world:

The Ahmadis. A messianic Muslim sect based in Pakistan, with perhaps eight million members in seventy countries, the Ahmadi movement was founded by Mirza Ghulam Ahmad, a Punjabi Muslim who began receiving divine revelations in 1876. "In order to win the pleasure of Allah," he wrote, "I hereby inform you all of the important fact that Almighty God has, at the beginning of this 14th century [in the Islamic calendar], appointed me from Himself for the revival and support of the true faith of Islam." Ahmad claimed to have been brought to earth as "the Imam of the age today who must, under Divine Command, be obeyed by all Muslims." Members of the movement are considered heretics by most Muslims and are persecuted accordingly. They are barred entry to Mecca. In the Ahmadi version of religious history Jesus escaped from the cross and made his way to India, where he died at the age of 120.

The Brahma Kumaris World Spiritual University. A prosperous ascetic meditation movement based in India, with some 500,000 members (mostly women) worldwide, the group was founded by Dada Lekh Raj, a Hindu diamond merchant who in the 1930s experienced a series of powerful visions revealing "the mysterious entity of God and explaining the process of world transformation." Its establishment was originally rooted in a desire to give self-determination and self-esteem to Indian women. Members wear white, abstain from meat and sex, and are committed to social-welfare projects. They believe in an eternal, karmic scheme of time that involves recurring 1,250-year cycles through a Golden Age (perfection), a Silver Age (incipient degeneration), a Copper Age (decadence ascendant), and an Iron Age (rampant violence, greed, and lust—our present state). The group is recognized as a nongovernmental organization by the United Nations, with which it often works.

Cao Dai. A syncretistic religion based in Vietnam, with more than three million members in fifty countries, Cao Dai combines the teachings of Confucianism, Taoism, and Buddhism and also builds on elements of Judaism, Christianity, Islam, and Geniism. The movement was formally established in 1926, six years after a government functionary named Ngo Ming Chieu received a revelation from Duc Cao Dai, the Supreme Being, during a table-moving séance. The movement's institutional structure is based on that of the Catholic Church: its headquarters are called the Holy See, and its members are led by a pope, six cardinals, thirty-six archbishops, seventy-two bishops, and 3,000 priests. Cao Dai is elaborately ritualized and symbolic—a blend of incense, candles, multi-tiered altars, yin and yang, karmic cycles, séances for communication with the spirit world, and prayers to a pantheon of divine beings, including the Buddha, Confucius, Lao Tzu, Quan Am, Ly Thai Bach, Quan Thanh De Quan, and Jesus Christ. Its "Three Saints" are Sun Yat-sen; a sixteenth-century Vietnamese poet named Trang Trinh; and Victor Hugo. The movement gained more adherents in its first year of existence than Catholic missionaries had attracted during the Church's previous 300 years in Vietnam.

The Raëlians. A growing new international UFO oriented movement based in Canada, with perhaps 55,000 members worldwide, primarily in Quebec, French-speaking Europe, and Japan, the group was founded in 1973 by Raël, a French race-car journalist formerly known as Claude Vorilhon. Raël claims that in December of 1973, in the dish of a French volcano called Puy-de-Lassolas, he was taken onto a flying saucer, where he met a four-foot humanoid extraterrestrial with olive-colored skin, almond-shaped eyes, and long dark hair. The extraterrestrial's first words, in fluent French, were "You regret not having brought your camera?" On six successive days Raël had conversations with the extraterrestrial, from whom he learned that the human race was the creation (by means of DNA manipulation) of beings known as the Elohim—a word that was mistranslated in the Bible as "God" and actually means "those who came from the sky." Past prophets such as Moses, the Buddha, Jesus, and Muhammad had been given their revelations and training by the Elohim, who would now like to get to know their creations on equal terms, and demystify "the old concept of God." To that end the Raëlians have raised the money to build "the first embassy to welcome people from space." (Originally Raël was told that the embassy should be near Jerusalem, but Israel has been less than cooperative, and a recent revelation has led Raël to investigate Hawaii as a possibility.) Raël has also recently attracted international attention by creating Clonaid, a company devoted to the goal of cloning a human being.

Soka Gakkai International. A wealthy form of this worldly Buddhism, based in Japan and rooted in the teachings of the thirteenth-century Buddhist monk Nichiren, Soka Gakkai has some 18 million members in 115 countries. It was founded in 1930 by Makiguchi Tsunesaburo and Toda Josei and then re-established after World War II, at which point it began to grow dramatically. *"Soka gakkai"* means "value-creating society," and the movements members believe that true Buddhists should work not to escape earthly experience but, rather, to embrace and transform it into enlightened wisdom. Early members were criticized for their goal of worldwide conversion and their aggressive approach to evangelism, a strategy referred to as *shakubuku,* or "break through and overcome." In recent years the intensity has diminished. The movement is strongly but unofficially linked to New Komeito ("Clean Government Party"), currently the third most powerful group in the Japanese parliament. It is also registered as an NGO with the United Nations, and recently opened a major new liberal-arts university in southern California.

The Toronto Blessing. An unorthodox new evangelistic Christian Charismatic movement, based in Canada, the movement emerged in 1994 within the Toronto Airport branch of the Vineyard Church (itself a remarkably successful NRM founded in 1974), after a service delivered by a Florida-based preacher named Rodney Howard Browne. To date about 300,000 people have visited the movement's main church. Services often induce "a move of the Holy Spirit" that can trigger uncontrollable laughter, apparent drunkenness, barking like a dog, and roaring like a lion. The group finds support for its practices in passages from the Bible's Book of Acts, among them "All of them were filled with the Holy Spirit and began to speak in other tongues as the Spirit enabled them" and "Some, however, made fun of them and said, 'They have had too much wine.'" The Vineyard Church no longer recognizes the Toronto Blessing as an affiliate, but the two groups, like many other new Christian movements, put a markedly similar emphasis on spontaneity, informality, evangelism, and a lack of traditional organizational hierarchy.

Umbanda. A major syncretistic movement of spirit worship and spirit healing based in Brazil, with perhaps 20 million members in twenty-two countries, Umbanda emerged as an identifiable movement in the 1920s. It fuses traditional African religion (notably Yoruban) with native South American beliefs, elements of Catholicism, and the spiritist ideas of the French philosopher Allan Kardec. In 1857 Kardec published, in *The Spirits' Book*, transcripts of philosophical and scientific conversations he claimed to have had (using mediums from around the world) with members of the spirit world. The movement grew phenomenally in the twentieth century and is sometimes considered the "national religion of Brazil," uniting the country's many races and faiths.

Religious Amoebas

Last April, hoping to learn more about such groups and the people who study them, I attended an academic conference devoted to new religious movements and religious pluralism. The event, held at the London School of Economics, was put together and hosted by an influential British organization called the Information Network Focus on Religious Movements (INFORM), in cooperation with an Italian group known as the Center for Studies on New Religions (CESNUR). The conference sessions were dominated by a clubby international crew of NRM scholars who travel around the world presenting papers to one another. The American, English, formerly Soviet, and Japanese contingents seemed particularly strong. People regularly referred to articles that they had published or read in the new journal *Nova Religio*, a major outlet for NRM scholarship. Much of the buzz in the corridors had to do with the French anti-cult legislation, which was soon to be voted on. Everywhere I turned I seemed to bump into avuncular bearded American sociologists. "I'm so damn sick of the cult-anti-cult debate, I could just puke!" one of them told me heatedly over dinner, gesticulating with his fork. I hadn't brought the subject up.

What made the London conference distinctive was its nonacademic participants. At the opening reception I drank orange juice and munched on potato skins with a tall Swedish woman who had introduced herself to me as a member of the International Society for Krishna Consciousness—a Hare Krishna. I was joined at lunch one day by a nondescript elderly gentleman in a coat and tie who turned out to be a wry Latvian neo-pagan. Among the others I came across were European Bahais, British Moonies, a Jewish convert to the Family (a sort of "Jesus Freak" offshoot formerly known as the Children of God), members of a small messianic community known as the Twelve Tribes, and several representatives from the Church of Scientology, including the director of its European human-rights office. (Scientology is trying hard to gain formal status as a religion in Europe and the former Soviet Union, but many countries—notably France, Germany, and Russia—consider it a cult to be eradicated.)

That sounds like an exotic cast of characters, but actually it wasn't. The NRM members I encountered at the London conference were no more or less eccentric, interesting, or threatening than any of the people I rode with every morning on the London Underground. I found this oddly oppressive; I thought I'd be getting strangeness and mystery, but instead I got an essential human blandness. The people I met were just people.

This was a point made explicitly by the conference's organizer, Eileen Barker, an eminent British sociologist based at the London School of Economics. Barker is a genial and apparently tireless scholar who is often credited with having popularized the academic use of the term "new religious movement." She made a name for herself in 1984, with her influential book-length study *The Making of a Moonie: Choice or Brainwashing?* (the answer was choice), and she now devotes most of her spare time to INFORM, which she founded. The group is dedicated to making available—to concerned relatives, government officials, law enforcement agencies, the media, representatives of mainstream religions, researchers, and many others—balanced, accurate, and up-to-date information on NRMs from around the world. Speaking at one of the conference sessions, Barker emphatically reminded her audience of "just how very ordinary the people in the cult scene are." When I asked her later about this remark, she elaborated.

"New religious movements aren't always as exotic as they are made out to be," she said. "Or, indeed, as they *themselves* would make themselves out to be. They're interesting in that they're offering something that, they claim, quite often correctly, isn't on sale in the general mainstream religions. So almost by definition there's a sort of curiosity value about them. They're comparatively easy to study—I knew pretty well all of the Moonies in Britain by the time I completed my study of them. They're interesting because you can see a whole lot of social processes going on: conversion, leaving, bureaucratization, leadership squabbles, ways in which authority is used, ways in which people can change, the difference that people born *into* a religion can make."

> *"New religious movements aren't always as exotic as they are made out to be."*—Eileen Barker, **London School of Economics**

I asked a lot of the scholars at the conference why they thought it was important to study new religious movements. Perhaps the most succinct answer came from Susan Palmer, a Canadian who in recent years has become an expert on the Raëlians (and whose ancestors were Mormon polygamists who fled U.S. persecution in the nineteenth century). "If you're interested in studying religion," she told me, "NRMs are a great place to start. Their history is really short, they don't have that many members, their leader is usually still alive, and you can see the evolution of their rituals and their doctrines. It's a bit like dissecting amoebas instead of zebras."

The ultimate dream for any ambitious student of NRMs, of course, is to discover and monitor the very early stirrings of a new movement and then to track it as it evolves and spreads around the globe. Everybody acknowledges how unlikely this is. But the idea that it *could* happen is irresistible. One scholar I met in London who admitted to harboring such hopes was Jean-François Mayer, a tall, bearded, boyishly enthusiastic lecturer in religious studies at the University of Fribourg, in Switzerland. For the past twenty years Mayer has been following a small French movement known as the Revelation of Arés. Founded in 1974 by a former Catholic deacon named Michel Potay, and based near Bordeaux, the movement describes itself as the corrective culmination of Christianity, Judaism, and Islam. "It is an NRM," Mayer told me, "that has all of the constitutive elements of a new religion of the book: new scriptures incorporating previously revealed scriptures, new rituals, and a new place of pilgrimage. When I study such a group, I see such obvious similarities with the birth of Christianity and the birth of Islam that for me it's fascinating and exciting. Sometimes I let myself think that I might be witnessing something similar at its initial stage." Even if the movement doesn't take off—which, Mayer readily admits, is likely—it is a perfect example of what many NRM scholars like to study.

What have the NRM scholars learned? The literature is copious and varied, but several ideas recur again and again. In an environment of religious freedom NRMs emerge constantly and are the primary agents of religious change. They tend to respond quickly and directly to the evolving spiritual demands of the times. It is often said that they are "midwives of new sensibilities." They exist at a

---

The people who join NRMs tend to be young, well educated, and relatively affluent.

---

high level of tension with society, but they nevertheless represent social and spiritual reconfigurations that are already under way— or, to put it differently, they almost never emerge out of thin air. Their views can rapidly shift from being considered deviant to being considered orthodox. The people who join NRMs tend to be young, well educated, and relatively affluent. They also tend to have been born into an established religious order but to profess a lack of religious belief prior to joining. They are drawn to new religious movements primarily for social reasons rather than theological ones— usually because of the participation of friends or family members. And (*pace* the anti-cultists) most of them soon leave of their own, free will.

This last phenomenon is profoundly symptomatic. Because the fact is that almost all new religious movements fail.

The Religious Marketplace

The sociologist Rodney Stark is one of the few people who have been willing to develop specific ideas about what makes new religious movements succeed. This is inherently speculative territory (as with stocks, past performance is no guarantee of future returns), but it also has the potential to be one of the most interesting areas of NRM scholarship, in that such ideas can be applied to all religious movements.

Stark, a professor of sociology and comparative religion at the University of Washington, is blunt, amiable, and a classically American maverick. He does scholarship with an often irreverent swagger. Knowing that he had written specifically on how and why religious movements succeed, I called him and asked him to summarize his thoughts on the subject. "The main thing you've got to recognize," he told me, "is that success is really about relationships and *not* about faith. What happens is that people form relationships and only then come to embrace a religion. It doesn't happen the other way around. That's really critical, and it's something that you can only learn by going out and watching people convert to new movements. We would never, ever, have figured that out in the library. You can never find that sort of thing out after the fact—because after the fact people *do* think it's about faith. And they're not lying, by the way. They're just projecting backwards.

"Something else: give people things to do. The folks in the Vineyard are geniuses at that. It's quite an adventure to go off somewhere and set up a new church for them. The Mormons are great at giving people things to do too. You know, they not only tithe money but they also tithe time. They do an enormous amount of social services for one another, all of which builds community bonds. It also gives you this incredible sense of security—I'm going to be okay when I'm in a position of need; there are going to be people to look out for me. That makes a difference. And if you want to build commitment, send your kids out on missions when they're nineteen! Go out and you save the world for two years! Even if you don't get a single convert, it's worth it in terms of the bonds you develop.

"You've also got to have a serious conception of God and the supernatural to succeed. Just having some 'essence of goodness,' like the Tao, isn't going to do it. It just isn't. It doesn't even do it in Asian countries, you know. They hang a whole collection of supernatural beings around these essences. So to succeed you do best by starting with a very active God who's virtuous and makes demands, because people have a tendency to value religions on the basis of cost."

This last idea is at the heart of much of Stark's work. It is a component of the major sociological model for which Stark is perhaps best known: the rational-choice theory of religion, which proposes that in an environment of religious freedom people choose to develop and maintain their religious beliefs in accordance with the laws of a "religious economy." This model of religious history and change, Stark feels, is what should replace the traditional model— which, he has written, is based on the erroneous and fundamentally secular idea of "progress through theological refinement." It's a controversial model (some find the science of economics only dimly enlightening even when applied to financial markets), but it has become a major force in recent theorizing about religion. Many of the presentations at the London conference used it as a starting point.

> ## [Religion] is a social rather than a psychological phenomenon.

The essence of the idea is this: People act rationally in choosing their religion. If they are believers, they make a constant cost-benefit analysis, consciously or unconsciously, about what form of religion to practice. Religious beliefs and practices make up the product that is on sale in the market, and current and potential followers are the consumers. In a free-market religious economy there is a healthy abundance of choice (religious pluralism), which leads naturally to vigorous competition and efficient supply (new and old religious movements). The more competition there is, the higher the level of consumption. This would explain the often remarked paradox that the United States is one of the most religious countries in the world but also one of the strongest enforcers of a separation between Church and State.

The conventional wisdom is that religion is the realm of the irrational (in a good or a bad sense, depending on one's point of view), and as such, it can't be studied in the way that other aspects of human behavior are studied. But Stark argues that all of social science is based on the idea that human behavior is essentially explainable, and it therefore makes no sense to exclude a major and apparently constant behavior like religion-building from what should be studied scientifically. The sources of religious experience may well be mysterious, irrational, and highly personal, but religion itself is not. It is a social rather than a psychological phenomenon, and, absent conditions of active repression, it unfolds according to observable rules of group behavior.

I asked Stark if he could give me an example of what's happening in the contemporary American religious marketplace. "Sure," he said. "I happen to have grown up in Jamestown, North Dakota. When I left, if you had asked me what the religious situation was going to be like a couple of generations later, I would have told you that it would have stayed pretty much the same: the Catholics would be the largest single group, but overall there would be more Protestants than Catholics, with the Methodists and the Presbyterians being the two largest. But that's not what happened at all. Today the Assemblies of God and the Nazarenes are the two biggest religious bodies in Jamestown. These are new religious movements. There were no Mormons in Jamestown when I was a kid, by the way, and now there's a ward hall. There were two families of Jehovah's Witnesses, and now there's a Kingdom Hall. Evangelical Protestants of all kinds have grown a lot. What's happened is that people have changed brands. They've changed suppliers. Writ small, this is what has happened to the country as a whole. There are new religious movements everywhere—and what this tells me is that in a religious free market institutions often go to pot but religion doesn't. Look at the Methodists! They were nothing in 1776, they were everything in 1876, and they were receding in 1976."

Stark has applied his ideas to the study of the history of Christianity. He suggests, in *The Rise of Christianity* (1996), that early Christianity was a rational choice for converts because its emphasis on helping the needy "prompted and sustained attractive, liberating, and effective social relations and organizations." People initially became Christians for a number of rational, nontheological reasons, he argues, and not, he told me, because "two thousand people on a Tuesday afternoon went and heard Saint Paul." People converted because Christianity *worked*. The Christian community put an emphasis on caring for its members, for example; that emphasis allowed it to survive onslaughts of disease better than other communities. People also converted, he writes, because, contrary to the standard version of events, Christianity's initial membership was not drawn predominantly from among the poor. Stark argues that in Roman society Christianity's early members, like members of most other new religious movements, were relatively affluent and highly placed, and thus weren't treated as a social problem to be repressed. In this view, although Christians were subjected to their share of anti-cult persecution, they were largely ignored by the Romans as a political threat and therefore were able quietly to build their membership. Early growth, Stark writes, involved the conversion of many more members of the Jewish community than has traditionally been acknowledged; Christianity offered disaffected Jews a sort of higher-tension new religion that nevertheless maintained continuity with some established Jewish orthodoxies. Why else—rationally speaking—would the Christians have held on to the Old Testament, a sacred text that in so many ways is at theological odds with the New Testament?

Stark has no shortage of critics. Bryan Wilson, a venerable scholar of NRMs based at Oxford, told me that the rational-choice theory of religious economics is "really rather ludicrous" and said that "most European sociologists of religion would quarrel with it." Steve Bruce, a sociologist based at the University of Aberdeen, in Scotland, has complained about the creeping prevalence of the theory, which he attributes (clearly with Stark in mind) to "the malign influence of a small clique of U.S. sociologists."

It does seem dangerously easy to approach any subject—love? music?—with a grand rational-choice framework in mind and then suddenly to see everything in terms of a marketplace of "products" subject to the laws of supply and demand. What does such an approach really say about specific situations? And what constitutes "choice" or "supply" anyway? How does being born into a religion, which is what happens to most people, affect the idea of a "free market"? These are questions that will be debated for years. In the meantime, one can safely say that, misguided or not, rational-choice theory is a serious attempt to grapple with the reality of continual and unpredictable religious change.

Future Shock

What new religious movements will come to light in the twenty-first century? Who knows? Will that raving, disheveled lunatic you ignored on a street corner last week turn out to be an authentic prophet of the next world faith? All sorts of developments are possible. Catholicism might evolve into a distinctly Charismatic movement rooted primarily in China and headed by an African pope. India's *Dalits*, formerly known as Untouchables, might convert en masse to Christianity or Buddhism. Africa might become the home of the Anglican Church and of Freemasonry. Much of the Islamic world might veer off in Sufi directions. A neo-Zoroastrian prophet might appear and spark a worldwide revival. Membership of the Mormon Church might become predominantly Latin American or Asian. Scientology might become the informal state religion of California. The Episcopalians might dwindle into something not unlike the Amish or the Hutterites—a tiny religious body whose members have voluntarily cut themselves off from the misguided world around them and have chosen to live in self-sustaining hamlets where they quaintly persist in wearing their distinctive costumes (ties with ducks on them, boat shoes) and in marrying only within the community. The next major religion might involve the worship of an inscrutable numinous entity that emerges on the Internet and swathes the globe in electronic revelation. None of these possibilities is as unlikely as it may sound.

One of the most remarkable changes already taking place because of new religious movements is the under-reported shift in the center of gravity in the Christian world. There has been a dramatic move from North to South. Christianity is most vital now in Africa, Asia, and Latin America, where independent churches, Pentecostalism, and even major Catholic Charismatic movements are expanding rapidly. The story of Christianity in twentieth-century Africa is particularly noteworthy. There were fewer than 10 million Christians in Africa in 1900; by 2000 there were more than 360 million. And something very interesting is happening: ancient Christian practices such as exorcism, spirit healing, and speaking in tongues—all of which are documented in the Book of Acts—are back in force. In classic NRM fashion, some of these Christianity-based movements involve new prophet figures, new sacred texts, new pilgrimage sites, and new forms of worship.

"New movements are not only a part of Christianity but an enormous part of it," I was told by David Barrett, the editor of the *World Christian Encyclopedia*, when I asked him about Christian NRMs. "According to our estimates, the specifically new independent churches in Christianity number about three hundred and ninety-four million, which is getting on for twenty percent of the Christian world. So it starts to look faintly ridiculous, you see, when the 'respectable' Christians start talking patronizingly about these new, 'strange' Christians appearing everywhere. In a very short time the people in those movements will be talking the same way about us."

One of the stock Northern explanations for these new movements has been that they are transitional phases of religious "development" and represent thinly veiled manifestations of still potent primitive superstitions. That's a line of thinking that Philip Jenkins—a professor of history and religious studies at Penn State, and the author of the forthcoming *The Next Christendom: The Coming of Global Christianity*—dismissed to me as nothing more than a "racist, they've-just-come-down-from-the-trees" kind of argument. Recent NRM scholarship suggests a less condescending view: in a lot of places, for a lot of reasons, the new Christianity works. Just as, in Rodney Stark's opinion, early Christianity

---

"African NRMs have been successful . . .
because they help people survive.*"*—Rosalind
I. J. Hackett, University of Tennessee–Knoxville

---

spread throughout the vestiges of the Roman Empire because it "prompted and sustained attractive, liberating, and effective social relations and organizations," these early forms of new Christianity are spreading in much of the post-colonial world in large part because they provide community and foster relationships that help people deal with challenging new social and political realities.

Rosalind I. J. Hackett, who teaches religious studies at the University of Tennessee at Knoxville, is a specialist in African religious movements. "African NRMs have been successful," she told me, "because they help people *survive*, in all of the ways that people need to survive—social, spiritual, economic, finding a mate. People forget how critical that is. In Western academic circles it's very fashionable these days to talk about the value of ethnic identity and all that. But that's a luxury for people trying to feed families. To survive today in Africa people have to be *incredibly* mobile in search of work. One of the very important things that many of these NRMs do is create broad trans-ethnic and trans-national communities, so that when somebody moves from city to city or country to country there's a sort of surrogate family structure in place."

Some of the most successful African Christian NRMs of the twentieth century, such as the Zion Christian Church, based in South Africa, and the Celestial Church of Christ, in Nigeria, are very self-consciously and deliberately African in their forms of worship, but a new wave of African NRMs, Hackett says, now downplays traditional African features and instead promotes modern lifestyles and global evangelism. The International Central Gospel Church, in Ghana, and the Winner's Chapel, in Nigeria, are examples of these churches; their educated, savvy, and charismatic leaders, Mensa Otabil and David Oyedepo, respectively, spend a good deal of time on the international preaching circuit. The emphasis on global evangelism has helped to spur the development of what Hackett has called the "South-South" religious connection. No longer does Christian missionary activity flow primarily from the developed countries of the North to the developing countries of the South. Brazilian Pentecostal movements are evangelizing heavily in Africa. New African movements are setting up shop in Asia. Korean evangelists now outnumber American ones around the world. And so on.

The course of missionary activity is also beginning to flow from South to North. Many new African movements have for some time been establishing themselves in Europe and North America. Some of this can be attributed to immigration, but there's more to the process than that. "Many people just aren't aware of how active African Christian missionaries are in North America," Hackett says. "The Africans hear about secularization and empty churches and they feel sorry for us. So they come and evangelize. The late Archbishop Idahosa [a renowned Nigerian evangelist and the founder of the Church of God Mission, International] once put it to me this way: 'Africa doesn't need God, it needs money. America doesn't need money, it needs God.' That's an oversimplification, but it gets at something important."

David Barrett, too, underscores the significance of African missionary presence in the United States. "America is honeycombed with African independent churches," he told me. "Immigrants from Nigeria, Kenya, South Africa, and Congo have brought their indigenous churches with them. These are independent denominations that are very vibrant in America. They're tremendous churches, and they're winning all kinds of white members, because it's a very attractive form of Christianity, full of music and movement and color."

Asian and Latin American missionaries of new Christian movements are also moving north. A rapidly growing and controversial Brazilian Pentecostal movement called the Universal Church of the Kingdom of God—founded in 1977 and often referred to by its Portuguese acronym, IURD—has established an aggressive and successful evangelistic presence in both Europe and North America. A revivalist, anti-institutional movement founded in China in the 1920s and referred to as the Local Church has made considerable inroads in the United States. El Shaddai, a lay Catholic Charismatic movement established in the Philippines in 1984 to compete with Pentecostalism, has now set up shop in twenty-five countries.

Another Christian group, the Light of the World Church, a Pentecostal movement based in Mexico, has spread widely in the United States in recent years.

The present rate of growth of the new Christian movements and their geographical range suggest that they will become a major social and political force in the coming century. The potential for misunderstanding and stereotyping is enormous—as it was in the twentieth century with a new religious movement that most people initially ignored. It was called fundamentalist Islam.

"We need to take the new Christianity very seriously," Philip Jenkins told me. "It is *not* just Christianity plus drums. If we're not careful, fifty years from now we may find a largely secular North defining itself against a largely Christian South. This will have its implications."

Such as? I asked.

Jenkins paused, and then made a prediction. "I think," he said, "that the big 'problem cult' of the twenty-first century will be Christianity."

Falun Gong: What's Behind the Movements?[2]

By Christopher Wanjek
Washington Post, November 20, 2001

The political leadership of China is not the only group alarmed by the spread of Falun Gong, a term used to describe both a set of slow, graceful exercises and the banned Chinese spiritual movement that practices them.

Teachers of qigong, a 5,000-year-old Eastern healing art that includes tai chi, acupuncture and other practices that have become popular in the United States, cannot understand the growing appeal of the exercises.

"I don't see how the Falun Gong exercises could work" to promote health, says Renxu Wang, a qigong master and retired Western-trained surgeon now living in Massachusetts. "Qigong strengthens the body. Falun Gong strengthens the soul for salvation . . . [by] adopting energy from different dimensions in the universe."

Perhaps we should start by defining some terms. Falun Gong is the exercise component of Falun Dafa, a political and spiritual movement that has been banned by the Chinese government at least partly because authorities are concerned that its spread could destabilize the government. Officially, Chinese leaders call Falun Gong a dangerous cult.

Falun Dafa's premise is that through a set of five exercises a practitioner cultivates an intelligent, golden-colored entity called the falun, which resides in one's gut (but in a different dimension) and spins continuously, absorbing energy from parallel universes, thereby making the body invincible to disease. Falun Gong's founder, Li Hongzhi, who lives in exile somewhere in Queens, N.Y., maintains that David Copperfield has some serious falun that allows him to walk through walls and perform magic.

While the vivid Falun Dafa imagery suggests a relationship to ancient forms of Eastern mysticism, the exercises were developed by Li in China in 1992. Which is to say, these exercises are no more ancient than step aerobics. Still, Falun Gong is beginning to attract people who have less interest in Chinese politics than in practicing the exercises.

---

2. Article by Christopher Wanjek from the *Washington Post* November 20, 2001. Copyright © Christopher Wanjek. Reprinted with permission.

At least a dozen indoor study groups meet in the Washington area, and there are many outdoor practice sites, including the Mall, Catholic University and the campus of the National Institutes of Health (NIH). The movement has reached into the suburbs, with practice groups massing at Montgomery Blair High School in Silver Spring and the Julius West Middle School in Rockville.

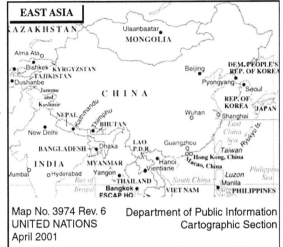

EAST ASIA

Map No. 3974 Rev. 6   Department of Public Information
UNITED NATIONS   Cartographic Section
April 2001

Yet seekers of the falun may not realize that the exercises are very different from other forms of qigong, which have been honed over centuries of practice.

"There are many differences between Falun Gong and qigong," says Wang. First, there's qi (pronouned "chee"), loosely defined as vital energy, the core concept of qigong. Through controlled breathing, practitioners of qigong direct vital energy within the body to locations that need it the most. In Falun Gong there is no breath work. Energy comes drifting in from forces that exist in different dimensions of the universe.

Qigong movements are precise, in order to maximize the flow of qi. Falun Gong practitioners worry less about the precision of their movements, Wang says, and indeed many practitioners render the poses very differently.

Further, qigong is practiced in many different forms to address many different ailments and goals; Falun Gong is a single set of exercises billed as a cure-all practice.

While the American medical establishment has not weighed in on Falun Gong, it is slowly warming to the more popular qigong practices known as "internal qigong": tai chi, acupuncture and meditation.

"Qigong can elicit the relaxation response," says Herbert Benson, an associate professor at Harvard Medical School and president of the Mind/Body Medical Institute in Boston. "Saying the rosary will do the same." Benson says that qigong-induced relaxation can slow one's metabolism, lower the heart rate and enhance resistance to disease.

Since 1990 the NIH has funded several small studies on the effects of qigong exercises for sufferers of neurological disorders, arthritis and other ailments. One study found that people over 70 years old gained more strength and cut their risk of accidental falls by nearly half after practicing tai chi. Larger studies are in the works.

> *The exercises are not meant to be strenuous; rather, they cultivate universal energy.*

Some practitioners make expansive claims about Falun Gong. In addition to providing the claimed link to universal energy fields and superhuman powers, they say, the exercises can cure everything from cancer to lifelong allergies.

The sitting pose, the "way of strengthening supernormal power" exercise, is similar to qigong meditation exercises that have been shown to lower blood pressure. The standing poses mainly stretch the upper body, similar to qigong poses that have been shown to improve circulation. The Falun Gong "penetrating the two cosmic extremes" exercise is quite invigorating. With this exercise, one's arms move slowly up and down like pistons.

The "Buddha showing the thousand hands" exercise is most reminiscent of tai chi, with arms stretched from side to side, like a hunter pulling back on a bow. The "falun standing stance" exercise can build strength in the arms and shoulders, for the arms stay suspended for several minutes above the head. Finally, the "falun heavenly circulation" exercise involves running one's hands up and down the entire body a few inches from its surface.

Falun Gong practitioners admit the moves are watered-down versions of qigong exercises, but that doesn't matter to them. The exercises are not meant to be strenuous; rather, they cultivate universal energy.

"If you do it from your heart, you will benefit," says Hailian Zhang, 34, who leads weekly group exercises on the Mall. By "heart," Zhang means "xinxing," a code of morality one must observe if the exercises are to have any benefit. Adhering to xinxing is yet another aspect that separates Falun Gong from qigong.

The stories of satisfied practitioners play out like late-night television testimonials. A retired white-collar worker from Beijing practicing on the Mall several weeks ago spoke of how Falun Gong had cured his skin allergies and chronic diarrhea, even though he doesn't believe much in rotating, multidimensional faluns. A Chinese woman in her fifties spoke of how Falun Gong helped her regenerate bone that had been removed in surgery. A self-described Christian said Falun Gong has helped control his diabetes.

"You just do the exercises, and one day you wake up and realize you don't have a particular [health problem] anymore," says Keith Ware, a Washingtonian in his forties who practices and teaches Falun Gong at home and on weekend mornings on the Mall, often with his wife.

The National Center for Complementary and Alternative Medicine at NIH and the qigong expert on the White House Commission on Complementary and Alternative Medicine Policy declined to comment on Falun Gong exercises. However, many health experts and some qigong teachers remain open to the idea that Falun Gong can provide some health benefits by reducing stress and boosting relaxation.

Yet some, as you can imagine, question the whole business of energy fields.

"There's nothing wrong with graceful exercise as a relaxation technique," says Stephen Barrett, a retired psychiatrist and editor of the Web site *Quackwatch*. "These practices can be mentally dangerous, though, when they instill false beliefs. False beliefs lead to bad decisions." He cites the possibility that a belief in the absolute power of Falun Gong could lead sick people to refuse standard medical treatments.

Movements like Falun Gong enter into the realm of quackery, Barrett says, when they consistently make health claims that cannot be verified scientifically. This includes healing by touch, raising the paralyzed, curing cancer at far higher success rates than conventional medicines, sending vibes across the sea to heal at a distance or living for several hundred years—all claims that have been made for Falun Gong.

"Some movement is better than no movement," Barrett said. "Socializing can have health benefits, too. People can do these things in a variety of ways."

The Church of the West[3]

ECONOMIST, FEBRUARY 9, 2002

In 1847, on the slopes where 1m visitors will descend to watch the 2002 Winter Olympics, 148 pioneers arrived by wagon to build the city of God. They created something extraordinary. Tolstoy called Mormonism "the American religion." Harold Bloom, a professor at Yale, argues that "the Mormons, like the Jews before them, are a religion that became a people."

In Utah, the Church of the Latter-Day Saints (as Mormons call themselves) is by far the most important public institution, with all-encompassing claims on the loyalty of its members far outstripping those of the state or nation, even though Mormons are among the most patriotic of Americans. Mormons account for 70% of Utah's 2.2m inhabitants. Yet all of the state's representatives in Congress, all of its Supreme Court, 90% of its legislature and 80% of its state and federal judges belong to the church. Not surprisingly, critics fear the Mormons are creating a theocracy.

Outside Utah, the number of Mormons has trebled in America over the past 30 years. The total for the whole country is now more than 5m (making them almost as numerous as the Jews). Outside America, where membership has increased even faster, there are now as many Mormons as in the United States, bringing the total to above 11m. Back in 1980, Rodney Stark, a professor at the University of Washington, predicted, to much derision, that there would be 2m Mormons in 2000. He now estimates 50m by 2040. If current growth rates continue, the Latter-Day Saints will be numbered in the hundreds of millions by 2080 and Mormonism will be, you might say, the first new world religion since Islam.

The hordes of sports fans gathering in Salt Lake City this week may be forgiven for ignoring this ferment. In the interest of good neighbourliness, the church has taken care not to preen itself. Yet the visitors will influence the church's future indirectly. "The Olympics", says Ted Wilson, a former mayor of the city, "means the refuge is over." In other words, Mormon Utah can no longer command the privacy it used to enjoy.

To their critics, the Mormons' phenomenal growth is a danger. They argue that the church's political power threatens the wall between church and state; that Mormons' cultural conservatism limits the rights of non-Mormons (look at the state's anti-alcohol

---

and anti-gambling laws); and that the inward-looking quality of the church (most Mormons mix with others of their faith) is divisive and menacing.

These charges are exaggerated. The alcohol laws are annoying rather than oppressive. The Mormons' undoubted conformity has not stopped the non-Mormon population of Salt Lake City becoming as diverse and lively as that of any other big city. But the charges raise a more interesting issue: the church's contradictory attitude towards its recent achievements. It is this that causes many of the difficulties the church now faces.

If you go to the Mormons' visitor centre at the heart of Salt Lake City, the smiling hosts will describe a mainstream American Christian church—faster-growing and more conservative than most, but otherwise nothing out of the ordinary. Its doctrines seem unexceptional. It lays great stress on the nuclear family. Its views on abortion, same-sex marriage and lifestyle are culturally conservative; Mormons do not drink alcohol, coffee or tea, and do not smoke or gamble. They also have an uninhibited attitude to capitalism, running plenty of for-profit firms.

Despite accusations of a "quasi-theocracy," the church is in some ways ostentatiously apolitical.

Despite accusations of a "quasi-theocracy," the church is in some ways ostentatiously apolitical. Its leaders, unlike those of many other churches, refuse to endorse candidates for office. It takes public positions only on moral matters, such as abortion. It insists on obeying the laws of even the dictatorial countries where its missionaries roam. One senior Mormon, Dallin Oaks, quotes scriptural authority for his view that "Latter-Day Saints obey the law, participate in the affairs of government at all levels and serve in the armed forces of their respective nations." In short, Mormons appear to be a mainstream evangelical church, upholding private property, traditional family values and the separation of church and state.

Yet, when they were founded in the early 19th century, the Mormons mounted radical challenges to each of these things. Early Mormons practised polygamy, which conflicts with the traditional nuclear family. Between 20,000 and 60,000 people still practise polygamy clandestinely, but the church long ago abandoned it and excommunicates its practitioners.

In the early years, the church was almost communist in its attitude to private property. It required Mormons to hand over their goods to the church, which then handed them back but gave the former owners only "stewardship" over them. This meant that the church's leaders could make discretionary demands on the faithful for the greater good. Like polygamy, this system was abandoned long ago, as the church's embrace of corporate capitalism shows. Yet vestiges remain.

Some conservative churches even now question whether Mormons are Christians at all.

The church is extraordinarily demanding of members' time and money. Mormons are supposed to "tithe"—that is, give 10% of their income to the church. Nearly two-thirds do so, accounting for most of the church's estimated income of $6 billion a year. They also voluntarily give anything up to 40 hours a week to church-run activities, an extraordinary commitment of time that helps to sustain one of the world's most impressive welfare services. At the local level, argues Dean May, a historian at the University of Utah, Mormons are far more "communal" in their attitudes than is normal in individualistic America.

Cannon to the Right of Him

More controversially, early Mormon doctrine contained such startling departures from Christian orthodoxy that some conservative churches even now question whether Mormons are Christians at all. The orthodox view of the afterlife is that good Christians spend eternity in the presence of God. Mormons believe in something different: "eternal progression" towards God. Their notion is that the soul exists throughout all time (before this earthly life as well as after it), with Latter-Day Saints advancing slowly to spiritual completion. The idea has something in common with eastern faiths; the lama in Rudyard Kipling's "Kim", with a reservation or two, would have nodded gently.

The logical conclusion of eternal progression is to muddy the difference—fundamental to other Christians—between God and man. The Mormons' founder, Joseph Smith, went so far as to say that "God himself was once as we are now, and is an exalted man." And if men have the capacity to be like God, that implies there could be a "plurality of Gods" (the Mormon phrase). To critics, this is mere polytheism.

Some Mormons want to play down parts of this doctrine, but eternal progression influences several beliefs that others find curious. As members of a relatively new church, for example, Mormons face the problem of how to treat people born before their prophet was, in 1805. They solve it by a doctrine of posthumous baptism: America's Founding Fathers and Shakespeare are among the millions accepted as Mormons.

More important, the notion influences the Mormon view of government. In the early years, church leaders were theocrats, not democrats, and saw no distinction between church and state. Joseph

Smith was running for president when he was murdered by a mob in Illinois. Brigham Young was governor of the Utah territory and president of the church.

Utah is no theocracy now but, unlike most churches, Mormonism retains a distinctive view of the state which derives from theology. Chris Cannon, a Mormon congressman, explains it as follows. Earthly life, Mormons think, is the time when the soul is tested. For the Test to mean anything, people have to be free agents; if they are not, the test will be meaningless. So, says Mr Cannon, "for Mormons, the question of what the government does is one of the most important we face." The government's role, he concludes, must be minimal, to leave people free to make their choices. As a good Mormon, who believes in proselytising, Mr Cannon is not just talking in the abstract: he wants this conception of the state to influence governmental reforms in places like Afghanistan, Pakistan and Iran.

Mr Cannon is also a conservative Republican, which may explain his "leave-us-alone" view of the state. Mormon Democrats (there are a few of them) reply that very poor people, and drug addicts, are hardly free agents; so these Mormons want a more active government.

In each of these matters, the church has made huge adjustments in the past decade or two. But in all of them, except polygamy, the basic ideas that set Mormons apart are still there. That reflects both the church's flexibility and its strength. But, as its membership continues to rise, the adjustment raises two big questions for the church and for the outsiders who are increasingly affected by what it does. How much further can it move away from what were once its fundamental beliefs before it loses its identity? And, if it cannot move away, or compromise, how will this affect its relations with non-Mormons?

The Trouble with Being So Big

The central challenge for the church is to keep alive its sense of being, as Mormons put it, "a peculiar people"—the chosen ones, rather like the Jews. For Mormons in Utah, this sense of being apart is bred in the bone—by the history of their great trek into the wilderness and, especially, by their history of persecution. It is hard for Mormons to forget that their founder was killed by a lynch mob and that the federal government once sent an army to exterminate them.

How do you maintain this sense of peculiarity when Utah's Mormons represent only 14% of the church's worldwide membership? The church's leaders try to answer that question by maintaining that there is a universal Mormon identity (something that all religions have had difficulty achieving, even when they have pursued it). How far the leadership can continue doing this as congregations abroad get ever huger is open to doubt.

The relationship between Mormons and other believers is no less tricky. For the moment, the fact that the Mormon church is such a hierarchical organisation (with power exercised by small groups of men who meet in secret) works in its favour. The leadership has been assiduous in trying to open up the church, admonishing Mormons against the dangers of clannishness. The real trouble comes from the bottom of the church, not the top: the conservatism of most church members and the inward-looking quality of Mormonism almost inevitably separate Mormons from others.

Last year the *Salt Lake Tribune*, the city's main non-Mormon daily, commissioned an opinion poll which found that two-thirds of those living in Utah recognised a cultural fault between Mormons and non-Mormons. Of course, the sheer size of the church in Utah contributes to the conflict: it is the 800-pound gorilla which doesn't have to do anything to seem threatening. But, as Mormonism spreads, that problem may spread too.

Throughout its history, outsiders have criticised the Mormon church as isolated, marginal and rigid. It has begun to slough off those qualities. But it is still unclear whether it can rid itself of the other feeling it elicits, however unfairly: hostility towards what is different.

Guatemala's New Evangelists[4]

BY RACHEL COBB
NATURAL HISTORY, MAY 1998

Wandering along the shore of volcanic Lake Atitlán, in the Guatemalan highlands, I come across two women kneeling in the sand with their backs to the lake, quietly praying in the shelter of some low cliffs. Copal, an incense of pine resin, burns in front of them, and as the wind blows, they struggle to light and relight small orange candles in the sand. They wear Mayan clothing typical for the locale—embroidered blouses, hand-loomed skirts, and bead necklaces. Behind them, at the water's edge, a young man and two children observe the ceremony in silence. Suddenly the two women turn to face the lake and the children and, holding their palms up, pray loudly. As they do, a woman of mixed Indian and European descent—a ladino—approaches from above along the low cliff and stares down at them. Without looking back, the two Mayan women abruptly stop their ceremony, gather up their belongings, and leave with the man and children.

I'm still trying to make sense of the scene that has unfolded and dissolved so quickly, when the ladino woman smiles at me. "*Brujeria* [witchcraft]," she comments about them. "Evangelical," I conclude about her. A chubby woman of about forty-five, Jovita Cabrera de Caranca has driven more than three hours from Escuintla with fellow members of her Assembly of God church for the baptism of a dozen young men and women. Jovita leads me to where her group is setting out loudspeakers for a service. Soon the pastor is preaching, thrusting his fist into the air, while local vendors wander through the crowd selling souvenirs and roasted peanuts with chili and lime. When it comes time for the baptism, everyone rushes to the shore for a good view. The candidates, aged fifteen to seventeen, tremble and cling to one another in the final moments before they are plunged into the lake. Afterward, over a picnic lunch, Jovita tells me she became an Evangelical Protestant in answer to God's call.

I have been coming to Guatemala for the past several years to learn more about people like Jovita. The first time I traveled to this country, in 1991, I heard emotional preaching and twangy electric guitar music coming from a cinder-block church on a muddy back street in Guatemala City. I also noticed brightly painted Evangelical churches even in small, remote highland villages. I saw preachers dressed in tuxedos, dramatically pointing to

4. With permission from *Natural History*, May 1998. Copyright © The American Museum of Natural History 1998.

heaven, mimicking the gestures of their counterparts in the United States. In a predominantly Catholic region, all this seemed out of place, a cultural export from home. I wanted to find out what was behind this phenomenon. At the time, I didn't know that Evangelical Protestantism had already swept almost a third of Guatemalans into its fold. Similar waves of conversion have taken place in many other Latin American countries.

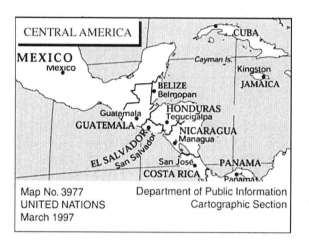

Map No. 3977
UNITED NATIONS
March 1997

Department of Public Information
Cartographic Section

In addition to Catholics, a wide range of Christian groups practice in Guatemala, including Baptists, Mennonites, Presbyterians, Methodists, Seventh Day Adventists, Jehovah's Witnesses, and a variety of Pentecostals. As David Stoll writes in *Is Latin America Turning Protestant?*, "While in the United States 'evangelical' connotes a theological conservative who emphasizes the Bible, personal salvation, and evangelism, in Latin America *evangélico* can refer to any non-Catholic Christian. The term includes the Mormons and Jehovah's Witnesses . . . as well as Protestants whose exegesis is unsuitably liberal." In Guatemala, converts come from all walks of life, but a great number have come from the Mayan community, the largest indigenous population in Latin America after Bolivia's. Twenty-two linguistically distinct Mayan groups exist today, descendants of the post-Classic population encountered by the sixteenth-century conquistadores.

When I was searching for a translator at the beginning of this trip, I met José Sanchez, the director of a language school in Antigua Guatemala, the old colonial capital. Speaking slowly and distinctly, he told me the story of his conversion. It happened in 1991, when he was drinking so much that his students began to comment. One of them, an American, confronted José and invited him to his church. José arrived hungover and thinking, "I need a beer," but during the service he thought, "This is my last chance." He went up to the altar and, in front of the congregation, asked Jesus Christ to be his savior. "I began a new life," he declared. He married, started a family, got a job at the American embassy, and later became the director of his own school. He was active in the church and taught Bible study classes on Saturday nights in his home.

Evangelical Protestants emphasize personal salvation, a direct relationship with God, and a literal interpretation of the Bible. They forbid smoking and drinking, a significant proscription in a country where alcoholism is widespread. Many of the converts I've met have converted in an effort to overcome a problem with alcohol. Evangelical Protestants' condemnation of alcohol consumption, gambling, adultery, and wife beating has strong appeal for women, giving them a new means of gaining control in a macho culture. Much-needed health clinics, houses, and schools are also provided by Evangelical Protestant groups. And on a spiritual level, the fastest growing groups, the Pentecostals, with their speaking in tongues and other outward signs of being touched by God, offer a type of mysticism that many are drawn to.

The translator I've hired is Cesar Perez. We have traveled to Lake Atitlán from Antigua Guatemala along the two-lane Pan American Highway, which runs through the highlands. Taking a turnoff, we headed down a mountain, past a road stand where watermelons stood upright like so many sculptures, pots of calla lilies beside them. Around a bend of the steep, winding road, shimmering Lake Atitlán suddenly came into view, and at the base of

---

The fastest growing groups, the Pentecostals, . . . offer a type of mysticism that many are drawn to.

---

the mountain we pulled into Panajachel, a favorite spot for tourists, aging hippies, and Guatemalans from the city. Panajachel was among the first places where Evangelical Protestantism took hold in Guatemala.

Catholicism, brutally imposed by the Spanish conquerors, is the principal rival faced by Protestant missionaries. But indigenous religious practices predating the Spanish Conquest still persist among the Maya, who largely follow a syncretic form of traditional and Catholic beliefs known as *costumbre* (custom). Religious traditions tied to the 260-day Mayan ritual calendar continue even within the *cofradías* (religious brotherhoods, or saint societies) that were introduced by the Spaniards. Traditionalists use copal, alcohol, candles, marimbas, and sometimes fireworks in their various prayer ceremonies for deities and ancestors or in celebrations of saints. Protestant missionaries first arrived in the 1870s, but not until a century later did widespread conversions take place. What helped open up the Maya to Protestantism was a long history of social inequality and political violence.

A key factor in this history was the expropriation of their land, which was the basis not only of their livelihood but also of their community. The process began following the Conquest—when the Spaniards gathered the Maya into some 700 concentrated settlements—and advanced in the 1870s and 1880s, as liberal reformers sought to modernize the country and develop the export of coffee. Communal property rights were abolished, and debt peonage laws were enacted, in effect forcing the Maya to work on the plantations, often far from home. Exploited and impoverished, the Maya saw their social order—and customs—fall into decline. The legacy has been the most uneven land distribution in all Latin America. Land reform that might have eased the deep social inequalities was squelched by a 1954 CIA-engineered coup. Organized resistance to the government mounted in the countryside and later developed into full-fledged civil war.

After a devastating earthquake in 1976, international aid started pouring in to rebuild the country, and so did Evangelical Protestant missionaries. Churches associated with Elim Ministries, Word Church, and Assemblies of God, among others, sprang up in areas hardest hit by the earthquake, which were largely populated by the Maya.

In 1982, General Efraín Ríos Montt seized power after a bloodless military coup. Guatemala's first Protestant leader, he brought two elders from his Word Church with him into the presidential palace. Although some of Guatemala's worst human rights abuses took place while Rios Montt held power, the Reagan administration and much of the religious right in the United States considered him an ally. He was deposed in 1983. Although severely battered by then, guerrilla forces continued fighting. After years of negotiations, a peace accord was finally signed in December 1996, ending Central America's longest civil war.

One afternoon in Panajachel, I meet two American Mormon missionaries, Elder Davis, twenty, and Elder Vantielen, nineteen. The Mormons (Church of Jesus Christ of Latter-Day Saints) claim some 165,000 members in Guatemala. Although it is not required, most men aged nineteen and women aged twenty-one are expected to serve as missionaries; for two years. Davis and Vantielen take me on one of their daily visits to people they hope to convert.

Just outside town, we approach an onion farmer methodically turning soil. He smiles and puts down his hoe to make small talk with us. With their close-cropped hair and crisp, white, name-tagged shirts, the elders stand in stark contrast to Juan Francisco Chiroy, who is all dense muscle wrapped in sun-browned skin. Juan Francisco attends the New Jerusalem Evangelical Church, but the Mormon elders patiently try to win him over.

Davis has a year's more experience and does most of the talking. He seems to understand that conversation with Guatemalans moves gradually, getting to the point almost as if by chance, but the silence during the pauses makes Davis nervous, and he fills in with exclamations of *"Excelente!"* and *"Calidad!* [Cool!]," rapidly snapping his fingers and shaking his wrist. After about twenty minutes, the elders flip open their notepads and schedule Juan Francisco for the following Sunday, an effort that seems out of place, given the fluid sense of time in these parts. Juan Francisco doesn't seem to mind their attention, but neither does he invite it. He politely goes along with the plans.

As we walk back to town, a woman from the Mormon church asks the elders to bless another woman's sick child, even though the child's mother is not Mormon. Inside the family compound, Davis tells me that I can watch but that I can't take pictures, because what is about to take place is sacred. They are going to call on the Holy Spirit to be present and cure this boy, and my taking pictures might disrupt that process.

A bare bulb lights the one-room house where the boy, who appears to be about ten, lies motionless in bed. His mother strokes his head. Davis and Vantielen speak gently to her for a few minutes. Then, guided by Davis, Vantielen moves closer to the mother and child, places his hands on their shoulders, and begins to pray. His prayers are quiet, a little unsteady. Within seconds the mother starts moaning and crying, "O Señor [Lord]! Por favor, Señor. . . ." Vantielen stumbles. Again he prays, and again she cries out. He stops. I see his face flinch a little as if he's trying not to laugh. Davis takes over, and the mother's cries continue as he anoints the child with oil. In a few minutes we are hurrying through the garden, and Vantielen is apologizing to me: "That's never happened! In our church one person prays and the others just listen. That's never happened! That was weird!"

A few days later, Cesar and I load up with food and water for the drive up to the northern part of Quiché Department into an area known as the Ixil Triangle, the mountainous region between the towns of Nebaj, Cotzal, and Chajul, where the Ixil language is spoken. During Guatemala's long civil war, this was a major battleground between guerrillas and the army. Virtually all rural settlements here were razed as part of the army's counterinsurgency strategy. Some were rebuilt as so-called model villages with straight, wide, easily patrolled streets.

We drive from the lake back up the mountain to where the road turns north, up hairpin curves into the touristy market town of Chichicastenango, on past the departmental capital of Santa Cruz del Quiché, and into more mountains. I have come to the Ixil Triangle in part to see the work of the Agros Foundation, which builds houses for people displaced by the civil war. Of the five communities they have helped build around the country, three are here. A couple of miles outside Nebaj, I drive up a dirt road into El Paraíso ("Paradise"), so named by those who live here. Children run alongside the pickup truck or jump onto the rear bumper for a ride. Tomás Godinez, the executive director of Agros in Guatemala, takes me to the freshly dug foundation where the new schoolhouse will be built. American volunteers and Maya from the village are measuring out rooms, digging, and hauling stones up the hill. It is late on the second day of work, and many volunteers are sunburned and tired. Some break off to play with the village children.

In an hour, the entire village of twenty-five families and the ten or so volunteers are gathered for a welcome meeting in a temporary schoolhouse, a structure with low wooden sides and a roof of draped blue plastic. Jacinto Perez, leader of El Paraíso's Committee (the decision-making body), explains the importance of this new community. "In the time of the violence, we lost everything we had—our animals, our crops, everything. The town of Nebaj is the only place that survived [in the Nebaj jurisdiction], the only community. In order to save our lives, many fled to the mountains, to the city, or to Mexico. But thankfully, we've been able to return to our community. Thanks to Agros and thanks to God, we have our houses now, which are the basis of our lives."

Afterward, while Tomás watches, I ask Jacinto about El Paraíso. What are the requirements to be accepted into the Agros program? just two, he says: you have to be displaced and you have to be Christian. By "Christian" he means Evangelical. Catholics are not permitted to live there. In a roundabout way, Jacinto acknowledges he converted to Evangelical Protestantism shortly before being accepted into the Agros program, and I can see this question embarrasses him, especially in front of the director. When I run into Jacinto a few days later, I press him again to tell me about his conversion. Anyone who tries this blunt approach with a Maya is likely

---

The missionaries I meet in the region are brave and unblinking in their belief that they are doing God's will.

---

to come up empty-handed, and I am no exception. He simply says, "That is how I want to worship God now."

Back at the hotel in Nebaj, I talk to Arondo Rivas, an eighteen-year-old who works as a receptionist. Several years ago, he converted to Evangelical Protestantism, along with the rest of his family. María, his mother, had no husband, no food to feed her children. She went to her sister's church one Sunday to pray, and a preacher from Texas, Brother Mike, asked, "Who is María? The Lord says she has nothing in her house to eat." Brother Mike promised that soon they would have food in the house, and the next day they did. He and other church members gave the family sixty-five quetzals; (about eleven dollars) to buy food.

"This is why I believe that God exists and that he sees us, but not those who don't believe," says Arondo, adding that his life has been transformed. He used to smoke cigarettes and "go in the streets with his friends," but now, he says, "I have felt the presence of God in my body, and it is beautiful." He reads the Bible every afternoon.

The missionaries I meet in the region are brave and unblinking in their belief that they are doing God's will. Ron and Vicky Fiedler found their calling after experiencing financial ruin in Dallas, Texas. "Lord Jesus, use us, use us, use us!" they begged, seeking meaning in their lives, and in missionary work they have found contentment. "We get to be here and we get to have all the fun," they say. "We get to be part of what God's doing." The Fiedlers have learned to get by month to month, not knowing where money will come from, living on faith.

The Fiedlers' friend Jerry Strahl is a "field associate" of Missionary Ventures. Together with his wife, he runs an orphanage for eight children and operates a farm with a fish pond. Jerry is tall and thin, with large, strong hands lined with dirt-filled cracks. Sometimes he is quiet, but when he is enthusiastic about something, the words flow in a jumble of Spanish and English. Jerry uses his everyday work as an entry into the lives of those he's trying to convert. Selling fish, he might interject something about "fishers of men."

"The agricultural teaching is just a way in to teaching the Bible," Jerry says. "We teach people what will grow and what won't grow. They don't know anything about corn," he adds, without a trace of irony. "There's something that you'd call hunger. There are some people who've never had an experience like this happen. They get a hunger for something, for the truth. When the Lord has something that fills your hunger, you want to eat it and it tastes good, so that's it. These people have got a hunger for the things of God."

Later, Cesar and I drive to Chajul to talk to Dwight Jewett, who has been working for almost twenty years for the Summer Institute of Linguistics (SIL), a sister group of Wycliffe Bible Translators, a California-based organization. SIL fieldworkers document the world's languages, particularly previously unwritten ones, and translate texts for native speakers to use.

In translating the Bible, Dwight has struggled to find Ixil expressions for concepts that are unfamiliar to those who speak the language. To translate "I love you" into Ixil, one might say, "I die regarding you." Any such translation can be tricky if one is trying to get across the idea of God's love for humankind. "I believe there is a sense in which we should have a fear of God, but we also must have a strong sense of the love of God," says Dwight, "and I don't see any of that in traditional Mayan religion."

"I see that as one of the major obstacles to development. . . . I really believe that before, they were afraid to change," he says. "Not only do they have the spirits of the hills and other natural objects, but they also have the spirits of ancestors." The fear of angering their ancestors, he believes, led the Maya to continue to do things the way they were done in the past. It took something as disastrous as war, he says, for them to finally open up to new religious ideas. "That's why I say political violence was a factor, because all of a sudden it didn't matter anymore what the spirits thought, because they're not helping, so there's an opening there for something new."

I hear of a Catholic priest who is doing remarkable work in the area. One morning, on my way to Cotzal to look for him, I drive through Pulay, a model village, and hear cries and shouts coming from inside a small wooden Pentecostal church. I park, pry open the creaky wooden door, and edge inside. About a dozen men and women stand close to the altar of the Complete Evangelical Church of God, singing, praying, and crying. Women, who on the street would be demure and reserved, are jumping up and down, stamping, their feet, and rhythmically bouncing their heads from side to side, shouting, "O Señor! O Señor!" One or two drop to the dirt floor in spasms, saliva dripping from their mouths. They clap as fast as possible, and I try to join in, feeling that my silence in this commotion is somehow noticeable.

Later that afternoon, after making an appointment with the Catholic priest in Cotzal, I return to talk to members of Pulay's Pentecostal congregation. Their six-hour prayer session is now over, and inside the unlit church, the pastor and two church elders sit next to the altar. I sit below in the first pew. I find myself answering, rather than asking, questions. I tell them I was raised in the Episcopal Church, thinking that puts me safely between Catholicism and Evangelical Protestantism. I explain that the Episcopal Church is a breakoff of the Catholic Church, older than the Pentecostal branches of Protestantism. No, they tell me, theirs is the first church, the church of God, founded fifty years after the death of Christ. Do I make the sign of the cross during services, they want to know. Yes, I answer. Smiling in satisfaction, the pastor turns to the others and mumbles something in Ixil that I can't understand, until I hear the word *católica*. Evangelical Protestants always seem to want to pin down my background in the first few minutes.

The next day, in the courtyard of the newly restored Catholic church in Cotzal, I meet Father Federico. Born in Germany, he has a brisk air, strong blue eyes, white hair, and a narrow beard that squares his jawline. He is gentle when he speaks to the Mayan men and women who work in his church, and I get the feeling that he is loved. Father Federico has worked here since 1989. He says that although a thousand people now attend Sunday Mass, when he arrived Catholics were "praying secretly or meeting in their homes." The Church had pulled out of the region, in 1980, after several priests and other clergy and catechists were killed.

In response to the desperate poverty of the Ixil Maya, priests who were in the region earlier, in conjunction with Catholic Action (a pastoral movement to foster greater orthodoxy among Catholics), had been moved to help organize health-care providers and start agricultural and craft cooperatives. Some called for resistance to social injustices, along the lines of what became known as liberation theology. They also spoke out against the army's increasingly ruthless counterinsurgency tactics. Army suspicion began to fall indiscriminately on priests, catechists, and association leaders, even on ordinary Catholics. In July 1980, after escaping an assassination attempt, Juan Gerardi, the bishop of Santa Cruz del Quiché, left his diocese and traveled to the Vatican to report on the violence. And that August, the Missionaries of the Sacred Heart, two of whose priests were murdered, issued a statement saying that they "left the area in solidarity with the bishop and in protest against five years of massacres by the army." While some Evangelical missionaries and leaders also lost their lives, by and large, they did not challenge authority.

The counterinsurgency penetrated communities through the organization of civil defense patrols, known as PACs, to root out guerrilla sympathizers. In Cotzal, the first PAC was formed with the help of an Evangelical pastor, Nicolás Toma. His brother was one of sixty-four men killed by the army in a massacre that took place on the morning of July 28, 1980. The massacre was a reprisal to a guerrilla attack on army barracks. Pastor Nicolás claimed that, caught between the army and the guerrillas, he was forced to choose sides. The information he provided helped identify the guerrilla infrastructure in and around Cotzal, and the PACs were instrumental in breaking the insurgency in the area.

It was about that time that Father Federico first visited Guatemala. He traveled north through Quiché and across the border into Chiapas, Mexico, where he saw Guatemalans arrive "marked by the massacres, by death, by violence." Guatemalan forces crossed the Mexican border and continued killing in refugee camps. "This experience had a very, very powerful effect on me," he says. "Since then, in all my work, the Quiché has always been, as they say, *el mundo de mis ojos* [die world to me]."

Speaking of Cotzal, he says, "Here, twenty-six of the twenty-nine small villages were leveled, practically on top of the people. We calculate about 1,200 civilians were killed, not counting the hundreds who fled to the mountains afterward and died of hunger . . . Many felt forced to change to another religion to save their lives. With an Evangelical identity card, they could pass freely [in and out of town]."

By 1989, when Father Federico came to Cotzal, the situation had eased, but he claims that "the Evangelicals, the military, and the civil patrollers didn't want the Catholic Church to reestablish itself in the parish." Shortly after his arrival, six Jesuits were killed in El Salvador. "The following Sunday, the commander said, in a meeting with 400 to 500 patrollers, 'In El Salvador they killed six priests, and here we don't respect them either.'"

Before long, Father Federico started roofing projects and then livestock projects. "They were always for everyone. The people were used to each church favoring only its own members," he asserts. "We didn't want to divide the villages by being able to recognize the Catholic houses by their roofs. That was, practically speaking, the point at which those who had opposed me before changed their viewpoint."

Six years ago, his church began to commemorate the 1980 massacre. Father Federico recalls that the widows in town came to him saying, "Father, we have to do something and ask God for forgiveness for the wrongs the army did to the sacred corn."

"In the time of the violence," he says, "the army destroyed the corn, they cut and burned the corn—everything, everything—to take the food from the guerrillas. That is the theory of Mao: to take water from the fish. The fish is the guerrillas and the water is the people. So they massacred the people . . . and they destroyed the food, the basic nourishment, which is corn. That, for the people, is criminal, because the corn is sacred. So the widows told me, 'Father, we have to do something.'"

They held a procession, one of the first great public processions in Quiché Department in many years. "The widows went to the locations where their husbands and fathers had been killed, and there, with the incense, with the smoke of copal, they brought the souls of their dead to the church." Then they pinned the names of the dead and "disappeared" onto the wall under a crucifix. "In the Mayan culture that is possible," explains Father Federico. "They [the souls] were restless; that's why to have their souls in the church was a great satisfaction and a great happiness."

Thinking back to the years of violence, Father Federico suggests that "the sects" (as some refer to Evangelical groups) provided a relief valve. "You can vent during the service, for example, with jumps, with songs, with shouts. It's a little like an escape," he says. "My theory has always been, when the military pressure diminishes—the fear, everything—they will lose their followers. [The people] now could say, 'Well, we've been through different times—more difficult, more violent—and to save our lives, we converted. And now that we live in peaceful times, we can return.' I don't know, I can't assess that yet. . . . Some always return."

The Expansion of Christianity[5]

An Interview with Andrew Walls

CHRISTIAN CENTURY, AUGUST 2–9, 2000

A former missionary to Sierra Leone and Nigeria, Andrew Walls taught for many years at the University of Aberdeen in Scotland. He is founder-director of the Centre for the Study of Christianity in the Non-Western World at the University of Edinburgh, and founding editor of the Journal of Religion in Africa. *He recently wrote* The Missionary Movement in Christian History *(1996). He is currently guest professor at Princeton Theological Seminary, and also teaches regularly in Ghana. We spoke to him about African Christianity and about the history of missionary expansion.*

In writing about the expansion of Christianity, you have drawn attention to the way Christianity has over the centuries established new centers of the faith in different cultures and in different parts of the globe. What is so significant about this pattern?

If you consider the expansion of Islam or Buddhism, the pattern is one of steady expansion. And in general, the lands that have been Islamic have stayed Islamic, and the lands that have been Buddhist have stayed Buddhist. Christian history is quite different. The original center, Jerusalem, is no longer a center of Christianity—not the the kind of center that Mecca is, for example. And if you consider other places that at different times have been centers of Christianity—such as North Africa, Egypt, Serbia, Asia Minor, Great Britain—it's evident that these are no longer centers of the faith. My own country, Scotland, is full of churches that have been turned into garages or nightclubs.

What happened in each case was decay in the heartland that appeared to be at the center of the faith. At the same time, through the missionary effort, Christianity moved to or beyond the periphery, and established a new center. When the Jerusalem church was scattered to the winds, Hellenistic Christianity arose as a result of the mission to the gentiles. And when Hellenistic society collapsed, the faith was seized by the barbarians of northern and western Europe. By the time Christianity was receding in Europe, the

---

churches of Africa, Asia and Latin America were coming into their own. The movement of Christianity is one of serial, not progressive, expansion.

Is this process more than an historical curiosity—does it have theological significance?

Well, this pattern does make one ask why Christianity does not seem to maintain its hold on people the way Islam has. One must conclude, I think, that there is a certain vulnerability, a fragility, at the heart of Christianity. You might say that this is the vulnerability of the cross.

Perhaps the chief theological point is that nobody owns the Christian faith. That is, there is no "Christian civilization" or "Christian culture" in the way that there is an "Islamic culture," which you can recognize from Pakistan to Tunisia to Morocco.

It seems that Christianity is able to localize itself or indigenize itself in a variety of cultures. Do you see this as in some way consistent with the Christian belief in the incarnation?

Yes. Christians' central affirmation is that God became human. He didn't become a generalized humanity—he became human under particular conditions of time and space. Furthermore, we affirm that Christ is formed in people. Paul says in his Letter to the Galatians that he is in travail "until Christ be formed in you." If all that is the case, then when people come to Christ, Christ is in some sense taking shape in new social forms.

I think cultural diversity was built into the Christian faith with that first great decision by the Council in Jerusalem, recorded in Acts 15, which declared that the new gentile Christians didn't have to enter Jewish religious culture. They didn't have to receive circumcision and keep the law. I'm not sure we've grasped all the implications of that decision. After all, up to that moment there was only one Christian lifestyle and everybody knew what it was. The Lord himself had led the life of an observant Jew, and he had said that not a jot or tittle of the law should pass away. The apostles continued that tradition. The obvious thing, surely, for the new church to do was to insist that the gentile converts do what gentile converts had always done—take on the mark of the covenant.

The early church made the extraordinary decision not to continue the tribal model of the faith. Once it decided that there was no requirement of circumcision and no requirement to keep every part of the law, then things were wide open. People no longer knew what a Christian lifestyle looked like. The converts had to work out, under the guidance of the Holy Spirit, a Hellenistic way of being Christian.

Think how much of the material in the Epistles needn't have been written if the church had made the opposite decision. Paul wouldn't have needed to discuss with the Corinthians what to do if a pagan friend invites you to dinner and you're not sure whether the meat had been offered in sacrifice the day before. That was not a problem for any of the apostles or any of the Christians in Jerusalem. They were not going to be eating with pagans in the first place, since observant Jews don't sit down at the table with pagans. But in Hellenistic Christianity this was an issue. These Christians were faced with the task of changing the Hellenistic lifestyle from the inside.

Early in your own career you were a teacher in West Africa. You have said that while teaching African Christians about the early church, you suddenly came to the realization that the African Christians were living in their own version of the early church. In a way, you were living amid the early church that you were teaching about. Tell us about this moment.

This was a very important realization. At the time I was still thinking of African Christian history as a sort of hobby, not part of the study of mainstream Christian history. I was wrong about that.

It became clear to me that we can better understand the early church in light of the recent experience of the churches in Africa and Asia. Our knowledge of the early church prior to the Council of Nicaea in 325 is fragmentary, but the fragments reveal many of the concerns African churches have today, from distinguishing between true and false prophets to deciding what should happen to church members who behave badly. Even the literary forms are often similar.

I think the experience of the African churches also brings into focus the period when Western Europe was converted to Christianity. We have a tendency to forget about this period, to jump from Augustine to Luther and forget about Bede and Gregory of Tours. During this period Christian missionaries had to explain Christianity to the inhabitants of Europe in light of the indigenous religions—the religions of the Goths, for example, or the Celts. And they had to answer practical moral questions, because the people who were abandoning their old gods needed to know what the new God demanded. Reading the pre-Nicene literature and the literature of the European conversion period in the light of modern African experience cast floods of light. African and Asian Christians can vastly illuminate "our" church history.

What are the theological questions that are urgent in Africa today?

Well, theology in southern Africa has had a political edge, because people have had to maintain their faith within a system of oppression which itself often had a Christian theological justification, as in South Africa. And throughout Africa, Christians have to ask questions about the nation state which Western Christians have never asked, because Western Christianity more or less grew up with the nation state.

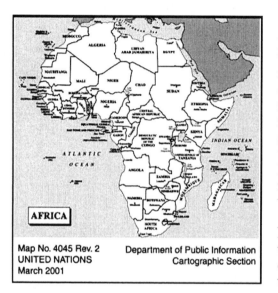

Map No. 4045 Rev. 2
UNITED NATIONS
March 2001

Department of Public Information
Cartographic Section

The nation state doesn't seem to operate well in parts of Africa. Sometimes the churches are the only form of civil society still operating in Africa. In that respect, too, Africa today resembles the pre-Carolingian stage of Europe, after the collapse of the Roman Empire, when the only institution that worked was the church.

The other important theological questions are cultural, and have to do with coping theologically with the African past.

What do you mean by "coping theologically with the past"?

Africans have a need to understand how God was at work among their own traditions. This question is alive for Africans just as it was for Greek converts in the ancient Hellenistic world. Do we have to reject our entire history and culture when we become Christians?

I think one can distinguish three stages in dealing with the non-Christian past: the missionary stage, the convert stage and the reconfiguration stage. African Christians are now in the reconfiguration stage.

We should remember that Paul was functioning in the missionary stage. He was himself a foreign missionary. He could use a Hellenistic idea like the *pleroma*, but he was still an outsider. Dealing with the Greek past became a much more pressing issue for converts of a later generation, such as Justin Martyr of the second century. Justin wanted to know how God had been at work among the pagan philosophers before the time of Christ. Were they totally without value? Did God have nothing to do with Socrates? Justin worked out the theory that the pagan philosophers who had been speaking according to reason, the logos, were in fact speaking also in accordance with the Logos. He found a way to reject part of his cultural tradition, affirm part of it and modify part of it.

The next stage of reconfiguring the past is represented by Origen, in the third century. He was not a convert; he grew up in a Christian home. But he also had a thorough Greek education. Origen was able to reconfigure the whole of the Greek tradition from a Christian perspective. He could do this because he was perfectly at home with the Christian tradition, whereas Justin was still uneasy within it. Justin was always afraid of demons, for example, whereas Origen wasn't afraid of the demons because he knew Christ had dealt with them.

What aspects of the African experience are being re-configured in Christian terms?

The role of ancestors and witchcraft are two important issues. Academic theologians in the West may not put witchcraft high on the agenda, but it's the issue that hits ordinary African Christians full in the face.

Of course, Western theology has made its peace with the Enlightenment, the fundamental assumption of which is that there is a firm line between the empirical world and the transcendent world or spirit world. If you're a rationalistic person of the Enlightenment, you'll say either that there's nothing on the other side of the line or that we can't know anything about it. Western Christians have particular points on which they cross the line—incarnation, resurrection, prayer, miracles and so on—but on the whole they still assume the existence of that firm division.

> *The world of most African Christians doesn't have this firm line between the world of experience and the transcendent world.*

The world of most African Christians doesn't have this firm line between the world of experience and the transcendent world. It's an open frontier which is being crossed all the time. They are very aware, for example, of the active forms that evil takes.

So what does a Christian theologian do when somebody says he's a witch? Our instinct in the West is to say, Oh no, of course you are not a witch. But what do you do when a person tells you she has killed somebody, that she hated some woman so much she wanted her baby to die—and then the baby dies. This can be a pressing pastoral issue in Africa.

When African Christians read the New Testament, they naturally see things that Western Christians miss. They can see, for example, that the New Testament plainly deals with demons, and that it also deals with healing—issues that Western Christians tend to think are part of an outdated world.

It seems that African Christians have two challenges: they are reinterpreting their traditional religious culture in the light of Christian teachings, and at the same time they are

responding to the pressure of the Enlightenment worldview and Enlightenment-sponsored technology.

Traditional and Enlightenment worldviews can live together very well. You can drive a car and watch television and still be very much aware of the objective force of evil and may want to call it witchcraft. And the reconfiguration process has a variety of solutions. African traditional universes have several components. Many recognize not only God, but also lesser divinities who are rulers of territories and of departments of life, as well as ancestors who are mediators. In African Christian thought, the God-component is enlarged—but what happens to the divinities? They are sometimes interpreted in terms of angels and ministers of God, sometimes in terms of demons and enemies of God. African Christianity has a lively sense of the demonic. Ancestor mediation produces still more complex theological questions. All three kinds of answers emerge within African Christianity. But Western theology is not very helpful in providing answers to such questions, because it doesn't even understand the questions.

John Mbiti has a wonderful story about the African student who goes home to his village with a Ph.D. in theology. This son of the village is greeted with a service of welcome and afterward a big party. During the party there's a shrieking and a howling and a banging in the tent—his sister has become possessed. Of course, the villagers immediately turn to the new Ph.D.—he's the expert, the one who has received the best theological training. But he's completely incapacitated for dealing with this African event.

The notion that the center of Christianity has moved to the southern world, to Africa and Asia, is familiar to U.S. Christians, but it doesn't seem to make much of a dent in how we operate or how we do theological education. How do you think this fact should influence us?

The center has changed, and though I wouldn't say there's no future for Western Christianity or no important task for Western theologians, it and they will be less and less significant for the future of Christianity. Already what they're doing is pretty parochial. The events that are shaping 21st-century Christianity are happening in Africa and Asia.

Part of what this change means is that the big ecumenical questions are no longer how Lutherans will get on with Baptists or Reformation churches with Rome. The urgent ecumenical question is how African, Asian, Latin American, North American and European Christians can live together in the same church, authentically expressing the same faith of Christ and love of Christ.

It seems to me that now, more than at any time in history, the church looks like the great multitude described in the Book of Revelation—a multitude from every tribe and nation.

Paul speaks of Jews and gentiles growing together, and he says that only when the two strands are one will they have grown into the full stature of Christ. At the time, no one had any idea how important the missions to the gentiles would prove to be. After the fall of Jerusalem, the church became as monocultural in a Hellenistic way as it had been in its earliest days in a Jewish way.

We live now at a time when the church is multicultural. I think that the fullness of the stature of Christ will emerge only when Christians from all these cultures come together. If I understand what Paul says in Ephesians correctly, it is as though Christ himself is growing as the different cultures are brought together in him.

IV. Religion and Ecology

Editor's Introduction

In 1941 T. S. Eliot opened his long poem "The Dry Salvages," the third of his "Four Quartets," with a passage suggesting that the modernist despair with which he had made his name might yield to something else—a convergence of religious (or at least mythic) consciousness with a renewed attention to nature:

> I do not know much about gods; but I think that the river
> Is a strong brown god—sullen, untamed and intractable,
> Patient to some degree, at first recognised as a frontier;
> Useful, untrustworthy, as a conveyor of commerce;
> Then only a problem confronting the builder of bridges.
> The problem once solved, the brown god is almost forgotten
> By the dwellers in cities—ever, however, implacable.
> Keeping his seasons and rages, destroyer, reminder
> Of what men choose to forget. Unhonoured, unpropitiated
> By worshippers of the machine, but waiting, watching and waiting.

Whatever one may think of Eliot's other political and cultural ideas, his sense that the natural world might yet have an important role to play in religion appears to have been accurate. In recent decades, scientists have helped alert the public to such environmental issues as global warming, sustainable development, and the extinction of species. Increasingly, religious leaders have begun to do the same; some have even asked whether certain religious doctrines may have contributed to the world's environmental problems.

In her article "Religion Goes Green: Ecology Joins Theology," Linda Ashton surveys a few of the varied religious organizations currently examining the ecological implications of their respective faiths. Among the groups discussed are Roman Catholics, Orthodox Christians, evangelical Christians, mainline Protestants, and Jews. Environmental engagement may be new for most of these organizations, but a growing number of religious leaders feel that reevaluating their traditions in light of modern ecology is a moral imperative.

This reevaluation has led some to investigate other faiths. In "Science, Religion, and Ecology Turn Eastward," Michael J. Strada argues that Western cultural and religious assumptions have in many ways contributed to the destruction of the environment. In particular, the dominant strain of Western monotheism, which depicts God as an otherworldy sovereign exercising dominion over Creation, has encouraged a condescending attitude toward the natural world. Eastern religions, on the other hand, emphasize the interdependence and interpenetration of the human, divine, and natural worlds. In Strada's view, recent scientific findings—among them the immense size of the

145

universe as measured by cosmologists and astronomers, the likelihood that life exists elsewhere in the cosmos, and the role of mass extinctions in biological evolution—warrant a critical reevaluation of Western cultural assumptions.

In "Religion, Modern Secular Culture, and Ecology," George Rupp concedes that Western monotheism, and especially the secular philosophies that Western monotheism spawned beginning in the late 17th century, are in large measure responsible for the current ecological crisis. Like Strada, he argues that Asian and indigenous religious traditions are, on the whole, more holistic in their fundamental outlook, and consequently, more ecologically responsible. However, Rupp warns against presenting any one tradition in "self-congratulatory terms" as consistently benign. For one, Western religions have their own traditions of affirming the natural world, just as non-Western traditions have included ecologically destructive elements. More importantly, Western individualism addresses "the crucial ethical question of how a more equitable sharing of limited resources may be attained"—a question which, Rupp observes, must go neglected in a strictly holistic outlook. Without offering much in the way of specifics, Rupp concludes by urging his readers to cultivate an ethos that would integrate sound ecological stewardship with a commitment to justice and equity.

Religion Goes Green:
Ecology Joins Theology[1]

BY LINDA ASHTON
HOUSTON CHRONICLE, NOVEMBER 11, 2000

When they're not saving souls, more of the religious faithful are trying to save the environment. They're lobbying for the Endangered Species Act, conducting energy audits and educating others about global climate change.

Around the nation, priests, pastors and rabbis are mixing theology and ecology, urging their congregations into earthly stewardship with passages straight from the Bible. Their message: From the Columbia River to the California redwoods and the hills of West Virginia, this planet is the handiwork of God, who wants us to take care of it.

"Our goal is to bring the mission of care for God's creation more fully to the heart of religious life," said Paul Gorman, director of the National Religious Partnership for the Environment, a network of environmentally aware Roman Catholic, Jewish, evangelical Christian and mainline Protestant organizations.

In the Northwest, seven Roman Catholic bishops from the United States and one from Canada will issue a pastoral letter early next year on the Columbia River.

"There are so many issues surrounding the river and its watershed. From the standpoint of the bishops, this was an opportunity to reflect on, from a spiritual standpoint, not only its beauty, but the way it brings people together," said Bishop William Skylstad of Spokane, Wash.

There is much symbolism in water for many different faithful, from purification to destruction. Indians of the Northwest have long incorporated the river into their religious beliefs.

Tsagiglalal, the "She Who Watches" ancient petroglyph carved into stone over the Columbia River Gorge, is one sacred site. Just up-river, at the Columbia's Stonehenge Memorial, Druids gathered in June at the summer solstice to welcome the new season.

The Seattle-based Washington Association of Churches, which has 1,600 congregations and parishes as members, has an environmental justice program that has met for "days of moral deliberation" on the Columbia River, said director John Boonstra.

---

1. Reprinted with permission of The Associated Press.

Wheat farmers, barge owners, fishermen, hydropower interests and others have examined not only the politics, economics and science of river management but also its spiritual value.

"Is there consensus? No. Should there be common ground? Yes," Boonstra said.

For many of America's religious, keeping the faith in the literal wilderness is relatively new.

The Rev. Chris Bender shares the word with the 35 families at his Assumption Greek Orthodox Church in Morgantown, W.Va. He got involved three years ago in the National Council of Churches' eco-justice working group.

"Once I got involved, I began to realize the nature and degree of the crisis facing us in the environment, and it became a very big part of my ministry," he said.

This fall, an interfaith educational campaign is under way in 16 states to educate people about global climate change.

Kicking off the effort recently in his state, the Rev. Fred Morris, head of the Florida Council of Churches, said, "If we genuinely believe in a creator God, then caring and protecting God's creation is an essential and central part of our religious life and activity."

Anne D. Burt, coordinator of the initiative in Maine, compared it to the stand that churches took on civil rights in the 1950s and '60s.

"This is the same thing," she said. "It is an issue of justice—it's an issue of the right relationship with the Earth."

In northern California, the "Redwood Rabbis" battled to save old-growth trees from logging in the Headwaters Forest. Last year, Pacific Lumber, owned by Maxxam Corp., agreed to sell two stands of redwoods to the U.S. and state governments to create a 7,470-acre reserve. Pacific Lumber also agreed to restrictions on cutting and land-management requirements for much of its other redwood inventory.

The rabbis had appealed to Maxxam owner Charles Hurwitz "on the basis of his faith," but it was unclear whether that was the deciding factor, said Mark X. Jacobs, director of the Coalition on the Environment and Jewish Life in New York City.

The coalition has focused on forest preservation and issues of global climate change, matters that have a very high level of interest among younger Jews, he said.

"This is a new area in Jewish life where younger people have an opportunity to exercise leadership," he said.

For Ronald J. Sider, a theology and culture professor at Eastern Baptist Theological Seminary in Philadelphia, activism has been a key part of the involvement of evangelical Christians in the environment.

In 1995, he led the Evangelicals for Social Action to Washington, D.C., to advocate for the Endangered Species Act, which caught some in the capital by surprise.

"Politically most everybody thought all evangelicals were part of the Christian Coalition and in the back pocket of the Republicans in Congress," Sider recalled.

But the mandate to support endangered species and the environment generally comes straight from Scripture, he said.

"We think that means we do not carelessly wipe out forever that which the creator has gently and lovingly shaped," Sider said.

Science, Religion, and Ecology Turn Eastward[2]

By Michael J. Strada
USA Today Magazine, September 2001

What passes for eclecticism in the science-religion dialogue is personified by Carleton University religion professor Ian Barber, 1999 winner of the Templeton Prize for Progress in Religion. Since 1965, he has been decrying that scientists know as little about religion as theologians do about science and prescribing more communication between the two groups as the antidote. He takes pride in observing that, 30 years ago, condescension typified relations between professional science and professional religion, whereas today, both sides are better listeners. Although significant, a richer dialogue between science and religion fails to expand the contemporary paradigm sufficiently. The vision of eclecticism associated with Barber falls short because it suffers from a blind spot—an ethnocentric, culture-bound, decidedly Western one. A plea is made here for a broader, environmentally friendly vision.

Among Western scientists, three common approaches to religion are discernible. The conflict thesis is epitomized by Cambridge University cosmologist Stephen Hawking, whose quest for a "Theory of Everything" considers the assumptions of each worldview as inimical to the other. Harvard University zoologist Stephen Jay Gould speaks for the peaceful coexistence thesis by arguing that, while the two domains cannot be synthesized, they need not come to blows, since neither represents a mortal threat to the other. The third nemesis—transcendence—finds fewer voices singing its praises. It seeks ways to rise above egocentrism to learn something from the other perspective, as advocated by the late Cornell University astronomer Carl Sagan.

Two scientific revolutions traditionally have been credited with transforming humanity's perception of itself: the Copernican revolution (Earth is not at the center of the universe) and the Darwinian revolution (humans obey the same evolutionary rules as other species). Paleoanthropologist Richard Leakey, however, maintains that a new insight needs to be added—the immense size of the universe—because of the redundancy of scale that favors life existing elsewhere.

---

2. Article by Michael J. Strada from *USA Today Magazine* September 2001. Copyright © Society for the Advancement of Education Inc. Reprinted with permission.

Today, astronomers measure the size of the universe as 20,000,000,000 light-years across. Current estimates suggest there are about 100,000,000,000 galaxies, each with about 100,000,000,000 stars. Under these circumstances, Sagan estimated that about 10,000,000,000 trillion planets may exist. There are more stars in the visible universe than grains of sand on Earth. Astronomer Frank Drake is similarly optimistic. Using what is known as the Drake Equation, he calculates that 50,000 intelligent civilizations may exist. While nothing like a consensus can be found, few scientists have assertively suggested that life elsewhere is unlikely. If intelligence is sprinkled around the Cosmos, it probably varies greatly. Therefore, why does monotheism's prime mover resemble the human race so snugly? As contextual background, Stephen Jay Gould suggests that "nothing is more unfamiliar or uncongenial to the human mind than thinking correctly about probabilities."

If intelligence is sprinkled around the Cosmos, it probably varies greatly. Therefore, why does monotheism's prime mover resemble the human race so snugly?

Tangible realities work better than probability as catalysts for human analysis of the chances of life elsewhere. For decades, the common presence of organic molecules—the building blocks of life—in space has been demonstrated by radio telescopes. Science reveals that Mars was once a wet world and now has polar ice caps—significant because, on Earth, water operates as the enabler of life. In 1996, scientists discovered a Mars meteorite containing organic matter. That same year, San Francisco State University astronomer Geoff Marcy won the race to verify the existence of an actual planet (Virginus 70) outside our solar system. Since Marcy's discovery, scores of new planets have been mapped. Some of them possess oxygen, methane, water, and temperatures favoring life as we know it. NASA head Dan Goldin is lobbying for funds to photograph such distant planets.

Only rigorous science can reveal what exists beyond Earth. Yet, if objectivity represents the heart of scientific method, then its soul consists of a certain attitude—skepticism. Science asserts that things are not always what they seem to be, making commonsensical understandings of the physical world inadequate. Sensory perception alone suggests that the sun revolves around the Earth; heavy bodies always fall faster than light ones; and ships made of iron must sink to the bottom of the sea. All of these perceptions, though, have been proven false, because science works via self-correction.

The 19th century witnessed profound self-corrections in both science and religion, stemming from Charles Darwin's Theory of Evolution. However, Darwin erred badly on some questions. As the product of a thoroughly Western (Christian, Victorian, British) culture, he believed implicitly in an upward, progressive slope to humanity's trajectory in the physical and social realms, including the Inevitability Myth regarding homo sapiens—since we are in fact here, predestination requires that we be here for a higher-order purpose. Thus, Darwin fell prey to exaggerating the potency of his central thesis (winners succeed and losers become extinct in the course of biological improvement). Extinction resulting from species failing competitively fit so easily with Western assumptions of competitive ascendancy that rarely did any scientist question this hypothesis.

Darwin's competitive motif tells only part of the evolutionary tale. Unavailable to him was vital knowledge about the role of mass extinctions. The Alvarez hypothesis from the father and son team of Luis (physicist) and Walter (geologist) Alvarez suggests that the great Crustacean extinction 65,000,000 years ago, ending the reign of dinosaurs, resulted from a large asteroid striking Earth. Mass extinctions are more frequent (every 30,000,000 years), and more decisive in evolutionary consequences, than previously believed. The Alvarez hypothesis made randomness part of the evolutionary dialogue, distinguishing between evolution during normal times (when competition matters) and mass extinctions (when survival depends on good luck, not good genes).

British ex-nun Karen Armstrong's history of monotheism (Judaism, Christianity, Islam) reveals considerable similarity among the three religions. Their historical and doctrinal overlap expresses itself concretely in the frequent head-bumping among them over turf in the city of Jerusalem. Armstrong advances a dynamic theory: Our views of God remain intact only if they continue to meet human needs; otherwise, adaptation inevitably follows. She traces the protracted competition between two distinct ideas of divinity—a transcendental God and a personal God. These two visions of deity are not created equal, though, since monotheism generally has invested its spiritual capital more heavily in the personal God than in its transcendental alter ego—especially when contrasted with Eastern religions. What results is a resilient anthropomorphism endemic to monotheism.

Monotheism's convenient anthropomorphism is multifaceted. The Biblical God exhibits all of the schizoid characteristics of human nature. In addition to compassion, we find no shortage of brutality, as when God commands Abraham to kill his only remaining son, Isaac. In the Hebrew tradition of Yahweh, His portrayal epitomizes the ultimate king, and Isaiah (a member of the royal family) found it natural to depict Yahweh as a king enthroned in His temple, much like the kings of Baal and Mardok. "By attributing their own human feelings and experiences to Yahweh, the prophets were creating a God in their own image," Armstrong maintains. The Hebrew

Yahweh is a prophet-meeting God-king who speaks, often practically and harshly, demanding obedient action that is never easy or calming. In Eastern religions, like Hinduism or Buddhism, encounters with a deity typically produce human enlightenment and spiritual peace, but this rarely occurs with the Biblical God.

No paucity of negative consequences have been traced to monotheism's penchant for anthropomorphism. One difficulty with a personal God is the Holocaust Dilemma: If God could not stop the Holocaust, He is impotent and useless. If He could have stopped the Holocaust and didn't, that makes Him even worse. In a classic double bind, the hands-on, personal God gets sullied by the unfathomable Holocaust. Another troubling argument stems from monotheism's historical track record of virulent religious intolerance, which is far less common in Eastern religions. Lastly, a sense of anthropomorphic sexism, inherently part of the Hebrew Yahweh, tends to denigrate ecology, since most of the values associated with modem environmentalism were considered feminine traits in Biblical times.

More than two millennia ago, Plato unequivocally stated that "All mankind, Greeks and non-Greeks alike, believe in the existence of gods." Even the quintessential pragmatist, Italian Renaissance philosopher Nicolo Machiavelli, accepted that, without religion, an orderly society would vanish into smoke. Russian novelist Feodor Dostoevsky's Grand Inquisitor mused that, "If there's no God, everything is permitted." Indeed, throughout human history, the institution of religion has accompanied all social development. From animism to polytheism to monotheism, a resilient spiritual dimension has pervaded human ritual. Humans apparently need spirituality.

Anthropologists suggest that religion persists because it has value to us, and such value can be either intrinsic, instrumental, or a combination thereof. Religion's staying power is illustrated poignantly in an Auschwitz Holocaust story related in journalist Bill Moyers' study on Genesis. Jews in this Nazi death camp held a mock hearing, placing God on trial for the Holocaust, asking the question, "Where was God?" Discovering no exonerating evidence, these Jews found God guilty and sentenced Him to death. Yet, later that same day, what did the same people do? They gathered for evening prayer. The struggle to understand continues because humans need religious ritual, even when mired in the despair of the Holocaust. An equally moving Holocaust story is told by survivor/author Elie Weisel. When he and the other remaining Jews were liberated from Buchenwald in the spring of 1945, what they did first was not to request water, food, or clothing, but to join together in circles, praying as one.

Part of religion's resilience is also attributable to the potency of myth. The Bible works as great literature because of dense, gripping stories that skim across millennia to engross culturally distinct Jews, Christians, and Muslims, and because Biblical stories feature universal themes. No scholar has depicted the Deity through the eyes of as many different cultures as author Joseph Campbell. In *The Hero with a Thousand Faces*, he tells readers that myth, "as a sacred narrative of the world and how we came to be in it,' presents a limited range of responses to the mysteries of life. For example, every society has an "origin myth" as its core story. "From behind a thousand faces, the single hero emerges, archetype of all myth," Campbell writes. Mythology serves as an embodiment of subjective truth, and his *The Power of Myth* demonstrates how myth links us to our past, and how religion and myth constitute different patches of the same spiritual quilt. Above all, Campbell hones in on this insight: Myth should not be considered anachronistic, because repetitive themes continue to affect how we visualize, and live out, life on Earth.

As comparative religionist Huston Smith argues, religion's challenge lies in discovering how to pluck its spiritual bounty without

---

Christianity's linear sense of time . . . , its creation story . . . , and its placing of humans in a special position over the rest of nature render it inimical to ecological integrity.

---

swallowing its considerable excesses, such as the materialistic preoccupations common to church bureaucracies. Few scholars can match Smith's insights, based not only on intellectual erudition, but on wide experience involving diverse religious practices. He sagely observes that, viewed panoramically, monotheism has functioned as both cause and effect of the scientific paradigm responsible for profound changes in the existence of humans and other species in our world. Humans' increased ability to comprehend the world scientifically has produced myriad benefits equated with the notion of competitive progress, but also significant liabilities, among them a proclivity for tunnel vision.

The volatile 1960s unleashed strong criticism of monotheism's contribution to environmental denigration. The classic piece setting the parameters of the dialogue was written by University of California medieval studies professor Lynn White, who took dead aim at Christianity as the culprit most responsible for the environmental crisis. He brands Christianity as the most anthropocentric religion. According to White, Christianity's linear sense of time (distinct beginnings and ends), its creation story (with humans made in God's image), and its placing of humans in a special position over the rest of nature render it inimical to ecological integrity. He does, nevertheless, identify St. Francis of Assisi as an unsung Church hero for advocating the equality of all creatures, including a doctrine tantamount to spiritual leprosy for Church fathers—the concept of an animal soul.

Other factors from Biblical times help to explain monotheism's blank stare regarding ecological consciousness. The first concerns how time is conceived. In ancient Hindu culture, time was considered cyclical, "a wheel of righteousness," as in nature's cycle of sunrise and sunset. This image of nature's cyclical clock provided no reason to consider humanity as anything but an integral part of the natural ecology. In the ninth century B.C., however, a shift took place among the Hebrews that continues to resonate today. Jews changed from the traditional cyclical metaphor to a linear metaphor of time, the etiology of which was inspired by human experience, not nature. Christians soon borrowed this concept, and Western imagery concerning time was fundamentally altered. Linear time encourages hierarchical thinking, assisting the myth that humanity stands not only apart from, but also above nature.

One other ancient shift, occurring shortly thereafter, likewise mitigated against a green conscience for Christianity. When Christ's followers first distinguished themselves from pagans, the word "pagan" meant "country-dweller," and the pagans' otherness was bound up with being a country bumpkin. Anything connoting rural life seemed alien to the early Christians, who lived in cities of the Roman Empire such as Antioch and Alexandria. Christianity had a decidedly urban style, and the stiffest opposition Christian proselytizers would encounter for more than a millennium was from the "tenacious nature religions of the peasantry," as Alan Watts wrote in *Nature, Man, and Woman*. Uniquely Christian as well is the way it bases its legitimacy on miracles bending the laws of nature to the will of God. While some other religions may sprinkle in miraculous events, their role is the crux of the matter only with Christianity.

Monotheism's condescending attitude toward nature appears even more hostile when contrasted with the environmentally friendly religions of the East. Western maximalism (bigger is better) contrasts sharply with Eastern minimalism (small is beautiful). Buddhism, for instance, is less didactic and more inferential than monotheism's big three religions. Buddha taught that the processes of nature are shaped by the morals of humans. Therefore, ecological problems can be alleviated by living simpler, gentler, more spiritual lives. Pollution in the environment is caused by the pollution of human hearts. Material excess often leads people away from living the existence of moderation practiced by the Buddha. Compassion and loving kindness for all living things are fundamental Buddhist values concerning nature.

Taoism can be traced back to the teachings of Lao-Tse (604–531 B.C.). It started out as a philosophy and was adopted as a state religion in 440 A.D., at which time Lao-Tse became venerated as a deity. Lao-Tse taught that Tao is the first cause of the universe and that our goal is to become one with the Tao. People must develop virtue through compassion, moderation, and humility.

Taoism's beneficence toward nature matches Buddhism's. Meaning "The Way," Taoism represents a depersonalized ethic demonstrating none of the anthropomorphism of a creator God.

In Taoism, nature is a living whole into which humanity, like everything else, must fit: "According to the Tao, there is a moral imperative to be virtuous toward nature." Taoism is based partly on the dialectical interplay of Tao's key cosmic principles—yin (dark side) and yang (light side)—which accounts for the rhythm found in the natural world. There can exist no unbridgeable gulf between humanity and nature, because absolutely everything is connected. The doctrine of Wu Wei advocates "acting in accord with nature, that is, in harmony with the Tao." All beings are embraced by Taoism's egalitarian ethic.

As mentioned earlier, Hinduism's sense of time remains cyclical, not linear. This contributes to Hinduism's organic view of nature, with humanity of it, in it, but not above it. Symbolic of Hinduism's cyclical mind-set is the doctrine of reincarnation of the soul. Reincarnation provides the vehicle for eventual perfection of the spirit and ultimate unity with the deity, or godhead. The main scriptures (the "Veda" the "Upanishad," and the "Bhagavad-Gita") teach tolerance and respect for life. The ancient Hindu religion continues to shape life in India and other Hindu cultures.

Eastern Insights

We must look to these Eastern religions for insights, because they enable more openminded approaches to the dilemmas of existence—especially environmental ones. One difficulty with looking East for enlightenment, though, is that understanding Eastern theologies is not easy. The extensive writings of Watts represents a resource noteworthy for making Eastern inscrutability accessible to the Western mind. Employing prose that stands up and performs poetically, he allows us to know something of Zen Buddhism, for example, without devoting a lifetime to unraveling its subtle paradoxes. While Buddhism and Christianity may differ greatly in form, they share many basic principles.

A similarly engaging contemporary meeting of Eastern and Western minds can be found in *The Monk and the Philosopher*, a tete-at-tete on metaphysics, morality, and meaning between French rationalist philosopher Jean-François Revel and his son, Matthieu Ricard, a Buddhist monk who works as a translator for the Dalai Lama. As the two men meet in an inn overlooking Katmandu, Western modes of thought take in Eastern modes of spiritual experience. The bond between father and son helps to bridge the gap, as they struggle to find commonality between Western theology and Buddhism concerning humanity's search for meaning.

One Eastern philosophy barely mentioned yet is Confucianism. In *Confucius Lives Next Door: What Living in the East Teaches Us About Living in the West, Washington Post* Tokyo bureau chief Thomas Reid explains the relevance of history to contemporary Asia. Confucian moral values still live throughout the East (not only China) and undergird responsible social behavior, ecological sensitivity, and the work ethic common to Asian societies. Even after 2,500 years, Confucius' timeless values of respect for elders, rising above sociopolitical hardships, group responsibility, and personal integrity, matter greatly. Reid emphasizes how similar are the moral statements shared by the ancient Greeks, Confucianism, and Christianity.

Hinduism and Taoism are the other Eastern religions vital for broadening the Western perspective. Since Western logic is vulnerable to the fallacy of single cause, the Occidental mind always wants to single out one factor causing a given result to occur. Westerners want to know which Eastern religion (Hinduism, Buddhism, Taoism, Confucianism) is the real answer to their problems. That they are all heuristic for the task strikes most Westerners as evading the question.

One of the most broad-minded Western scientists today is biologist Edward Wilson, who condemns the tunnel vision characteristic of those who stay within the comfortable boundaries of single academic disciplines. His highly interdisciplinary approach remains praiseworthy, but his faith in science may be excessive. Wilson pays homage to monotheism's Biblical tradition as the wellspring of Western science, and he laments Oriental philosophy having missed the scientific boat: "It abandoned the idea of a supreme being with personal and creative properties. No rational author of Nature existed in their universe; consequently, the objects they meticulously described did not follow universal principles." This condescending attitude belies the blind spot of even the most eclectic Western scientists, such as Wilson. Maybe he has it backwards; maybe it is really the West that has paid too high a price for its strident scientism.

Similarly trained in Western science, physician Andrew Weil nevertheless manages to go beyond those intellectual parameters, advancing an intellectual paradigm that he calls "integrative." Weil traces how fundamental differences between Eastern and Western philosophy manifest themselves in the science (and art) of medicine. Owing to a proscription against cutting up cadavers, for thousands of years Chinese medicine focused on function (immunity, potency, energy) and developed means—like herbalism and acupuncture—to help the body's natural healing properties do their work. Western medicine concentrated on structure (circulatory system, liver, skeleton) and developed means, like surgery, to remove infected tonsils or cancerous tumors. Both approaches offer benefits, and Weil's eclecticism enables him to segue between Oriental and Occidental techniques in ways that unidimensional healers of either stripe cannot.

Weil's eclecticism in medicine understands the luminous insight derived from ecological studies in recent decades—everything is linked in an organic whole. Such holism needs to saturate the triptych where religion, science, and ecology converge if what passes for philosophical eclecticism is to grow beyond its Western blind spot. Such expansion, one might argue, will blossom from Western consciousness grounding itself in Eastern religions since they embrace nature as a living whole wherein everything must fit. Despite failing the test for a green conscience, monotheism's track record for flexibly adapting to new human needs is impressive, which provides reason for hope. Today, humanity's changing needs begin with valuing nature as a sacred trust.

Religion, Modern Secular Culture, and Ecology[3]

By George Rupp
DÆDALUS, Fall 2001

As an occasional participant in the meetings that led to this issue of *Dædalus*, I have been invited to sketch the historical, religious, and academic context that these deliberations on religion and ecology presuppose. I can summarize that context in two countervailing points: virtually all of our religious and cultural traditions have contributed to the gravity of the ecological threats we face; at the same time, both our religious traditions and our universities can marshal substantial resources for addressing those threats more effectively than has been the case so far. The challenge is to move from point one to point two.

Almost thirty-five years ago, Lynn White wrote an arresting essay entitled "The Historic Roots of our Ecologic Crisis," an article that was published in *Science* and has received widespread attention over the years from scientists as well as humanists. It is worth returning to White's article more than three decades later because it continues to be instructive, not only through its telling insights but also through its equally revealing omissions. White correctly identifies the dominant strain or core structure of Western theism that represents God as transcending the world and humanity as exercising dominion over the natural order. Where White falls short is in failing to notice how other elements in the structure of biblical religion in effect counterbalance the invitation to exercise human sovereignty over nature. Two such elements are crucial: the affirmation of creation as the handiwork of God and therefore as good; and the record of humanity's fall and consequent need for redemption.

That nature is God's creation and therefore good calls for respectful care and stewardship. White is aware of what he terms "an alternative Christian view," which he delineates almost exclusively with reference to Saint Francis of Assisi. But he does not interpret the theme of care and stewardship for the divine creation as a central element in the structure of Jewish and Christian religion.

---

3. "Religion, Modern Secular Culture, and Ecology" reprinted by permission of *Dædalus*, Journal of the American Academy of Arts and Sciences, from the issue entitled, "Religion and Ecology: Can the Climate Change?" Fall 2001, Vol. 130, No. 4.

Similarly crucial for counterbalancing the motif of human sovereignty over nature is the biblical story of fall and redemption. The destiny of the faithful is, after all, not to be realized in worldly rulership. Especially in much of Christian piety, the human vocation is to be a pilgrim who is only passing through the fallen world and therefore is to tread lightly over the earth on the way to redemption in heaven.

This otherworldly orientation can, of course, cut both ways. It may lead to a disengagement that is, paradoxically, friendly to the environment from which it is estranged. But it may also result in the exploitation of the fallen world precisely because it is viewed as lacking intrinsic value. Thus, even very traditional Western religious worldviews have a deeply equivocal relationship to our ecological crisis.

What is noteworthy, though, is that the force of the structural elements outlined by White become only more pronounced as increasing numbers of people find the traditional narrative of fall and

---

Very traditional Western religious worldviews have a deeply equivocal relationship to our ecological crisis.

---

redemption less and less compelling. If salvation in heaven is not the central goal of human life, then the prospect of sovereignty over the natural world takes on greater urgency. And if the evident evil in worldly affairs is to be overcome apart from any redemptive divine action, then vigorous human effort will be required.

Similarly, if God as creator is believed to have established a general order to nature but is no longer thought to intervene in particular events, then human will and intelligence can seek to understand and in time even attempt to control the natural world. And if even the limited role attributed to this remote deity is no longer attractive or persuasive, then human effort is all the more crucial. Thus the rise of science and a correlative retreat by traditional theism from at least the late seventeenth century on accentuated precisely the anthropocentric elements that White identifies as characteristic of Jewish and Christian religion.

To put the point bluntly, it is only when the transcendent God of biblical religion is no longer thought to intervene in the world either as creator or as redeemer that the full force of claims for human dominion over nature becomes evident.

In the twentieth century this unrestrained human self-assertion over nature reached what remains its starkest expression in the literary and philosophical movement called existentialism. Like most broad cultural trends, existentialism has many variants that certainly do not agree in all their details. But the early thought of Martin Heidegger exerted enormous influence on the movement as a whole and in many respects illustrates its central tendencies. For Heidegger, the human self is, to use his metaphor, "thrown" into an indifferent universe from which it must seize and shape whatever meaning can be attained. There is no created order to discover. Nor is there any redemptive community. Instead the self-reliant individual must establish authentic existence in stark opposition both to nature and to the mores of any and all forms of conventional social life—in particular the mass culture of modern society.

Existentialism offers a convenient illustration of both the glory and the travail of modern Western individualism. Its summons one to authenticity, to self-actualization over against a conformist society and an indifferent nature; it resonates with the energy and initiative and independence of our most individualistic traditions. But existentialism also exemplifies the willful self-assertion and arrogance that all too frequently characterize Western attitudes both toward nature and toward the cultures of others.

There are, of course, substantial cultural resources for enriching this environmentally inhospitable and religiously impoverished individualism. The essays on religion and ecology in this issue collect and present impressive evidence of the vitality of those resources. Especially noteworthy are the contributions from a remarkable range of Asian traditions—from Hindu, Buddhist, Taoist, Shinto, and Confucian thought and practice. Indeed, one of the most remarkable achievements of this collection is the depth and variety of representation of those various traditions. But that very achievement at the same time demonstrates how diverse each community is, how disparate its historical impacts have been, and how untenable it is to present any tradition in self-congratulatory terms as consistently and effectively unified in its ecological orientation.

The result is that neither Asian traditions nor the relatively fewer environmentally friendly themes of Jewish, Christian, and Muslim action and reflection nor the orientations of indigenous communities in Africa, Oceania, and the Americas are by themselves adequate for addressing the environmental challenges we face. We cannot select and emphasize only environmentally friendly motifs from multiple traditions. Nor can we simply embrace a unified position that affirms the whole of reality just as it is. Instead we must grapple with the fact that modern Western individualism and its institutional expressions in social, political, and economic life have become major historical forces across cultures—forces that we cannot ignore or wish away but rather must engage and incorporate into an ecologically responsible stance appropriate to the centuries ahead.

One of the settings in which we must grapple with this ecological crisis is our universities. It is scarcely surprising, in view of the history of their development, that modern research universities exemplify an advanced form of the very individualism that we must overcome. This is so not only because individual members of at least Western academic institutions are in their personal styles highly individualistic—though that is certainly often true; more important, it is because universities, in developing academic disciplines as central to the organization of domains of knowledge, exhibit a pattern that parallels the role of individualism in the broader society.

Disciplinary specialization is a significant achievement of the research university. It has been remarkably effective in generating understanding of both specific data and general explanatory hypotheses. But this attainment of analytical rigor has as its correlate a depth of specialization that renders connections with other disciplinary approaches difficult at a time when we are becoming more and more aware that many challenging intellectual problems, certainly including issues at the heart of our ecological crisis, do not fall neatly within the domain of a single discipline.

This state of affairs predictably has led to calls for interdisciplinary investigation. While completely understandable, such calls are problematic in ways that parallel the invocation of one or another religious or cultural tradition as the answer to our ecological crisis. Just as we cannot simply return to a state of innocence that antedates the historical emergence of modern Western individualism, so we cannot embrace a synthetic interdisciplinary approach that fails to incorporate the analytic strengths and achievements of disciplinary specialization.

What is required is therefore not interdisciplinary study but rather multidisciplinary investigation comparable in rigor and depth to specialized research within single disciplines. Such investigation offers the prospect of moving forward on two crucial fronts. The first requires us to understand and then also to demonstrate in compelling ways how current patterns of advanced industrial societies are not sustainable indefinitely—or even for very long. The second calls for participation in developing alternative technical approaches and economic incentives that allow and encourage movement away from unsustainable current practices.

Progress on both fronts clearly requires joint efforts on the part of scientists and engineers on the one hand and policy professionals on the other. That such joint efforts are being launched is promising. But the interests that favor continuation of current patterns of consumption are extremely powerful. Consequently, any campaign to conserve our environment must be solidly based on compelling scientific evidence and cogently expressed in terms of economic incentives and policy requirements.

Along with marshaling scientific, technical, and policy capabilities for addressing ecological issues, we must also enlist the full range of the world's cultural resources. This process must recognize the extent of pluralism not only among traditions but also within each of them. Because there are multiple voices within each of a rich variety of communities, effective collaboration across traditions entails greater complexity than has often been supposed—but, paradoxically, may also be more readily attained, at least in partial and stepwise fashion.

Pluralism within traditions testifies to the capacity for change in what remains a continuous line of development. Thus even the communities most inclined to invoke authoritative figures or texts in fact regularly take into account new data and respond creatively to the demands of novel situations. This capacity for change opens up opportunities for collaboration across traditions, as minor or even submerged motifs in one community gain a higher profile through interaction with other communities in which those motifs are more prominent.

To take a critical instance, in seeking to counter the Western tendency toward unrestrained individualism, a major resource is the insistence of many religious and cultural traditions that humans in the end are parts of a larger whole to which their personal interests and ambitions are subordinate. In Western religious and cultural traditions, this holistic affirmation has not been a dominant theme insofar as God has been construed as outside the world, and it has been muted still more as the divine has been relegated to the margins of natural life and human affairs. But even in Western traditions, there is a persistent testimony that God is intimately involved with the world and indeed incorporates the world into the divine life.

This testimony is not confined to Francis of Assisi and a few other revolutionary figures, as Lynn White suggests in referring to "an alternative Christian view." Instead, it is a recurrent even if not dominant motif in the Bible and in Western theology and philosophy. In regard to this theme, Psalm 139 speaks for much Jewish and Christian piety:

> Where can I go from your spirit?
> Or where can I flee from your presence?
> If I ascend to heaven, you are there;
> if I make my bed in Sheol, you are there.
> If I take the wings of the morning
> and settle at the farthest limits of the sea,
> even there your hand shall lead me,
> and your right hand shall hold me fast.
> If I say, "Surely the darkness shall cover me,
> and the light around me become night,"
> even the darkness is not dark to you;
> the night is as bright as the day,
> for darkness is as light to you.

> (Ps. 139:7–12)

And for Christian theology, the central teaching of the incarnation affirms that the divine is integrally related to the human, that a deity who is distant cannot be the God who loves and embraces the world in Christ.

Modern secular appropriations of Western religion illustrate the persistence of this holistic affirmation. Spinoza and Hegel are probably the most influential examples of philosophers who sought to restate the truths of Jewish and Christian religion in secular terms after the erosion of belief in a God outside the world. But instead of retreating to the remote God of Deism, Spinoza and Hegel insisted, each in his own way, that any coherent conception of God must include all of reality in the divine.

This holistic strain in Western traditions may attract attention out of proportion to its historical prominence in the context of interaction among religious traditions, especially once the interaction has moved beyond self-congratulatory representation to a search for common ground. This seeking common ground does not imply an attempt to find a least common denominator to which the various religious traditions can be reduced. Instead, the aim is to enrich and develop further the resources in each community for resisting unrestrained individualism through the affirmation of an inclusive reality into which personal interests and ambitions must be integrated.

We in the West have much to learn from religious and cultural traditions that locate the human within nature and do not authorize the exploitation of nature to serve narrow human interests. At the same time, all of us as humans now confront ecological challenges that require vigorous effort to redirect the environmental impact of our species. Consequently, the energy and imagination that have contributed to the threats we face may also be a major resource for countering those threats.

In this respect, modern Western individualism in both its secular and its religious expressions may play a constructive role in ongoing deliberations on religion and ecology. While the recognition that the human is integral to a larger whole is crucial for cultivating an ecological ethos, this insight alone is not enough. In particular, this holistic affirmation of all that is does not directly address the crucial ethical question of how a more equitable sharing of limited resources may be attained.

Here again, each tradition can bring impressive resources to bear. But along with counterparts from other traditions, Western religious and secular perspectives certainly can and should play a role in the common cause of restoring ecological balance while at the same time advancing toward a more equitable sharing of the earth's scarce resources. Only this joining of environmental concern with a commitment to justice is worthy of the best in each of our diverse traditions.

To integrate an ethos of care for the earth as our common home with an ethic that engages the issue of equity would be an optimal outcome for a series of deliberations on ecology and religion. This volume has certainly not yet achieved that integration. But in marshaling resources both from the academy and from an impressive range of religious traditions, it at least moves in the right direction.

V. Religion and Gender

Editor's Introduction

Most world religions, like the societies in which they are practiced, have discriminated against women in one way or another. According to one Buddhist tradition, for example, the historical Buddha originally refused to ordain women; he relented only after Ananda, an early male disciple, prevailed on him to reconsider. To this day, while it is generally not possible to be ordained as a woman in Japan, Cambodia, Laos, or Myanmar, female ordination is practiced in Sri Lanka, Taiwan, China, Hong Kong, and South Korea. The article "Thai Monk Blazes Path For Equality For Women" profiles Chatsumarn Kabilsingh, the first female monk to be ordained as a novice in the Thai branch of Theravada Buddhism.

If religion has colluded in relegating women to a second-class social status, however, it has also played a part in promoting sexual equality. The Islamic faith, which has been used by some to justify the subjugation of women, is an instructive example, as illustrated by Priya Malhotra's article "Islam's Female Converts." Each year in the United States alone, some 20,000 Americans embrace Islam; about 7,000 of those converts are women. Islam offers these women many things: for some, the religion represents a compelling alternative to what they see as the empty materialism of secular culture; others are attracted to the strong emphasis on family; finally, some view the modest dress stipulated by their religion as a liberation from the sexual objectification of women. Moreover, as one Islamic scholar points out, Islam has a long tradition of empowering women. As early as the seventh century, Islamic law recognized a woman's right to arrange her own marriage and to own and inherit property. Given the patriarchal character of pre-Islamic Arab society, these were genuine advances; indeed, similar rights were not codified in the West until the 19th century.

In many religious traditions, as in secular society, the rise of feminism over the last few decades has encouraged women to embrace roles traditionally reserved for men. Nina Siegal, in her article "New Fields and Strict Judaism Coexist," profiles several Orthodox Jewish women pursuing careers outside of the traditional fields of social work and teaching. While religious duties sometimes conflict with the demands of the working world, notes Siegal, many women have devised innovative ways of balancing the two.

The final article in this section, "Reconciliation," by Vanessa E. Jones, examines a movement in the black church to encourage the full participation of gays and lesbians. According to Jones, homosexuality is a controversial subject in black churches—and one that is not often discussed in public. As is the case with most other Christian churches (indeed, with most religious institutions in general), the black church has a long history of homophobia. That history is additionally complicated by the impact of racism on sexual attitudes. While some African-American gays and lesbians have abandoned the black church in favor of white denominations that accept their sexuality, a growing number are expressing frustration at having to choose between their racial and sexual identities. Moreover, many feel a special connection with the traditions of the black church. The particular church examined in this article, Boston's Union United Methodist Church, accepts gays and lesbians as members; however, it does not marry gay couples, nor does it ordain gay clergy.

Thai Monk Blazes Path for Equality for Women[1]

NEW YORK TIMES, OCTOBER 14, 2001

Chatsumarn Kabilsingh gave up her husband, family life and a distinguished career to walk the path of Buddha.

It has led her into a sharp conflict over the lowly and unequal status of women in Buddhist practice in Thailand, reviving a fight faced by her mother four decades ago.

Ms. Kabilsingh, a 57-year-old former professor, carries a new name—Dhammananda, or the joy of righteousness—given to her after ordination as a novice monk in February. The ordination, in Sri Lanka, put her on a collision course with a Buddhist hierarchy in Thailand that believes that only men can enter the monkhood.

Conservative monks and laymen accuse Dhammananda of intentionally creating problems that will further erode a religion plagued in this predominantly Buddhist nation by numerous sex and money scandals in recent years.

"This is a conflict between ignorance and right understanding," said Dhammananda, quoting Buddha as saying the health of the religion depends on four pillars—male and female monks, male and female lay people.

"I just want to live a quiet and peaceful life by following the Lord Buddha's footsteps," she said in an interview. "My ultimate hope is the same as that of other Buddhists—going to Nirvana."

Adhering to the strict practices of the Theravada school of Buddhism, she gets up daily at 5 a.m. to meditate, pray and study scriptures. She takes no solid food after noon.

Having taken vows of celibacy, she is divorced from her husband and lives apart from her three sons. Dhammananda, who holds a doctorate in religion, also gave up her status as a leading Buddhist scholar, having written and translated more than 40 books on the religion.

In the afternoons, people seek her advice on personal and spiritual problems. Several women have inquired about becoming monks, and in June, Chamnean Rattnaburi, 41, was also ordained in Sri Lanka.

If Dhammananda continues her practice, she will become a full monk in two years, although she will probably not be recognized as such in her homeland.

---

1. Reprinted with permission of The Associated Press.

THAILAND

Map No. 3853
UNITED NATIONS
October 1994

Department of Public Information
Cartographic Section

Theravada scriptures, as interpreted in Thailand, require that for a woman to be ordained a monk both a male and female monk must be present at the ceremony.

Since there are no women who are monks in Thailand, ordinations for women cannot take place "and only the Lord Buddha can change that," said Visith Pongpatanajit of the Religious Affairs Department.

Women can be ordained as monks in Sri Lanka, Taiwan, China, Hong Kong and South Korea, with most of these countries dominated by the Mahayana school of Buddhism. Female ordination is not practiced in Japan, Cambodia, Laos or Myanmar, formerly Burma.

Currently, the only path for women wishing to develop their spirituality within Thailand's formal religious structure is to become a nun. But these women with shaved heads and white robes are little better than servants for the monks, cleaning and cooking in exchange for monastic shelter and food provided by the men.

"This is very old thinking," said Thongbai Thongpao, a human rights lawyer, noting that the Sangha Council, the country's ruling Buddhist body, has made changes only to rules for men in line with a changing, modernizing world. "Many religions change to give women equal rights."

Mr. Thongbai, who is a senator, said the issue of women in the monkhood could also be viewed as a conflict between traditional religious belief and the equal rights granted women under Thailand's new, reformist constitution.

Phra Dhepdilok, vice abbot of the Bowon Niwet Monastery, dismisses Dhammananda's ordination as just "revenge for her mother."

Forty years ago, Thailand's religious establishment refused to recognize the ordination of Dhammananda's mother, Voramai Kabilsingh, in Taiwan. But it did not stop the construction of Thailand's first temple for women in the monkhood on the family's land west of Bangkok. This is where Dhammananda now lives, as does her mother.

That conflict was swept under the rug, but resurfaced when Dhammananda decided to follow her mother's footsteps.

"I hope that allowing female ordination will shore up women's status in religion, and most of all, help strengthen the religion," she said.

Dhammananda has no plans to seek official recognition as a monk.

"The recognition comes after trust," she said. "I will prove that female monks are really a boon to Thai Buddhism. This is my mission in life."

Islam's Female Converts[2]

By Priya Malhotra
Newsday, February 16, 2002

"Allahu akbar [God is great], Allahu akbar!" called Muhammad Hannini as about 15 worshipers gathered Sunday in a mosque in the basement of a home in Richmond Hill, Queens. Instantly, they knelt and touched their heads to the floor, a gesture symbolizing submission to God in Islam.

The eight women bent in prayer a few feet behind the men were dressed in scarves and long dresses or ankle-length skirts. "You should see my humanity, my compassion, my devotion to God coming through the surface, not my body," said Sunni Rumsey Amatullah, who became Muslim a quarter century ago.

The women say they consider the veil and modest dress symbols not of oppression but of liberation. They say the emphasis on the female body in the Western world, with all its manifestations in popular culture, has led to the sexual objectification of women. And, despite their own often problematic relationships with men, they say their religion treats each gender equally, though not identically.

Like Amatullah—who was born Cheryl Rumsey in Jamaica, Queens, and raised Episcopalian—these women are among the estimated 20,000 Americans a year who since the mid-'90s have adopted Islam, a religion that has been receiving much attention since the Sept.11 terrorist attacks.

Despite the persistent image of the oppressed Muslim woman, about 7,000 of those converts each year are women, according to the report of a study led by Ihsan Bagby, a professor of international studies at Shaw University in Raleigh, N.C. The study was financed in part by the Council on American-Islamic Relations, based in Washington. About 14,000 of the total number of converts in 2000, the report found, were African-American, 4,000 were white and 1,200 were of Hispanic descent. (Members of the Nation of Islam were not included in the study.)

What is the religion's draw for women? "The tightly structured way of life, the regular set of responsibilities, where you know what you believe and you know what you do, attracts some women," said Jane I. Smith, professor of Islamic studies at Hartford Seminary in Connecticut and author of *Islam in America* (Columbia University Press).

---

2. Article by Priya Malhotra from *Newsday* February 16, 2002. Copyright © Priya Malhotra. Reprinted with permission.

With laws for almost every aspect of life, Islam represents a faith-based order that women may see as crucial to creating healthy families and communities, and correcting the damage done by the popular secular humanism of the past 30 or so years, several experts said. In addition, women from broken homes may be especially attracted to the religion because of the value it places on family, said Marcia Hermansen, a professor of Islamic studies at Loyola University in Chicago and an American who also converted to Islam.

Next Saturday, the women, along with Muslims around the world, will celebrate the festival of Eid ul-Adha marking the end of hajj, the annual pilgrimage to Mecca. They "don't see the structures as repressive," Hermansen said. "They see them as comforting and supportive."

Choosing Islam can also be a type of "cultural critique" of Western materialism, she said. "Islam represents the beautiful, traditional, grounded and authentic."

With laws for almost every aspect of life, Islam represents a faith-based order that women may see as crucial to creating healthy families and communities.

"It is Allah talking to you directly," said Amatullah, 50, the director of an HIV prevention program at Iris House, a health-care organization in Harlem. She said she converted after leading a wildly hedonistic lifestyle for several years. "It's a spiritual awakening. What happens is you're in a fog and you don't know you are in a fog, and when it clears up you say, 'Hey, I thought it was clear back there,'" she said. "My friend's husband gave me the Quran in my early 20s, because he thought I was too wild."

At first, Amatullah said, she paid little attention, but she was profoundly affected when she started delving into the book. Still, it took about five years and a great deal of contemplation, she said, before she became truly interested in Islam and came to believe the Quran was the divine truth. She said she also was impressed by the rights women had under Islam in seventh-century Arabia, a time when women in most other cultures had virtually no power over their lives.

"Islamic law embodies a number of Quranic reforms that significantly enhanced the status of women," according to John Esposito, a professor and director of the Center for Muslim-Christian Understanding at Georgetown University and author of *Islam: The Straight Path* (Oxford University Press). "Contrary to pre-Islamic Arab customs, the Quran recognized a woman's right to contract her own marriage.

"In addition, she, not her father or male relatives, as had been the custom, was to receive the dowry from her husband. She became a party to the contract rather than an object for sale," Esposito wrote. "The right to keep and maintain her dowry was a source of self-esteem and wealth in an otherwise male-dominated society. Women's right to own and manage their own property was further enhanced and acknowledged by Quranic verses of inheritance which granted inheritance rights to wives, daughters, sisters and grandmothers of the deceased in a patriarchal society where all rights were traditionally vested solely in male heirs. Similar legal rights would not occur in the West until the 19th century."

Esther Bourne, a 46-year-old accountant in Manhattan, was raised Catholic by her American mother after her British father died when she was 6. Spiritually inclined from a young age, she said she first read the Quran in her mid-20s, because her former husband, a Muslim, owned a copy. "I would go in and out of it," she said.

By her mid-30s, after ending an abusive relationship and enduring the tragic death of a man she loved dearly, Bourne said she began a spiritual quest that included classes on Islam at a mosque on Manhattan's Upper East Side. "When the teachers would explain, my heart just accepted it," she said. "The heart believed it."

In 1992, at the age of 36, Bourne took her shahada, the profession of faith that is the first of the five pillars of Islam. "I don't have panic anymore, and if some misfortune happens, I just accept the decree from Allah," Bourne said.

"You slowly adjust yourself to an Islamic way of life, thinking about God, doing good deeds," Amatullah said. "Some days I do it better than others."

Amina Mohammed, a 58-year-old dental assistant at the Veterans Administration hospital in St. Albans, has been a Muslim for more than 20 years. She was born Doris Gregory, the daughter of an American Indian mother and a Jamaican father, and was raised as a Lutheran. She said she stopped going to church when she was 16.

Two years later, she began an active spiritual quest by reading about Buddhism, Hinduism and American Indian religions, but, she said, none of them was what she was looking for—a way to pray to one God in one form. "I was so disappointed," she said. "I knew that there was a correct religion, but I just hadn't found it. But I believed in God—I was no atheist."

In her mid-30s, after two failed marriages and two daughters—who are now 27 and 33—she said she felt a desperate need for spiritual direction and coincidentally was exposed for the first time to Islam. "This is what I had always felt in my heart," she said.

For about three years she studied the religion; she began to cut down on dating and to cover her head occasionally. Then she went to a mosque in Manhattan and "saw women from different countries and from different races praying together," she said. "I thought this is how it should be on earth."

Amatullah, who lives in St. Albans, has been married and divorced three times since she converted to Islam. Her first husband was from Sudan, the second was from Egypt and the third was Italian-American; all were Muslim. Allah gives both men and women the right to divorce, she said, and she initiated each split.

Although the Quran does not prohibit women from gaining an education or having a career, the converts said, it is a woman's primary responsibility to take care of her children.

"Look at the Western society of today with the breakdown of family, the mother being out of the home and the children being alone," said Bourne, who is single and has a 28-year-old son. "I had problems because I practically had to raise my son alone."

Their faith, the three converts said, has not been shaken by the Sept. 11 attacks, carried out by men who said they were acting as Muslims. The distortion of Islam by extremists and terrorists, the women stressed, should not lead to the condemnation of a great religion.

"To kill innocent lives," Amatullah said, "is anti-Islamic."

New Fields and Strict Judaism Coexist[3]

BY NINA SIEGAL
NEW YORK TIMES, JANUARY 4, 2001

When Yitta Halberstam Mandelbaum was growing up in Borough Park, Brooklyn, in the late 1950s, she figured there were two careers for Orthodox Jewish girls: teaching and social work. But Yitta's father, a traditional Hasidic man whose dark curls dangled from beneath his black hat, planted his daughter in the biography section of the local public library and encouraged her to dream.

When she started writing poetry at age 8, he helped her send her work to poetry journals and Jewish magazines. By 9, she had been published. When Mrs. Mandelbaum signed her first book deal in 1995, she placed her contract on her father's grave to include him in her proud moment.

Mrs. Mandelbaum is now a best-selling author who has appeared on several national talk shows and traveled across the country to lecture. She said she never imagined that her career would take her so far from Borough Park. Yet she still regularly attends services at her synagogue, where she sits with the women, separated from the men by a curtain.

Yitta Mandelbaum has found herself in a fast-widening circle of Orthodox Jewish women who have chosen atypical careers without trading in their strict religious practices. Across the spectrum of Orthodox Judaism, more observant women are stepping out of traditional jobs.

"In the past, Orthodox women were expected to be schoolteachers; that was pretty much the extent of their professional opportunities," said Ari L. Goldman, author of *Being Jewish* (Simon & Schuster, 2000). "Now you have women who are doctors and lawyers, judges, politicians, musicians and even blue-collar types like bus drivers and paramedics."

That Orthodox women work is nothing new. Many Modern Orthodox women have already entered professional fields. Even in some ultra-Orthodox households, women have long been the primary wage earners so their husbands can devote more time to Torah study and prayer. But until recently, Orthodox Jewish women generally chose jobs in nurturing professions like teaching, social work and nursing. Or they worked in sales at Jewish-owned businesses that closed to observe the Sabbath and holidays.

---

3. Article by Nina Siegal from the *New York Times* January 4, 2001. Copyright © *New York Times*. Reprinted with permission.

These jobs were chosen because they were compatible with the demands of an Orthodox household—caring for the children so their husbands could focus on the Torah, preparing kosher meals and observing the Sabbath.

But now, said Sylvia Barack Fishman, a professor of contemporary Jewish life at Brandeis University, growing numbers of Orthodox women are balancing religious life and increasingly demanding duties in the workplace.

"This is a profound change," Dr. Fishman said, "because she's working at very high-status jobs and yet still running this very traditional household, where there is complete Sabbath observance every week. She may litigate cases, but she is still coming home and setting the Sabbath table, and going to the ritual cleansing once a month and keeping up the traditional duties."

Dr. Fishman noted that although many Modern Orthodox women work, in the past few chose to do so while their children were

---

Although there are no statistics on how many Orthodox women are working, their growing numbers have begun to force Jewish institutions to shift and bend.

---

small. It is much more likely, she said, that those women will now work full time through their childbearing years. And, she said, although Hasidic women are still less likely to work while they have young children, more are looking for work after their children grow up.

Although there are no statistics on how many Orthodox women are working, their growing numbers have begun to force Jewish institutions to shift and bend. The largest Zionist women's group in the United States, Americans for Israel and Torah, is a 75-year-old charity that operates largely on volunteer help from its 82,000 members. "Our whole organization has had to change with the times," said Marvin S. Leff, its executive director. "Most of our chapters used to meet in the daytime. Now at least half have to meet in the evenings or weekends because so many women are working."

And the increase in working women has also led to shortages in professions that have defined Orthodox Jewish communities. "The change is causing a real crisis in Jewish early childhood education," said Cheryl Wadler Meskin, director of the early childhood department of the Board of Jewish Education of Greater New York. "We have no teachers coming into the pool anymore because women are choosing other professions."

At the same time, she added, Jewish parents are placing their children in preschool at younger ages, bringing the average age of the school population down. "The aging down of children is in direct correlation with mothers' going back to work," Mrs. Meskin said. "And we are bursting at the seams with children and no faculty to serve them."

And the number of working Orthodox women will probably continue to grow. Karen Bacon, the dean of Stern College for Women, the women's undergraduate division of Yeshiva University in New York, where Jewish religious study is part of the required curriculum, said the continued growth in enrollment (up to 964 this year over 761 last year) and new interest in unusual majors (studio art, psychology, communications, finance and accounting, pre-med, dentistry and veterinary sciences) were a sign that increasing numbers of Jewish women intended to juggle religious and secular aspirations.

Yitta Mandelbaum has observed the shifts firsthand. "I've seen tremendous change over the last two decades," she said. "It's very clear that feminism has impacted even the ghetto Jew. And I'm definitely from the ghetto, Borough Park."

When Mrs. Mandelbaum began traveling for work, her husband, Mordechai, and her youngest son, Eli, went with her. But now she travels alone, toting her kosher food in a suitcase and saying her prayers in hotel rooms. When she returns to Borough Park, she and her husband prepare for the Sabbath together, and invite needy people into their home to share their meal. "When I'm home, I'm home," she said. "My presence is felt."

After graduating from Brooklyn College, Mrs. Mandelbaum worked at *Seventeen* magazine, becoming, she said, the publication's first Hasidic staff member. But she said concerns about the moral content of the magazine drove her away. Later, she yearned to write a novel. But she hit a wall. A Judaic rule called loshon hora, which literally means "bad words," forbids Orthodox Jews to speak or hear gossip or derogatory comments about other people.

The rule is variously interpreted, but to Mrs. Mandelbaum it meant she could not write anything unflattering about Jews. "I was stymied," she said. "A novel is based on conflict, between good and evil. I thought, 'I'm not going to write a boring book, without conflict.'"

Instead, she took a different route, writing *Small Miracles: Extraordinary Coincidences from Everyday Life* (Adams Media Corporation, 1997), and a series of inspirational, but nondenominational, books under the same rubric, with Judith Leventhal, another Orthodox Jew.

Other Orthodox women have also shown creativity in melding their careers and their faith. Chasidah B. D. Avraham, 37, a Hasidic woman who lives in Crown Heights, worked for several years as a trucker, hauling overnight freight for Federal Express. A member of the Chabad-Lubavitch community, Ms. Avraham likes to pray with other Hasidic Jews on the Sabbath.

Whenever she was on the road, she took a directory listing the names of Lubavitcher, or Chabadnik, families in the United States. On Thursday nights, the end of her weekly shift, she would contact a family, drive to the family's home and spend the Sabbath praying with the family.

"I know every Chabadnik family in the United States now," Ms. Avraham said. "All you know about them when you arrive is that they're Chabadniks. But you meet them and it's like you've never left home."

There are still certain types of professions that ultra-Orthodox women simply cannot go into. For example, an Orthodox woman cannot be a singer, unless she performs only for other women. Under Jewish law, women's singing voices are not supposed to be heard by men.

"The reasoning is obvious," explained Rabbi Meir Fund of the Flatbush Minyan, an Orthodox and Hasidic synagogue in Brooklyn. "There's an element of seductiveness in being a performer, and assuming a role that is publicly seductive is antithetical to Orthodoxy."

But Orthodox women still express themselves through the arts.

Deborah Drattell, a Modern Orthodox woman who grew up in the Jewish community of Manhattan Beach, is a composer in residence at the New York City Opera. Her opera trilogy, *Central Park*, which she composed in collaboration with the playwright Wendy Wasserstein, was performed at Lincoln Center last season, and she is now working on a second project with Ms. Wasserstein.

"I do the only thing you really can do in this business that doesn't conflict with the Sabbath," she said recently. Aside from the fact that she cannot attend the premieres of most of her own operas, which usually take place on weekend nights, she said her religious practice rarely comes into conflict with her work.

Another woman, Georgie (she uses only one name), set up a business in Borough Park that allowed her to express her creative side. She is one of the most sought-after wig makers and hairstylists among ultra-Orthodox women, who are required to cover their hair once they marry.

"When I was growing up, the parents all wanted their daughters to become secretaries," Georgie, 51, said. "I refused to learn how to type, because I didn't want to be a secretary in the worst way. I always had a terrible weakness for fashionable things. Hairdressing gives me such adrenaline. I pick up a comb and all of a sudden the whole world opens up."

Although the growing numbers of working Orthodox women are not universally embraced in the community (girls at yeshivas are still told that the most honorable profession for an Orthodox woman is homemaker), others welcome the change.

"Not too long ago, it was argued by Reform Jews that full-fledged Orthodoxy was incommensurate with the modern world," said Rabbi Fund. "I think we've come to the realization now that that is not true. Halakhic observance is not about seclusion. It's about having the highest values for living in the world."

Reconciliation[4]

By Vanessa E. Jones
Boston Globe, January 30, 2002

It happens every week. During his Sunday sermon at the Union United Methodist Church, the Rev. Martin McLee invites casual visitors to walk to the chancel if they would like to become members of the church. On a recent Sunday, that exhortation was met with an awkward lack of movement. Then Shamalie Graham stirred and gently nudged her partner, Pamela Johnson, into the aisle.

For months, Johnson had occasionally visited the South End church, which two years ago emerged as the first black church in Boston to become what the denomination calls "reconciling" by welcoming "the full participation of all black lesbians and gay men, and all other homosexual persons who confess Jesus Christ as Lord and Saviour." Johnson had always hesitated about becoming a tithe-paying member, aware that United Methodists regard homosexual sex as a sin, forbid gay and lesbian marriage, and don't ordain homosexuals.

On this snowy morning, Johnson overcame her trepidation. Propelling her toward the chancel was grief over the news she'd received by telephone earlier that morning: Her grandmother had died. For the last hour she had basked in the warm words of McLee, who spoke of Johnson's loss during the service and encouraged the congregation to "surround this wonderful sister with your steadfast love." Johnson reached the front of the church, turned her tear-stained face toward the crowd as Union's newest church member, and proudly stated, "I'm a lesbian, and I love the Lord."

An increasing number of black gay, lesbian, bisexual, and transgendered people who previously sought spiritual refuge in predominantly white denominations or alternative religions are demanding to be more than silent presences in churches that reflect their heritage. Those involved in the struggle call the issue "explosive" and "dangerous." After all, much of the black church and some of its followers have branded homosexuality an "abomination" and a threat to the black family—often using the Bible to reinforce their positions. Last year the Rev. H. Beecher Hicks Jr., pastor of Metropolitan Baptist Church in Washington, D.C., spoke out from the pulpit, calling homosexuality sinful.

4. Republished with permission of *Boston Globe*, from "Reconciliation" by Vanessa E. Jones, January 30, 2002. Copyright © 2002. Permission conveyed through Copyright Clearance Center, Inc.

"This issue has caused as much of a firestorm as race and women's ordination," says Kelly Brown Douglas, author of *Sexuality and the Black Church: A Womanist Perspective* and religion professor at Goucher College in Baltimore. "Once again, we're being called to look into the real meaning of our faith. We're being challenged, and all too often the church fails the test."

> *Historically black houses of worship . . . are now beckoning gays and lesbians into their pews.*

A small number of black pastors are now perusing their Bibles and deciding that the Good Book doesn't prohibit the acceptance of alternative lifestyles. In addition to Union, historically black houses of worship such as Trinity United Church of Christ in Chicago and National City Christian Church in Washington, D.C., are now beckoning gays and lesbians into their pews. Programs such as the annual National Black Religious Summit on Sexuality in Washington educate pastors about homosexuality at a grass-roots level.

"We recognize that there's a great resistance in the church because of ignorance and what they've been taught," says Carlton Veazey, president of the Religious Coalition for Reproductive Choice, organizer of the Black Religious Summit. "But we see ministers, younger ones especially, dealing with this issue in a very honest and straightforward way. So I think that the perception of the black church is changing as it relates to homosexuality."

Of course, homophobia isn't unique to the black church. Many white Baptist, Catholic, and fundamentalist Christian churches scathingly condemn gays and lesbians. A recent Gallup Poll revealed that 43 percent of Americans still think homosexuality is not an acceptable lifestyle. In the black church, the subject remains a dirty-laundry topic that people don't want aired. It's so sensitive that those working for acceptance speak carefully, reluctant to erase progress by joining what McLee calls the "beat down the black church bandwagon." Many black pastors in Boston didn't return calls about the subject.

The black church's disapproval of homosexuality is a vestige of its discomfort with sexuality, Douglas writes in her book: "Because white culture racialized sex and 'sexuated' race by equating blackness with sexual deviance, the black community has been diligent in its efforts to sever the link between such deviance and blackness."

Silence, or a Search

Johnson grew up in the Columbus Avenue AME Zion Church in the South End, where she performed in plays as baby Jesus three times and was treated with respect as the granddaughter of an elder church member. When it came to her sexuality, however, she remembers "an overriding sense of needing to stay silent," she says. "I've never heard any active speaking out against homosexuality. It was simply ignored, and it wasn't included in those unions sanctified by God."

Church is also in the blood of Douglas Brooks, who four months ago invited Johnson to Union and stood by her side as she became a member. His parents were leaders of the African Methodist church he attended in Macon, Ga. Reflecting on the experience now, Brooks says the church "wounded" him by forcing him to keep silent about his sexual preferences.

The pressure to stay silent turns some black gays and lesbians into spiritual wanderers.

"That's the source of pain," says Brooks, 39, a Jamaica Plain resident who joined Union in 1998. "The very place where one should have been able to go to receive the solace and the consolation from the worldly pains was not available. I couldn't go to my pastor and say, 'This is what people say about me,' for fear he might say, 'Well, they're right, and on top of that you're going to hell.'"

That's what Darnell McCarter, 51, heard after she refused to hide her sexuality from the pastor of her Methodist church in New York City. She remembers being told, "'You need to change your sexuality. You're wrong. You're going to hell.' It was like I was committing a Godly sin."

The pressure to stay silent turns some black gays and lesbians into spiritual wanderers in search of a religion that accepts their sexuality. Johnson meditated and joined a lesbian circle honoring Shiva and Oshun. While living in Provincetown, Brooks attended a Unitarian Universalist church where, he says, "there was some room for my Christianity, but not a lot. It just wouldn't have been acceptable to have a sermon on Jesus more than once every two to three months."

The conundrum this group faces, says Johnson, is that "you sometimes have to choose to worship in community groups that don't necessarily reflect you in order to feel good about coming to worship on Sunday. You sometimes need to make a choice between your racial identity and your sexual identity."

That becomes tiring, says McLee. "The whole notion of making up your own faith is kind of wearing away because that doesn't have any lasting strength. Folks want to have a connection with God in a communal way that has some tradition, and what better way to do that than in a denominational church setting?"

Union began offering that environment two years ago, when the congregation unanimously voted to become reconciling. The move had been spearheaded by one of the church's oldest members, Hilda Evans, 76, who had watched as the South End welcomed a growing number of gay residents. Her question—"What is the church's stance on homosexuality?"—spawned a committee whose members for two years perused the Bible and read reports to educate themselves on the subject.

Another question on Evans's mind was "What would Christ say about this if he were in church today? Would Christ turn them away?"

Since the committee answered the latter inquiry with a resounding "No," other local black pastors have approached McLee about the issue "off the record in a very clandestine way," he says, chuckling. "Our Baptist brothers, they're not trying to have that dialogue. It's too hot an issue for a lot of pastors to deal with openly, but there are several pastors who feel a compassion for folk who can't find life in the church."

A Church in Transition

Union doesn't keep records of members' sexual orientation, but based on anecdotal evidence, McLee says "there's been a huge, marked increase" in gay and lesbian membership since the church became reconciling. New members are not only black. Michael Hight, 37, of Somerville, took the membership walk along with Johnson just a few weeks after his partner, David Rudewick, became a member. Says a beaming Rudewick of the congregation, "They don't see me as sex. They see me as a beautiful person."

Since joining the church, gay and lesbian Union members aren't sitting around singing "Kumbaya." There's still work to be done, they say, concerning the denomination's stance on homosexual sex, unions, and ordination. Bill Bows, who joined Union in July specifically because it is reconciling, says of the United Methodist position, "It makes me feel sad, but then I just focus on my spirituality and I try to keep in mind how I could possibly be hurting anyone by my feelings."

However, McLee, who was thoughtful enough to purchase a book of short stories by lesbian writers for Johnson days after she became a member, defends the denomination's stance.

"There are people who would love to make us an example of what a church should be: marrying gay folk, having gay clergy," he says. "That's the Church of Christ. That's the Unitarian church. That's not who we are."

Bibliography

Books

Armstrong, Karen. *A History of God: The 4,000-Year Quest of Judaism, Christianity and Islam*. New York: Ballantine, 1994.

Barker, Eileen. *The Making of a Moonie: Choice or Brainwashing?* Oxford: Blackwell Publishers, 1984.

Barrett, David B., George T. Kurian, and Todd M. Johnson, eds. *World Christian Encyclopedia: A Comparative Survey of Churches and Religions in the Modern World*. New York: Oxford University Press, 2001.

Becher, Jeanne, ed. *Women, Religion, and Sexuality: Studies on the Impact of Religious Teachings on Women*. World Council of Churches, 1991.

Bergen, Peter L. *Holy War, Inc.: Inside the Secret World of Osama bin Laden*. New York: Free Press, 2001.

Berger, Peter L., and Jonathan Sacks, eds. *The Desecularization of the World: Resurgent Religion and World Politics*. Grand Rapids: Wm. B. Eerdmans Publishing Co., 1999.

Capps, Walter H. *The New Religious Right: Piety, Patriotism and Politics*. Columbia, SC: University of South Carolina Press, 1990.

Davis, Philip G. *Goddess Unmasked: The Rise of Neopagan Feminist Spirituality*. Dallas: Spence Pub., 1999.

Finke, Roger, and Rodney Stark. *Acts of Faith: Explaining the Human Side of Religion*. Berkeley: University of California Press, 2000.

Hutton, Ronald. *The Triumph of the Moon: A History of Modern Pagan Witchcraft*. New York: Oxford University Press, 2001.

Jaffrelot, Christophe. *The Hindu Nationalist Movement in India*. New York: Columbia University Press, 1995.

Jenkins, Philip. *The Next Christendom: The Coming of Global Christianity*. New York: Oxford University Press, 2002.

Kinsley, David R. *Hinduism: A Cultural Perspective*. Upper Saddle River, NJ: Prentice Hall, 1993.

Lavey, Anton Szandor. *The Satanic Bible*. New York: Avon, 1989.

Marty, Martin E. *A Short History of Christianity*. Minneapolis: Fortress Press, 1987.

Neusner, Jacob. *The Way of Torah: An Introduction to Judaism*. Belmont, CA: Wadsworth, 1997.

Qutb, Sayyid. *Milestones*. Chicago: Kazi Publications, 1993.

Raël. *The True Face of God*. Vaduz: The Raelian Foundation, 1998.

Ranke-Heinemann, Uta. *Eunuchs for the Kingdom of Heaven: Women, Sexuality and the Catholic Church*. New York: Doubleday, 1990.

Rashid, Ahmed. *Jihad: The Rise of Militant Islam in Central Asia*. New Haven: Yale University Press, 2001.

Rashid, Ahmed. *Taliban: Militant Islam, Oil and Fundamentalism in Central Asia*. New Haven: Yale University Press, 2001.

Schimmel, Annemarie. *Islam: An Introduction*. Albany, NY: SUNY Press, 1992.

Sharma, Arvind, ed. *Hinduism and Secularism: After Ayodhya*. New York: St. Martin's Press, 2001.

Smith, Huston. *The World's Religions: Our Great Wisdom Traditions*. San Francisco: Harper San Francisco, 1992.

Smith, Joseph, trans. *The Book of Mormon: Another Testament of Jesus Christ*. 1830. Salt Lake City: The Church of Jesus Christ of Latter-Day Saints, 1981.

Sri Rahula, Walpola. *What the Buddha Taught*. New York: Grove Press, 1986.

Starhawk. *The Spiral Dance: A Rebirth of the Ancient Religion of the Great Goddess*. San Francisco: Harper San Francisco, 1999.

Stark, Rodney. *The Rise of Christianity: How the Obscure, Marginal Jesus Movement Became the Dominant Religious Force in the Western World in a Few Centuries*. New York: HarperCollins, 1997.

Swidler, Arlene, ed. *Homosexuality and World Religions*. Harrisburg: Trinity Press International, 1993.

Walls, Andrew. *The Missionary Movement in Christian History: Studies in the Transmission of Faith*. Maryknoll, NY: Orbis Books, 1996.

Ware, Timothy, and Kallistos Ware. *The Orthodox Church*. New York: Penguin USA, 1993.

Zaleski, Carol, and Philip Zaleski, eds. *The Book of Heaven: An Anthology of Writings from Ancient to Modern Times*. New York: Oxford University Press, 2000.

Additional Periodical Articles with Abstracts

More information on the role of religion in politics and society can be found in the following articles. Readers who require a more comprehensive selection are advised to consult *Readers Guide to Periodical Literature*, *Readers Guide to Abstracts*, *Social Science Abstracts*, and other H.W. Wilson publications.

Religions for Peace. Michael Amaladoss. *America*, v. 185 pp6–8 December 10, 2001.

Amaladoss discusses whether religion can help in peacemaking. In his view, religions cannot claim innocence in the ongoing conflict among peoples. The destruction of places or peoples in the name of religious faith is common in many places today. There cannot be any lasting peace without religion, however. For true peace, people need a sense of human, moral, and spiritual values, as well as recognition, respect, and acceptance of the dignity of persons-in-community and their cultural and religious identities. An appreciation and search for the common good, local and universal, leading to justice and equality is also required for real peace. A purely nonreligious, secular order could not deliver this.

Notes from a Community—Catholic and Gay. Eric Stoltz. *America*, v. 178 pp10–13 March 28, 1998.

The writer discusses the spiritual and religious life of the gay community in Los Angeles's Miracle Mile. Gay people have found salvation in community, so it is only fitting that they seek salvation as a community. In the Miracle Mile congregation, which is predominantly gay, there is no anger, resentment, or embodiment of the liberal agenda. Rather, people are faithful to their Catholic heritage and struggle to live in accordance with the Gospel, an aspect of the homosexual lifestyle that is not reflected in the media.

Soji-ji. John Lowe. *The American Scholar*, v. 70 pp87–93 Winter 2001.

Lowe describes staying at Soji-ji in Japan, one of two training monasteries where the sons of Zen priests from Soto temples all over the country train for six years.

The Scholars and the Goddess. Charlotte Allen. *Atlantic Monthly*, v. 287 pp18–22 January 2001.

Wicca appears to be the fastest-growing religion in the United States. Many of its adherents came to the religion after reading Starhawk's *The Spiral Dance: A Rebirth of the Ancient Religion of the Great Goddess*, which posits that the nature-attuned, woman-respecting, peaceful, and egalitarian culture on which it is based has existed for more than 35,000 years. Overwhelming evidence exists to indicate that Wicca is a distinctly new religion and that various assumptions informing the Wiccan view of history are deeply flawed, however. Allen discusses the theories about Wicca's founding that were advanced in Philip G. Davis's *Goddess Unmasked: The Rise of Neopagan Feminist Spiritu-*

ality and Ronald Hutton's *The Triumph of the Moon.*

Worship without Walls. Robert C. Fuller. *The Boston Globe*, pD1 December 23, 2001.

Fuller points out that almost half of all Americans have no association whatsoever with organized religion. While one in four of these "unchurched" Americans consider themselves to be secular humanists, most label themselves "spiritual, but not religious." According to Fuller, this "religion without churches" is likely to influence the nation's religious life in the decades to come.

What Scholarship Reveals about Politics and Religion. *The Chronicle of Higher Education*, v. 47 pp7–9 September 8, 2000.

Wolfe discusses academic theories about the relationship between politics and religion.

Methodists Protest Church Policy on Gays. *The Christian Century*, v. 117 p786 August 2, 2000.

United Methodist churches in western America have approved a statement that urges the full inclusion of gays and lesbians in the church. This statement echoes a declaration by New England churches that protested the decisions by the church to prohibit same-sex unions and the ordination of gays. Meeting in Casper, Wyoming, between July 12 and 15, 2000, delegates from United Methodist churches in 12 western states pledged to work for the "full participation at all levels in the life of the church and society" for gays and lesbians.

Americans See Religion As Gaining Clout in Public Life. Jane Lampman. *Christian Science Monitor*, p3 December 7, 2001.

Lampmann reports on a poll that shows most Americans believe religion is gaining influence in public life.

Buddhism and the "Subversive Science." David P. Barash. *The Chronicle of Higher Education*, v. 47 pp13+ February 23, 2001.

According to Barash, people who follow ecological thinking also embrace, perhaps unwittingly, the ancient Buddhist spiritual tradition. Ecological thinking parallels the fundamental insight of Buddhism that all things are interconnected and interdependent.

The Darwinian Universe. John F. Haught. *Commonweal*, v. 129 pp12–18 January 25, 2002.

Haught discusses the ways in which the work of Charles Darwin has become more compelling than ever for those who continue to believe that science is both authoritative and fundamentally damaging to religion. Darwinian evolution can easily be reconciled with theology without any editing, however. A biblical understanding of God as the power of the future is consistent with evolution and logically anticipates the type of world Darwinian biology presents. An image of God fully open to the data of evolutionary science and the human yearning for authenticity lies beyond both scientific materialism and "intelligent design."

Religion, Politics, and the State: Cross-Cultural Observations. N. J. Demerath and Karen S. Straight. *Cross Currents*, v. 47 pp43–57 Spring 1997.

Demerath and Straight examine four types of situations implied at the intersection between the religious and the secular and between politics and the state. They identify these four situations as involving religious politics with a religious state, secular politics with a secular state, secular politics with a religious state, and religious politics with a secular state. They contend that of these four combinations, a religious state combined with religious politics is the most potentially violent but that a secular state with secular politics may provide stability at the price of cultural vacuity. They conclude that the coupling of a secular state with religious politics, although rare, is arguably the most promising type for promoting both structural stability and cultural vitality.

The Living Cosmos of Jainism: A Traditional Science Grounded in Environmental Ethics. Christopher Key Chapple. *Daedalus*, v. 130 pp207–24 Fall 2001.

According to Chapple, Jainism perceives the cosmos as living, inspiring an ecologically sensitive response on the part of its adherents. The Jaina definition of life extends far beyond the standard dictionary usage, maintaining that the manifold parts of the world contain "touch, breath, life, and bodily strength." This belief can prompt a greater cognizance of human reciprocity with the things of the world through the senses. Jainism's cosmological perspectives, contemporary science's insights, and an increasing awareness of the beauty and fragility of the natural order all can help create a vital shift in consciousness that values life in its many forms. Chapple discusses two primary concepts of Jaina teaching—unique cosmology and the innate sensuousness of the nonsensate world—in light of contemporary Western ecological thinkers Brian Swimme and Thomas Berry.

Where Do We Go from Here? Bill McKibben. *Daedalus*, v. 130 pp301–6 Fall 2001.

Part of a special issue on the attitudes of world religions to nature. According to McKibben, historians of religion and theologians have explored old texts and traditions in search of sources for a new environmental ethics. The fine work of these historians has yielded much that is useful and reveals that myriad clues and suggestions about how humans might live more lightly on the planet are clear in various traditions. The deepest religious insights on the connection between God, nature, and humans may not materialize, however, until religious people, complying with the terms of their traditions, join movements working to incorporate these new understandings into their responsibilities. The very process of engagement will inspire new thinking and understanding.

How Hindu an India? *The Economist*, v. 360 pp29–30 August 18, 2001.

The tension between Hindutva, or the quest for Hindu-ness, and secularism represents India's main ideological conflict. Support for Hindutva is strongest in the state of Gujarat, where the Hindu-nationalist Bharatiya Janata Party (BJP), which governs India at the head of a 19-party coalition, rules alone with a decisive majority. Many suspect that the rhetoric of the party in Gujarat is the type that the party would spread across India if given the opportunity. BJP ideologies threaten India's secularism and worry minorities, but the party's coalition partners, who are dependent on minority votes, have obliged the BJP to restrain its ideas. Secularists hope that, outside of Gujarat, the rest of India is too democratic and diverse to be swayed by Hindutva.

Women and the Ministry. *Journal for the Scientific Study of Religion,* v. 36 pp565–627 December 1997.

This special issue includes articles on clergywomen of the pioneer generation, conflicts over women's ordination, the factors that influence the rate at which clergy find their first parish positions, and worries regarding the "feminization" of the clergy profession.

Stars of David: Kabbalah Learning Center in Los Angeles. Stacie Stukin. *Los Angeles*, v. 43 pp94+ December 1998.

Stukin reports that while it is popular among celebrities, the Kabbalah Learning Center in Los Angeles has come under criticism. The center, just south of Beverly Hills, advocates a mixture of the ancient Jewish practice of Kabbalah, or mysticism, along with New Age, self-help, and astrological methodologies aimed at eradicating negativity. The controversial organization has received a public-relations boost thanks to its championing by a number of celebrities, including Madonna and Roseanne. Nonetheless, critics claim that the center divides families, pressures students to make extravagant donations, and preys on the weak. National cult expert Rick Ross says the center seems to be a mind-control cult that is more interested in money than spirituality.

Acknowledging That God Is Not Limited to Christians. Joseph C. Hough Jr. and Gustav Niebuhr. *New York Times* online January 12, 2002.

In an interview with Gustav Niebuhr, Joseph C. Hough Jr., the president of Union Theological Seminary in New York, argues that toleration alone, when based on the assumption that some religions are more "authentic" than others, is not sufficient in a world of religious pluralism. Rather, for Hough it is essential for Christians to know "that we have seen the face of God in the face of Jesus Christ. It is not essential to believe that no one else has seen God and experienced redemption in another place or time."

A Monastery That Embraces the Old and Thrives on the New. Dean C. Smith. *New York Times* online January 12, 2002.

Smith reports on Mepkin Abbey, a Trappist monastery 30 miles north of Charleston, South Carolina that has experienced a dramatic change of fortune in the last decade. While the abbey appeared headed for decline 10 years ago, it now receives more than 15,000 visitors per year. At the same time, the monastery strictly upholds the Rule of St. Benedict, a code of chastity, physical labor, and prayerful silence.

Radical New Views of Islam and the Origins of the Koran. *New York Times* online March 2, 2002.

Stille reports on the recent efforts of some scholars to apply the techniques of textual analysis to the Koran.

A Desire to Duplicate. Margaret Talbot. *New York Times Magazine*, pp40+ February 4, 2001.

As Talbot reports, human cloning could begin with a grieving family hoping to replace a lost child and a genetics-obsessed sect dreaming of reaching immortality. The science-loving, alien-fixated Raelian sect, for whom cloning is a central tenet, has tapped into a wellspring of desire for human cloning whose fulfillment would surely take many people off-guard. In June 2000, an American couple whose ten-month-old baby boy had died offered to finance the Raelians in an all-out effort to clone the boy from cells they had frozen. Although not likely to succeed, the fact that at least 50 female followers eagerly volunteered as egg donors and surrogate mothers means the Raelians cannot be ruled out.

Lives of the Saints. Lawrence Wright. *New Yorker*, v. 77 pp40–57 January 21, 2002.

Wright reports on the Salt Lake City–based Church of Jesus Christ of Latter-Day Saints. Having entered the 20th century as the most persecuted creed in the United States, the LDS Church begins the 21st century as perhaps the most robust religion in the country. The number of its adherents, or Mormons, in the United States has increased by almost 225 percent over the course of the past 30 years to more than 5 million. This is at a time when the memberships of more traditional denominations, such as Methodism and Episcopalianism, have sharply declined. Mormons, like the Jews, undertook an exodus that forged their early identity as a scorned people and believe that they are God's chosen. They are a missionary people, the majority of them first-generation converts. Wright discusses the origins and evolution of the church and the hosting of the 2002 Winter Olympics in Salt Lake City.

China Wakes up a Tiger: China's Repression of Falun Gong. Mahlon Meyer. *Newsweek*, v. 137 pp32–3 February 5, 2001.

In Meyer's view, China's repression of Falun Gong could turn a spiritual movement into a political opposition. Falun Gong is a movement dedicated to a diverse mix of mysticism, meditation, and slow-motion exercise. It has no political agenda, and its sole charismatic figure—Li Hongzhi, the 49-year-old founder—lives quietly in exile in America. Despite this, there has been an ongoing brutal crackdown on people who, in most other countries, would be considered harmless idealists. This is because, with the Chinese Communist Party ideology in tatters, the government feels threatened by any organization that can attract millions of people to a set of ideals. By repressing Falun Gong, however, the party risks labeling millions of Chinese as enemies of the regime and politicizing a movement that originally had nothing to do with politics.

In Bad Faith. Ivan Oransky. *Salon.com* online April 26, 2001.

Oransky discusses scientific research indicating that religious involvement or spiritual belief can lead to concrete medical benefits, including decreased risk of stroke, heart disease, and depression. The author concedes there is some evidence of a link but adduces several criticisms of the studies conducted to date.

The Great Chupacabra Conspiracy. Robert Sheaffer. *Skeptical Inquirer*, v. 25 pp19–21 March/April 2001.

Sheaffer discusses recent reports in a number of paranormal fields: During the last 12 months or so, certain South American countries have supposedly endured a blitz of attacks by "chupacabras," the ferocious "goat suckers" that torment Hispanic farmers and ranchers; UFO specialist Joel Carpenter has found a similarity between the side mirrors used on trucks in the 1920s and 1930s and the images purported to be of UFOs that are shown in a couple of celebrated photographs taken by the late Paul Trent on May 11, 1950; and acts of harassment carried out by Scientologists against their critics have continued in great number.

Cults, Violence, and Religious Terrorism. Jean Francois Mayer. *Studies in Conflict and Terrorism.* v. 24 pp361–76 September/October 2001.

Mayer examines the idea of whether violence committed by religious groups should be regarded as a specific subcategory of terrorism that has distinctive patterns. He contends that a single, unitary phenomenon cannot be created by the fact that violent actions were committed by various groups often labeled as "cults." He concludes that the distinguishing factor of such violence is the situation in which cult groups have to operate in relation to the rest of the society.

Health and Fulfillment on the Run: Falun Gong Followers in the United States. Barry Hillenbrand. *Time*, v. 157 p35 July 2, 2001.

It is not easy to generalize about the Falun Gong movement's U.S. followers, writes Hillenbrand, but devotees all seem to share similar stories about the joy that Falun Gong has brought to their lives. Part religion, part health regime and holistic exercise, some practitioners took up Falun Gong because they were convinced of its healing power, and others came to it as a natural progression from tai chi and yoga. Whatever their motivation, many seem to agree with government statistician Gary Feuerberg who says that Falun Gong is very powerful and makes the devotee a better person.

Helping "Two People Who Love Each Other." Linda Kulman. *US News and World Report*, v. 128 p50 April 10, 2000.

Reform rabbis have voted to recognize same-sex gay unions. Lawmakers in Vermont recently took the first step toward giving legal recognition to same-sex unions. The resolution that the yearly meeting of the Central Conference of American Rabbis, representing 1.5 million Jews, passed by a huge margin recently stated that gay couples are "worthy of affirmation through appropriate Jewish ritual." The debate on gay unions was also likely to dominate the 2000 United Methodist, Presbyterian, and Episcopal Church conventions.

The Varieties of Muslim Experience: Not All Muslims Are Fundamentalist. Stephen Schwarz. *Weekly Standard*, v. 7 pp18–22 October 15, 2001.

According to Schwarz, the Council on American-Islamic Relations (CAIR) has been the most adroit group at importing the rhetoric and deceit characteristic of Islamic fundamentalism into the U.S. public sphere. Created in the mid-1990s to define the position of U.S. Muslims in politics and international relations, CAIR pretends to represent all Muslims in their "relations to America," even though its Islam is fundamentalist and anti-Western. Keenly aware of Americans' desire to be amiable and of U.S. journalists' wish to be politically correct, CAIR has framed its assault on American public opinion in terms of sensitivity: that it is hurtful to "the Muslims" for the U.S. media to describe any among them as fundamentalist or terrorists. The writer discusses a number of moderate groups who have rejected Wahhabism, a radical strain of Islam, including most Muslims on the Indian subcontinent and the traditional but tolerant Sufi Muslims.

Hindu Nationalism Clouds the Face of India. H. D. S. Greenway. *World Policy Journal*, v. 18 pp89–93 Spring 2001.

Greenway reports that Hindu nationalists believe that for 1,000 years India has been a single cultural unit that assimilated all its invaders and that other religious groups are converts of, or scions of, a basic Hindu entity. He states that the battle between secularism and a Hindu-based sense of Indian exceptionalism is not new, as a militant organization, founded in 1925, was dedicated to overthrowing the secular programs of the National Congress. However, he contends that secularists are not bowing to the pressure from Hindu nationalists; therefore, it is likely that secularism will continue at the political center. Nevertheless, he contends that the face and customs of India will continue to change as a result of capitulation of Hindu nationalism.

Index